SHEFFIELD HALLAM UNIVERSITY
LEARNING CENTRE
CITY CAMPUS, POND STREET,
SHEFFIELD S1

D0527721

_ ___ Series

Commercial

ONE WEEK LOAN

chapter 9
chapter 10
2 7 OCT 2009

LAW

Cavendish
Publishing
Limited

Sheffield Hallam University
Learning and Information Services
WITHDRAWN FROM STOCK

London • Sydney • Portland, Oregon

Q&A Series

Commercial Law

THIRD EDITION

Paul Dobson, LLB, Barrister
Code Administrator for the Direct Selling Association

and

Jo Reddy, LLB, LLM, Barrister

Cavendish
Publishing
Limited

London • Sydney • Portland, Oregon

Third edition first published in Great Britain 2003 by
Cavendish Publishing Limited, The Glass House,
Wharton Street, London WC1X 9PX, United Kingdom
Telephone: + 44 (0)20 7278 8000   Facsimile: + 44 (0)20 7278 8080
Email: info@cavendishpublishing.com
Website: www.cavendishpublishing.com

Published in the United States by Cavendish Publishing
c/o International Specialized Book Services,
5804 NE Hassalo Street, Portland,
Oregon 97213-3644, USA

Published in Australia by Cavendish Publishing (Australia) Pty Ltd
3/303 Barrenjoey Road, Newport, NSW 2106, Australia

© Dobson, P, Reddy, J   2003
First edition   1994
Second edition   2000
Third edition   2003

All rights reserved. No part of this publication may be reproduced, stored in a
retrieval system, or transmitted, in any form or by any means, electronic, mechanical,
photocopying, recording, scanning or otherwise, without the prior permission in
writing of Cavendish Publishing Limited, or as expressly permitted by law, or under
the terms agreed with the appropriate reprographics rights organisation. Enquiries
concerning reproduction outside the scope of the above should be sent to the
Rights Department, Cavendish Publishing Limited, at the address above.

You must not circulate this book in any other binding or cover
and you must impose the same condition on any acquirer.

British Library Cataloguing in Publication Data

Dobson, AP (Alan Paul), 1945–
Commercial law – 3rd ed – (Q&A series)
1 Commercial law – England
I Title II Reddy, KJ
346.4'2'07

Library of Congress Cataloguing in Publication Data
Data available

ISBN 1-85941-740-X

1 3 5 7 9 10 8 6 4 2

Printed and bound in Great Britain

CONTENTS

TABLE OF CASES

NB: CCLR denotes Consumer Credit Law Reports which were published until 2000 in *Consumer Credit Control* by Bennion and Dobson, but are now published as part of Sweet & Maxwell's *Encyclopedia of Consumer Credit Law.*

TABLE OF STATUTORY INSTRUMENTS

CHAPTER 1

GENERAL QUESTIONS

Introduction

This chapter contains two questions which are not confined to one particular part of the syllabus but are broader. Such questions are often included in examinations in order to test your knowledge of recent developments in the subject or simply to give you an opportunity, which most questions in law papers do not, to demonstrate a joined-up, wide knowledge of the syllabus. The second question is a general question, such as one sometimes finds in examinations, which invites the examinee to take an overview of the subject and to do so from a particular perspective. For that type of question, one needs to have a good knowledge of the whole area of sale of goods and related law.

Checklist

For the particular questions here, you will need to know:

- the common law and legislation relating to exclusion clauses and contracts generally;
- the law of sale of goods, including recent developments;
- recent developments in consumer law;
- proposed or pending changes in the law, particularly European initiatives.

Question 1

In recent times, a constant stream of Directives, initiatives and proposals relating to consumer law has been emanating from the organs of the European Community. The result is that businesses dealing with consumers will incur considerable compliance and other costs, and they need to keep under review their trading practices to ensure compliance with a branch of the law that is changing quickly.

Explain and discuss.

Answer plan

This question is designed to test your knowledge of current developments in consumer law. It is not quite a 'write all you know about the topic' type of question. It clearly requires you to concentrate on laws which are created by the European Community, and needs an examination of recent laws and also proposed ones which have yet to be enacted. One way to deal with the question is as follows. First, deal with European Directives on consumer law which have recently been implemented. Secondly, deal with any recent Directives which have yet to be implemented. Thirdly, deal with proposed Directives and Regulations. It is a good idea to begin your answer by identifying the main Directives and proposals which are to be discussed. It is important, however, not just to write down all you know about the law or proposed law in question. You must deal with the likely or possible costs to business. That is explicitly asked for by the question.

Answer

There does indeed appear to be something near to a torrent of Directives and other initiatives coming out of Brussels. This is no doubt largely due to the fact that currently the development of consumer policy within the European Community is a priority of the European Commission. Directives actually issued in recent times include those on: Distance Selling (1997); Injunctions (1998); Amendments to the Product Liability Directive (1999); Aspects of Sale of Goods and Consumer Guarantees (1999); and E-Commerce (2000). Even more recently, there have been consultations over:

- the extent to which differences between the national laws of contract hinder or deter cross-border sales within the Community;
- proposed revisions to the Consumer Credit Directive;
- a proposed general duty to trade fairly;
- a proposed European Regulation on Sales Promotion.

This answer will begin by discussing Directives recently implemented in the UK, and will then deal with the other developments just mentioned.

Distance Selling Directive

The Distance Selling Directive was implemented in the UK by the Consumer Protection (Distance Selling) Regulations 2000. With very few exceptions, they apply to 'distance contracts'. These are business-to-consumer sales of goods or services where the supplier makes exclusive use of distance communication up to and including when the contract is made. Thus, sales made by mail order, telephone, fax and over the internet are all within the definition, which basically catches all sales where there is no face to face contact with the customer prior to and at the time of the making of the contract. These Regulations introduced significant improvements in the rights of consumers under distance contracts. They require the giving of specified information to the consumer before the contract is made, and the giving of specified information (much the same as the pre-contract information) in durable form – which really means in a written document or (it is probably sufficiently durable) in an email sent to the consumer. The requirement of pre-contract information requires businesses which sell by telephone to be very careful to ensure that the information is given either by an automated voice prior to the consumer being put through to a real interactive human being or else by the latter person (or by a combination of both). Equally, care must be taken by those who sell goods or services to customers over the internet in the design of their websites. It is thought that very many distance selling businesses are still failing to comply with the Regulations. The rights given by the Regulations also include a cooling-off period, during which the consumer has the right to cancel a distance contract. The cooling-off period is seven working days, where the first of the seven days is either the day after the contract is made (in the case of services) or the day after the goods are delivered (in the case of goods). Information about the consumer's right of cancellation is part of the specified information which must also be given pre-contract and in durable form. Other rights created by the Regulations include:

- a rule that, unless otherwise agreed, a distance contract must be performed within 30 days;
- with a few exceptions, if, in relation to a distance contract, fraudulent use is made of a payment card (whether a credit card, debit card or store card), the card-holder is entitled to be reimbursed or to have his account re-credited.

A further change effected by the Regulations relates to unsolicited goods sent to a consumer. Whereas previously such goods were deemed to have been an unconditional gift to the consumer if, after six months, they had not been collected by the sender, now they are deemed immediately to have been an unconditional gift. Beneficial as these new Regulations undoubtedly are to consumers, there is no doubt that they pose significant compliance requirements on businesses selling by distance contracts.

Injunctions Directive

This Directive was first implemented in UK law by the Stop Now Orders (EC Directive) Regulations 2001. It has not, however, created any increase in either compliance requirements or the costs imposed on business. This is because it does not create any additional requirements for businesses. Rather, it is aimed at securing better enforcement of requirements imposed by other pieces of legislation. Thus, the Regulations give the Office of Fair Trading (OFT) and other designated bodies (including enforcement bodies in other Member States of the European Community) the right to issue 'stop now' orders to traders who have been found to be in breach of the laws created to implement a whole range of European Directives aimed at consumer protection. Those Directives include those on misleading advertising, doorstep selling, consumer credit, package travel/holidays, unfair contract terms, timeshares, distance selling and consumer guarantees. Subsequently, in the UK, the Stop Now Orders (EC Directive) Regulations 2001 will be superseded by the Enterprise Act 2002, when it is brought into force. Whereas the Regulations (like the Injunctions Directive itself) are confined to the enforcement of laws which enact one of the Directives aimed at consumer protection, the Enterprise Act 2002 effectively extends that new enforcement regime to traders who, in the UK, breach any law (domestic or European) designed to protect consumers. It could simply be the law of contract. The new regime, when it is brought into force, will thus remedy the shortcomings of the enforcement machinery previously contained in Pt III of the Fair Trading Act 1973. Under this, the OFT could not take enforcement action unless it could establish the trader's persistence in a course of conduct contrary to the law and, even then, could not apply to the court for an order without first using its best endeavours to secure from the trader an undertaking of future good conduct. Better enforcement of the law in favour of consumers under these provisions is welcomed and does not impose costs on business other than on those who are not complying with existing law.

Product Liability Directive Amendment

The Product Liability Directive was implemented in the UK by Pt I of the Consumer Protection Act 1987. It creates strict liability for personal injury (and damage to non-business property exceeding £275) caused by defective products. As originally enacted, the Directive allowed Member States to exclude from liability the producers of game and primary agricultural products. This was largely thanks to the strength at that time of the farming lobby in France and other Member States. The Directive did, however, impose liability on the secondary producers (that is, those who put agricultural produce through some sort of industrial process, such as canning, bottling, cooking, etc). Such secondary producers would, whenever possible, impose contract terms on the farmers from whom they purchased, thereby giving themselves the right to claim indemnity from the farmers in the event that the secondary producer was found liable in respect of a defect in the produce which was present when the farmer sold it. The amendment to the Directive was implemented in the UK by amendments made in 2000 to Pt I of the Consumer Protection Act 1987. These removed the previous exemption from liability for the producers of game and primary agricultural products. This change to the law affected only a small section of business (farmers) and, even then, barely affected them, since they were generally liable in the way already explained for damage caused by defective produce supplied by them. The compliance costs are thus virtually nil, and liability costs in the event of a claim are in most cases unaffected.

E-Commerce Directive

This was implemented in the UK by the Electronic Commerce (EC Directive) Regulations 2002. These provide basic protection for those receiving an 'information society service'. This certainly includes those who receive electronic commercial communications (other than fax and telephone messages) as well as those accessing commercial websites, etc. The Regulations apply irrespective of whether the recipients are consumers. The requirements must be complied with by those who provide the information society service, which includes all those who sell goods or services over the web, including via email, by telephone text messaging, etc. In this part of this answer, such people will simply be termed 'traders'. Those receiving the electronic commercial communications or accessing traders' websites will be referred to as 'customers'. The Regulations are not confined to the situation where services are themselves provided electronically (for example, by being downloaded). They apply where the trader is using electronic means to sell or advertise goods or services which are to be supplied by any means (whether over the internet, in person, by post or by any other method). Equally, mere brand advertising (for example, over the internet) is also caught.

The requirements of the Regulations cover such things as:

- giving the customer specific information which is directly and permanently accessible, such as the trader's name, geographic address, electronic address, whether prices include delivery and tax, etc;

- identifying the sender of any commercial communication (for example, an email seeking to promote a sale) and indicating that it is a commercial communication;

- identifying any unsolicited commercial email as such;

- giving clear instructions as to the technical steps to follow to make a contract and to correct any input errors;

- making any terms and conditions provided by the trader available in a way that allows the customer to store and retrieve them;

- giving prompt electronic acknowledgment of an order.

Undoubtedly, the Regulations impose compliance costs on businesses which advertise or sell goods or services over the internet. However, these costs are necessary in order to provide an essential level of consumer/customer protection. Furthermore, those traders who were already doing business with consumers over the internet will already have been required to comply with the Consumer Protection (Distance Selling) Regulations 2000 (discussed above), and much of the specified information required by the two sets of regulations is the same.

Directive on Aspects of Sale of Goods and Consumer Guarantees

This Directive has been implemented in the UK by the Sale and Supply of Goods Regulations 2002, which come into force on 31 March 2003. These regulations have made changes to the Sale of Goods Act 1979. The changes affect the rights of buyers who are consumers (that is, who are buying for purposes outside their businesses). The changes have the following effects:

- liability is imposed on the seller for pre-contract public statements by others (for example, in advertisements put out by the manufacturer);

- a rule is created (by a new sub-s (4) to s 20 of the Sale of Goods Act) that in the case of a consumer purchase, the risk (of accidental loss or damage to the goods) does not pass to the buyer until delivery;
- the range of remedies available to the consumer buyer is expanded to include repair and replacement of goods which do not conform with the requirements of the implied terms in ss 13–15 of the Sale of Goods Act;
- contractual effect is given to the terms of any guarantee of goods sold and delivered to a consumer.

The changes made to the Sale of Goods Act are reflected in similar changes made to other Acts of Parliament regulating the supply of goods to consumers: the Supply of Goods (Implied Terms) Act 1973 and the Supply of Goods and Services Act 1982. The changes created by these provisions are not very extensive. The requirement to give the consumer a replacement or to repair non-conforming goods is not burdensome on business, since it will often make commercial sense anyway for the seller to offer just such a remedy. Furthermore, if such a remedy is either impossible or disproportionate, the seller will not be required to provide it. Where a seller is liable in respect of pre-contract statements put out by the manufacturer (or distributor/importer, etc) or under a guarantee given by that other person, the seller will often be able to recover the cost from the latter. The situations where the cost ultimately falls on the seller are likely to be relatively rare – for example, where the manufacturer who gave the guarantee has become insolvent.

Other European initiatives

Duty to trade fairly

In 2001, the European Commission issued a consultation document which sought to address certain legal barriers to cross-border trade within the Community – in particular, cross-border trade where a business in one Member State sells to a consumer in another. The Consultation Paper recognised that in the area of consumer protection, there had been a series of Directives, which had been 'minimum' Directives – that is, Directives which laid down minimum levels of consumer protection to be provided in each Member State, but which allowed Member States to impose more stringent levels of protection. The result had been that the laws in different Member States had imposed varying levels of legal control. For example, the Doorstep Selling Directive had required Member States to provide a mandatory cooling-off period (of at least seven days) for agreements made at the consumer's home during (or as a result of) an unsolicited visit by a salesperson. However, in some Member States, the law now provides for a longer period and, in others, the requirement to provide a cooling-off period applies also to agreements made when the consumer solicited the visit to his house. The Consultation Paper also recognised that the various Directives relating to consumer law had been made piecemeal and that a number of them dealt only with particular sectors or practices: for example, Doorstep Selling, Timeshares, Broadcasting, etc. The Commission therefore is proposing that there should be one main over-arching Directive requiring traders to trade fairly (or not to trade unfairly) with consumers. This Directive would be supported by codes giving guidance as to good/bad practice which would help in applying it. This is, of course, all part of the drive to harmonise the law within the European Union and thereby to remove barriers to trade. The consultation exercise has revealed that big business (represented in Britain, for example, by the CBI) is against any such development in the law, but that small to medium sized businesses find the legal differences between the different Member States to be a barrier to cross-border trade.

General contract law

In another consultation paper in 2001, the European Commission enquired about the extent to which differences in the basic law of contract of the Member States are barriers to cross-border trade. The result of this exercise could be a proposal for some (or indeed a great deal of) harmonisation of the contract law of the Member States.

Consumer Credit Directive

In a consultation exercise in 2002, the European Commission published a draft revised Consumer Credit Directive. This is likely to lead to some significant changes to this particular area of law. In particular, the draft would totally ban all unsolicited doorstep selling of credit or of goods and services on credit. It would also apparently curtail to some extent liability under s 75 of the Consumer Credit Act 1974 (colloquially known as 'connected lender liability') by, for example, not applying that liability in the case of purchases paid for by credit card. It would also amend the rules for the calculation of the Annual Percentage Rate of Charge (the APR).

Proposed Regulation on Sales Promotion

In 2001, the Commission proposed that there be a European Regulation on Sales Promotion. A regulation is directly applicable law which therefore will become part of the law of each Member State without any further implementation by those States. The purpose of the Regulation will be to harmonise rules on the advertising and promoting of products, so as to allow pan-European marketing campaigns. It will prevent Member States outlawing or placing restrictions on certain practices, such as offering discounts (for example, money-off coupons or 10% extra free).

There is no doubt that at least some of the above proposals will come to fruition. For sure, some revised version of the Consumer Credit Directive will appear in due course. Whether there is to be a European general duty to trade fairly or if there are to be major pan-European developments in contract law remains to be seen.

Ultimately, of course, one recognises that it is consumers themselves who pay in higher prices for any extra costs imposed on businesses. Surely the increase in prices occasioned by the developments discussed above is worth paying for what are mostly very necessary pieces of consumer protection. Certainly, as the question suggests, in order to ensure compliance, businesses will have to keep abreast of changes as they arise.

Question 2

'Despite developments in recent times, the law of sale of goods is still permeated with the following key concepts: freedom of contract, privity of contract and *caveat emptor*.'

Discuss the extent to which this is true.

Answer plan

This question is a generalised one of a type often treated by students as one to tackle as a desperate last resort. Being generalised, it requires a good overall knowledge of the subject. In this particular question, three different concepts are expressly referred to and therefore it is required that each be addressed. There is every reason to take a straightforward approach and deal with one concept at a time.

Answer

Freedom of contract

The law of sale of goods was originally developed by judges in deciding cases. In the first Sale of Goods Act of 1893, Parliament set out to incorporate this common law into statute form and the 1893 Act, in its preamble, described itself as an Act to codify the law. Most of the provisions of the 1893 Act are now contained, often word for word, in the current 1979 Act. There is no doubt that the freedom of contract philosophy underpinned much of the common law development, this philosophy being that the parties were free to decide for themselves what contract to make and what terms to incorporate into it. The law set out to provide for what would be the position if the parties had not themselves determined what it should be. Thus, throughout the 1893 Act, one finds provisions such as 'unless otherwise agreed' and also a general provision (now to be found in an amended form in s 55 of the 1979 Act) that where any right or liability would arise by implication of law, it can be negatived by express agreement between the parties. This was the embodiment of the freedom of contract principle. The amendment now found in s 55 relates to the rules on exclusion clauses. Since the original Act of 1893, it had become clear that the freedom of contract principle could be abused by a party who was in a very strong bargaining position and who could insist on (often quite harsh) terms being in the contract. This was particularly true of standard form contracts made between a business and an ordinary private consumer and was not confined to contracts of sale of goods. It occurred in hire purchase contracts and such contracts as those to buy railway tickets or to park one's car in a car park. The abuse often took the form of an insistence on the incorporation of clauses excluding liability towards the consumer. After initial legislative attempts to control these exclusion clauses in particular contracts (for example, hire purchase agreements), Parliament enacted general legislation on exclusion clauses in the Unfair Contract Terms Act 1977. This Act has introduced a very clear restriction on the freedom of contract principle in the following ways. First, it deals with the terms as to title, description, quality and sample implied by ss 12–15 of the Sale of Goods Act (and by other Acts in relation to other contracts involving the passing of property or the hire of goods). It distinguishes between consumer deals and non-consumer deals and, broadly speaking, it makes it impossible to exclude or restrict liability for breach of the implied terms as to title and, where the buyer is a consumer, makes it impossible to exclude or restrict the other implied terms just referred to. Where the buyer is not a consumer, a clause purporting to exclude or restrict liability for these latter terms is subject to a test of reasonableness, which is also the position with any other exclusion clause using standard terms.

The Unfair Contract Terms Act deals only with exclusion clauses. With that important exception, the freedom of contract principle remains largely intact. Thus, for example, whether an express term is a condition or a warranty is a matter the parties are free to determine. A term as to the time of delivery will normally be construed by the courts as a condition, but it is still open to the parties expressly to state otherwise. Similarly, the rules in ss 17–20 on the passing of property and risk apply only where the parties have not expressed a contrary intention.

A further significant inroad into the principle has derived from the 1993 European Directive on Unfair Contract Terms. This was implemented in Britain by the Unfair Terms in Consumer Contracts Regulations 1994, which have since been replaced by the 1999 Regulations of the same name. These apply with certain exceptions to any term (in a consumer contract) which, contrary to a requirement of good faith, causes a significant imbalance in the parties' rights and obligations to the detriment of the consumer. It is not just exclusion clauses which can be declared 'unfair' and thus of no effect; provided it is not a core term (for example, in a sale of goods contract, a term which states the price), almost any term is subject to this possibility. An important feature of this piece of legislation is that it gives the Director General of Fair Trading the duty to consider complaints about unfair terms and the power to bring court proceedings seeking an order or injunction to prevent a trader from using unfair terms (see, for example, *Director General of Fair Trading v First National Bank* (2000)). These Regulations apply, of course, only to contracts between a business and a consumer – the typical example where there is a substantial imbalance of bargaining power between the parties.

In 2002, the Law Commission published a Consultation Paper in which it proposed that the two pieces of legislation referred to above (the Unfair Contract Terms Act 1977 and the Unfair Terms in Consumer Contracts Regulations 1999) be: (a) combined; and (b) re-written to make the language more accessible and user-friendly. The Consultation Paper also proposed, however, that the latter Regulations be extended to apply not only to business-to-consumer contracts but also to business-to-business contracts. That would mean that in a business-to-business contract, it would not just be exclusion or limitation of liability clauses which would be challengeable under the legislation. Any standard term (other than a core term) in a business-to-business contract would be open to challenge as being unfair/unreasonable. Arguably, this is necessary since, even in business-to-business contracts, there is no guarantee that there is a level playing field. There can, in such a contract, be a great disparity between the bargaining power of the two parties. The proposal would involve a further inroad into the freedom of contract principle, but this may be necessary in order to redress an imbalance in bargaining power.

To sum up: the freedom of contract principle is, and is likely to remain, largely intact except for those instances where legislation proves necessary in order to protect a weaker party (often a private consumer) from the abuse of power that that principle would otherwise allow to the stronger party.

Privity of contract

This is still a central element of sale of goods law. Thus, the implied terms which create strict liability generally apply only as between seller and buyer. This has two effects. First, a buyer (let us call him Harry) who has bought, say, a defective car which is not of satisfactory quality can in general sue only his seller for breach of the implied term as to satisfactory quality. Although his seller can then sue the person from whom he bought the car, Harry cannot take the shortcut of himself suing someone further up the distribution chain. This could leave Harry without a remedy in the situation where his seller has become bankrupt. There is, however, one important inroad into this principle of privity of contract which could assist Harry if he had used credit to purchase the car. This can be found in s 75 of the Consumer Credit Act 1974 which would allow a buyer to bring the claim for the seller's breach of contract (or misrepresentation) against the creditor. This is a section which can apply where the creditor is someone different from the seller, where the credit agreement was a regulated debtor-creditor-supplier agreement within the meaning of the Consumer Credit Act and where the cash price of the item exceeded £100 and did not exceed £30,000.

The second effect of the doctrine of privity is that only a party to the contract can sue on it. So, if Harry and his wife are both injured because the car is not of satisfactory quality, his wife will not (unless she was a joint purchaser) be able to seek a remedy by relying upon the implied (or express) terms in Harry's contract. There is now an important exception to this second effect of the doctrine. Thus, a third party can now enforce a contract where the third party is able to rely on the Contracts (Rights of Third Parties) Act 1999. This enables a third party to enforce a term of a contract if either: (a) the contract expressly provides that he may; or (b) the term purports to confer a benefit upon the third party. To be able to enjoy this right, the third party must be expressly identified in the contract by name or as a member of a class or as answering a particular description. This statute is too recent to have generated any case law, but its effect is clearly very limited and does not extend to anyone who is neither expressly given a right in the contract nor purported to be given a benefit by the contract. Harry's wife is unlikely to be able to rely upon it unless, perhaps, the contract expressly referred to the fact that Harry was buying it as a present for his wife. Even that may not be sufficient, for it is arguable that even then the contract does not purport itself to confer a benefit on Harry's wife, but rather to put Harry in a position where he can confer a benefit upon her by making a gift to her.

There is now, however, a different way – that is, outside the law of contract – where a buyer (or indeed a consumer who, like Harry's wife, was not a buyer) may be able to have a remedy against someone for damage caused by defective goods. This is by relying on Pt I of the Consumer Protection Act 1987. This introduces a regime of strict liability into the law of tort to enable a claim to be brought against the manufacturer (or importer into the European Union). This is not so much an inroad into the doctrine of privity of contract as the provision of a way round it. The consumer brings the claim outside contract altogether. This is not, however, a complete solution to the problems presented to consumers by the doctrine, because although the 1987 Act allows an action for damage caused by the defective product, it does not allow a claim to be brought in respect of damage to that product or in respect of the fact that the product is worth less than it should be; to put it another way, the 1987 Act does not provide for a claim in respect of loss of bargain. A buyer of a defective product which has caused no damage is left with only the possibility of a claim against the seller or (if the purchase was financed by the relevant kind of consumer credit agreement) against the creditor under s 75 of the Consumer Credit Act. The only way round that restriction at present is if someone else, for example, the manufacturer, has given a guarantee which could then be relied upon. Any doubts about the enforceability of such guarantees (for example, on grounds of lack of privity of contract) will be removed once the Sale and Supply of Goods Regulations 2002 come into force on 31 March 2003. These regulations implement the 1999 European Directive on Consumer Guarantees. They also, in reg 16, make the seller liable to the consumer in respect of a guarantee given by the manufacturer (or any other third party, such as an importer or distributor).

Caveat emptor

The notion 'buyer beware' is to some extent tied up with the earlier two concepts already discussed. The freedom of contract principle means that the buyer can, if he can make the seller agree, have all sorts of protections and guarantees built in as express terms of the contract. Of course, the reality is that this seldom happens and that therefore the buyer receives only such legal protection as is automatically built into the contract. This amounts to the following: the ability to rely upon any misrepresentation which was one of the causes that induced him to make the contract; the ability to rely upon any express term of the contract (for example, as to the date of delivery); the ability to rely upon the terms implied into the contract by ss 12–15. The latter include the terms as to satisfactory quality and fitness for purpose, which constitute the buyer's principal legal protection as to the quality of the goods he is buying, and which are implied only where the seller is selling in the course of a business. Thus, the notion 'buyer beware' is particularly strong where the buyer buys from his neighbour, or at the church fête, or as a result of replying to a small advertisement in the newspaper, or in some other way from someone who is not selling in the course of a business.

The buyer's ability to rely upon any misrepresentation, express term or implied term of the contract is backed up by the provisions in the Unfair Contract Terms Act and the Unfair Terms in Consumer Contracts Regulations, discussed above. As we saw, the consumer/buyer is guaranteed the benefit of the implied terms and, so far as liability for misrepresentation or breach of an express term is concerned, any exclusion clause will need to satisfy the requirement of reasonableness. Thus, so far as the consumer/buyer is concerned, there is quite a degree of protection. It is fair, however, to say that the buyer does need to 'beware' in some sense. He really needs to ask questions and also to let the seller know for what purpose(s) he wants the goods. This is because the seller is liable for any misrepresentation, but this does not extend to making him liable for not making a statement and, turning to s 14 of the Sale of Goods Act, there can be no liability for the goods not being reasonably fit for a particular purpose if the buyer has not made known to the seller what that purpose was.

It also should be pointed out that the consumer's legal protection is no longer confined to the contractual liability of the seller. As we have seen, there can be strict liability under the Consumer Protection Act 1987 for damage caused by defective goods – although, as observed, there is no liability under that provision for loss of bargain.

In conclusion, the notion *caveat emptor* still applies so that the wise buyer still asks questions, makes tests and makes known why he wants the goods. The notion is less strong in the case of a consumer/buyer. The privity of contract doctrine has been relaxed for consumers (or made circumventable) in certain circumstances (see s 75 of the Consumer Credit Act and the provisions of the Consumer Protection Act). Also, the Contracts (Rights of Third Parties) Act 1999 has created an exception for the third party upon whom the contract purports to confer a benefit. The principle of freedom of contract is still intact, but is subject to some exceptions (see the Unfair Contract Terms Act 1977 and the Unfair Terms in Consumer Contracts Regulations 1999). The common theme is that these three notions, each derived from a body of commercial law developed largely to regulate the position between merchants, have had to be qualified to some extent in order to achieve justice for consumers.

CHAPTER 2

DESCRIPTION AND QUALITY

Introduction

The questions in this chapter relate to the statutory implied terms as to description, quality and fitness for purpose, to exclusion clauses and also to product liability. In some courses, the law of trade descriptions is dealt with in questions which also raise contractual issues (for example, under s 13 of the Sale of Goods Act 1979). This has not been done in this book because a number of sale of goods courses do not include trade descriptions in their syllabuses. There is, instead, a discrete question here on trade descriptions.

Checklist

The following topics should be prepared in advance of tackling the questions:

- the statutory implied terms in ss 13 and 14 of the Sale of Goods Act 1979;
- the same terms implied by the Supply of Goods and Services Act 1982;
- terms as to the provision of services implied by the Supply of Goods and Services Act 1982;
- rules in s 30 of the Sale of Goods Act 1979 as to delivery of the wrong quantity;
- remedies for breach of the implied terms;
- acceptance within the meaning of ss 35 and 35A of the Sale of Goods Act 1979;
- collateral contracts;
- product liability under Pt I of the Consumer Protection Act 1987;
- the law on exclusion clauses – in particular, the provisions of the Unfair Contract Terms Act 1977;
- misrepresentation;
- trade descriptions.

Question 3

Pomp Ltd is a British manufacturer of Pomp electrical switches. It supplies them to, among others, Cleopatra Cie, an Egyptian company which makes Cleo refrigerators in Cairo. These refrigerators are imported into Britain by Needle plc and supplied to the retail market through a distribution system. A year ago, Joan bought a Cleo refrigerator for £250 from Harry's electrical shop in London. Yesterday, the Pomp switch in the refrigerator smouldered and set fire to the refrigerator. Joan was badly burnt in putting out the fire, but managed to limit the damage so that, apart from her burns, the only damage done was that the refrigerator was a write-off and Joan's kitchen carpet (worth £250) was burnt and has had to be replaced.

Advise Joan, bearing in mind that Harry's shop has stopped trading since Harry became bankrupt last week.

How, if at all, would it affect your advice if the Pomp switch which caused the fire was a replacement one supplied and fitted three months ago by Harry's electrical shop after Joan had complained about the refrigerator not switching on at a sufficiently low temperature?

Answer plan

This question demands a discussion of product liability. A claim by Joan under the Sale of Goods Act 1979 is clearly ruled out by the statement that Harry has become bankrupt, but this must be stated in your answer. That leaves the answer to deal with two possible grounds of liability, at common law for negligence and for product liability under the Consumer Protection Act 1987. Some, maybe many, commercial law (or consumer law) courses are taken by students after they have taken basic subjects such as tort. It is therefore not always easy to know how much basic tort law, such as negligence, to include in an answer. In a question such as this, as a priority, make sure that you deal fully with the issues raised under the statute and also ensure that you do cover in some way the negligence issues. It is a matter to some extent of your own judgment as to how much space you can afford to give the negligence issues.

Most commercial law courses will not specifically include coverage of conflict of laws issues; thus, in this answer, those problems in relation to Cleopatra Cie are no more than hinted at.

Answer

The claim which Joan may very well have for breach of express or implied terms in her sale of goods contract with Harry is clearly not going to yield much if anything for her, since Harry is bankrupt. Nor can Joan bring that claim against the manufacturer or importer or anyone else earlier in the distribution chain, since there is no privity of contract between her and any of them. Thus, any claim against one of the other parties will have to be a claim in negligence under the principle in *Donoghue v Stevenson* (1932) or a product liability claim under Pt I of the Consumer Protection Act 1987.

Negligence

Joan has a claim in negligence against anyone in respect of whom she can establish three things: (1) that that person owed her a duty of care; (2) that that person (or one of his employees in the course of his employment) failed to take reasonable care; and (3) that that failure to take care caused her damage which was of a foreseeable type occurring in a generally foreseeable sort of way. Given that the source of the damage was an apparently defective electrical switch, it is unlikely that those three elements could be shown except in relation to Pomp Ltd which manufactured it, or possibly Cleopatra Cie which incorporated it into one of its machines. The principal difficulty in the case of Pomp Ltd would be proving a failure to take reasonable care, since clearly Pomp Ltd owed a duty to the ultimate consumer to take care in the design (or in its adoption) and manufacture of the switch. Whether reliance on the doctrine of *res ipsa loquitur* would help Joan prove negligence would depend very much on what evidence of care and systems is put forward by Pomp Ltd. So far as Cleopatra Cie is concerned, there is no doubt in English law that a duty of care in the manufacture of machines was owed to the ultimate consumer, and little doubt that this extends to taking reasonable care to ensure that only safe components are used. The difficulties with a claim in negligence against Cleopatra Cie are: (1) getting an English court to take jurisdiction; (2) proving that the duty just outlined was broken, that is, that Cleopatra Cie failed to take reasonable care; and (3) the fact that, even if the claim were successful, damages would be recoverable only for Joan's burns and the damage to the carpet. Damages would not be recoverable in respect of the loss of the refrigerator itself, just as damages would not have been recoverable by Mrs Donoghue for the value of the ginger beer, this loss being an unrecoverable economic loss (*Murphy v Brentwood* (1990)). Thus, so far as negligence is concerned, Joan's best bet is a claim against Pomp Ltd, in which case, Joan will face the difficulty of proving a failure to take reasonable care. In the event of such a claim succeeding against Pomp Ltd, it is debatable whether the damages would include compensation for the loss of the refrigerator. On the one hand, that is damage caused 'by' and not 'to' the item (the switch) manufactured and put into circulation by Pomp Ltd. On the other, the switch was clearly designed to be incorporated into and subsequently supplied as a component of another item.

Product liability

Joan's best claim may well be one in respect of a defective product under Pt I of the Consumer Protection Act 1987. She has, it seems, been the victim of two defective products, a switch and a refrigerator. They almost certainly were defective, that is, not as safe as persons generally are entitled to expect (s 3). Liability is strict and therefore negligence does not have to be proved. Nothing given in the problem suggests that any of the defences in s 4 will apply, unless perhaps the damage was entirely attributable to something in the refrigerator design, as opposed to something in the switch. In that case, there would be no liability under Pt I in respect of the switch, but only in respect of the refrigerator (s 4(1)(f)).

In the problem, there is no one who is an 'own brander'. So, the persons potentially liable (see s 2) are the manufacturers, that is, Pomp Ltd and Cleopatra Cie, and the importer into the European Community, Needle plc. The problem does not precisely state that Needle plc imported the refrigerators direct into Britain from Egypt. If, in fact, someone else imported them from Egypt into another country of the European Community, for example, France, and Needle plc only imported the goods from France into Britain, then Needle plc would not be liable. Instead, liability could be fixed on whoever imported them into France. It will now, however, be assumed that Needle plc did import them from Egypt directly into Britain.

Pomp Ltd as producer can be held liable in respect of the defective switch, and Cleopatra Cie as producer can be held liable in respect of the defective refrigerator. Needle plc as the importer can be held liable in respect of both. Given the possible difficulties of proceeding against a foreign company, with maybe no presence in Britain or even in the European Community, it may make sense therefore for Joan to contemplate claims only against Pomp Ltd and Needle plc. These claims would certainly include a claim in respect of Joan's personal injuries, that is, her burns. So far as property damage is concerned, no claim can succeed unless the property damage claimable amounts to more than £275 (s 5(4)). This means that Joan's claim can succeed only if she is able to claim for both the loss of the refrigerator (£250) and the damage to the carpet (£250). If she is able to claim both, then she is entitled to recover the whole of the £500, that is, including the first £275. There is nothing (apart from the need to exceed £275 in total property claims) to rule out her claiming for the carpet, which is clearly property for private, as opposed to business, use. However, Joan cannot claim for the damage to the refrigerator. So far as the claim (against Needle plc) in respect of the defective refrigerator is concerned, the damage to the refrigerator is unrecoverable (s 5(2)). It can be observed that although Pt I of the Consumer Protection Act talks about liability for defective products, it defines 'defective' in terms of safety and thus, in truth, creates liability for *dangerous* products. It creates a liability for damage caused by them, but not for damage caused to themselves. The position is exactly the same when one considers the claim against Pomp Ltd (and also Needle plc) in respect of the defective switch. Any argument that the damage caused by the defective product (here, the switch) to other things includes the damage to the refrigerator is ruled out completely by s 5(2). This sub-section prevents recovery of damage for loss or damage to any product (here, the refrigerator) which has been supplied with the defective product (here, the switch) comprised within it. Thus, the damage to the refrigerator is not recoverable and thus it follows that the damage to the carpet is also ruled out because it does not exceed £275 in value.

In conclusion, therefore, it appears that in respect of her burns, Joan has a good claim under Pt I of the Consumer Protection Act 1987 against Pomp Ltd and Needle plc. The claim against Needle plc may be a little more secure in that, even if Pomp Ltd were able to show (under s 4(1)(f)) that the defect was not in the switch but in the unsuitability of the refrigerator for the particular switch, Needle plc would be still be liable as the importer into the European Community of the defective refrigerator. It seems, however, that any claim in respect of the carpet would have to be brought in negligence.

Contributory negligence

It is possible, if unlikely, that in trying to put out the fire, Joan was herself negligent. It is unlikely since instinctive reactions in the heat (literally perhaps) of the moment are not normally regarded as amounting to contributory negligence (*Jones v Boyce* (1816)). If she were contributorily negligent, then her damages for her burns, whether under the common law of negligence or under the Consumer Protection Act (see s 6(4)) would be reduced proportionately. It does not follow, however, that any damages (that is, assuming they are recoverable) for the damage to the carpet or refrigerator would also be reduced, since although it is very likely that any negligence of Joan in choosing to fight the fire may have been one of the causes of her being burnt, it is unlikely that that negligence caused the damage to the refrigerator and the carpet. Indeed, her fighting the fire, far from being a cause of property damage, almost certainly prevented more occurring.

The rider

There are two possibilities. The first is that the switch was defective. The second is that the refrigerator was defective, a defect wholly attributable to its design, making it unsuitable for a switch which presumably was listed as one of its replacement parts. If the second possibility is the reality, then Pomp Ltd will not be liable, but the advice given above as to the liability of Needle plc for product liability will remain unaltered. It seems more likely that the first possibility is the reality. In that case, Pomp Ltd will remain liable for product liability, but Needle plc will not be liable at all, since presumably Needle plc did not import into the European Community the replacement switch which Joan fitted and which caused the damage. Furthermore, Pomp Ltd's liability can now include liability for the loss of the refrigerator, since Joan's refrigerator was not supplied to her with that switch comprised within it. This means that Pomp Ltd's liability under the 1987 Act will include liability for the refrigerator and the carpet, the two together amounting to property damage exceeding £275.

Question 4

Consultants plc recently bought two used cars, each six months old, for its executives to drive. Conrad, managing director of Consultants plc, first saw the two cars at Daley's Garage a month ago when he noticed that one, a Roadster, had an engine oil leak and the other, a Speedster, had a water leak in the boot. He did not, however, look in the boot of the Roadster. Daley assured him: 'They are good little buses; you can rely upon them.' After test driving both cars, Conrad, on behalf of Consultants plc, signed two contracts of purchase, one for each car. Conrad left the Roadster with Daley to have the oil leak repaired and drove away in the Speedster. Two weeks later, he returned the Speedster for its boot leak to be repaired and collected the Roadster. The next day, he discovered: first, that the Roadster had a water leak in its boot; secondly, that the engine oil leak had not been repaired and was irreparable (meaning that a new engine was necessary); and, thirdly, that soon after delivery to its first buyer, the Speedster had been in an accident and subsequently treated by its owner's insurance company as a 'write-off'. Upon learning these facts, Conrad informed Daley's Garage that he was rejecting the cars and he demanded the return of the purchase price to Consultants plc.

Advise Consultants plc.

Answer plan

This question follows a certain style of setting questions, which involves a lot of points being included. The question is testing your ability to spot each of the issues raised as well as your ability to deal with them. Thus, a good answer must acknowledge each of the points raised and must not concentrate on some of the issues to the exclusion of the others.

The issues raised in this question are:

- liability for breach of the conditions as to satisfactory quality and fitness for purpose;
- liability (for an express term and/or misrepresentation) arising out of the statement about the cars being 'good little buses', etc;
- the remedies available to the buyer and, in particular, whether there has been acceptance of the goods so as to preclude rejection.

A sensible order of treatment is: implied conditions in s 14; express term/misrepresentation; remedies.

Answer

This question raises issues of liability for express and implied terms of the contract, for misrepresentation and the extent of any remedies available to Consultants plc. There may be liability in respect of the implied conditions as to satisfactory quality and fitness for purpose, liability for breach of an express term that the cars were 'good little buses', and liability for misrepresentation arising out of the same assertion by Daley. These possible liabilities will be considered, as will the remedies which may be available to Consultants plc. It is to be observed that a separate contract was signed in relation to each car and, therefore, presumably the parties intended two distinct contracts. This answer will proceed upon that assumption. Consultants plc was not a 'consumer' as defined in the Sale and Supply of Goods Regulations, which implement (as from 31 March 2003) the European Directive on Consumer Guarantees. Thus, the new rights as to repair and replacement do not fall to be discussed in this answer.

Satisfactory quality

This condition, in s 14(2) of the Sale of Goods Act 1979, is not implied as regards any defect specifically drawn to the buyer's attention before the contract was made or, given that Conrad made a pre-purchase examination of the cars, as regards any defect which 'that' examination ought to have revealed. The engine oil leak in the Roadster and water leak in the boot of the

Speedster both appear to be defects falling into one or both of these categories, most clearly the latter category, since we are told that Conrad noticed them. Assuming the water leak in the Speedster can be repaired, it seems clear that in respect of that leak, no reliance can be placed by Consultants plc upon s 14(2). The engine oil leak of the Roadster has turned out, however, to be irreparable without a complete engine replacement. This suggests that the true nature and/or extent of the defect was not something which was either drawn to Conrad's attention or which ought to have been revealed by his pre-contract examination of the car. Neil LJ in *R and B Customs Brokers v United Dominions Trust* (1988) indicated, *obiter*, that a defect which the buyer is aware of, but which he reasonably (and mistakenly) believes will be rectified at no cost to himself is not excluded from the effect of s 14(2). It seems therefore that Consultants plc can rely upon the condition in s 14(2) as regards the engine oil leak in the Roadster. The condition as to satisfactory quality might also apply to the water leak in the boot of the Roadster and to the fact that the Speedster had been an insurance 'write-off'. The first of these *might* be a defect which Conrad's pre-purchase inspection *ought* to have revealed. It seems clear that that inspection did not in fact reveal it because Conrad did not in the course of that inspection look into the boot of the Roadster. In *Thornett and Fehr v Beers* (1919), it was held that a buyer who had, before the purchase, inspected the outside of some barrels but not the inside was precluded from relying on the condition as to merchantable (now, satisfactory) quality as regards defects which would have been revealed if he had inspected the inside. It is submitted, however, that a minor change to the wording of s 14(2) effected in 1973 (to the then Sale of Goods Act 1893), namely, the change from 'such examination' to 'that examination' has reversed the effect of the 1919 case. Thus, Consultants plc is precluded from relying on those defects which ought to have been revealed by the examination which Conrad actually made, but is not prejudiced by him having made a less extensive examination than he might have made. Put another way, the leak in the Roadster's boot was not a defect which ought to have been revealed by the examination which Conrad actually made.

So, do the engine oil leak and boot leak in the Roadster make the car of unsatisfactory quality and does the fact that the Speedster was an insurance 'write-off' make the Speedster of unsatisfactory quality? When, in 1994, the expression 'merchantable quality' was replaced by 'satisfactory quality', the definition of that expression was also revised. Section 14(2A) now requires us to ask in each case whether the car reached a standard that the ordinary person would regard as satisfactory, taking account of any description given to the goods, the price and any other relevant circumstances. Undoubtedly, one of the relevant circumstances is the fact that in each case, the car was not new but was six months old. Section 14(2B) lists a number of aspects of the quality of the goods, including their 'fitness for all the purposes for which goods of the kind in question are commonly supplied'. This is, however, so close to the former definition of 'merchantable quality' that a number of earlier decisions are clearly still relevant in applying the statutory definition (of satisfactory quality) to motor vehicles. Thus, the purposes for which a car is bought include not merely the purpose of driving it from place to place, but of doing so with the appropriate degree of comfort, ease of handling and pride in its outward and interior appearance (*Rogers v Parish* (1987)). This general approach applies also to secondhand cars and the question is whether, in this case, the defects were sufficiently serious to render even these secondhand cars of less than satisfactory quality. A secondhand car which, unknown to the buyer at the time of the contract, had been an insurance 'write-off' has been held for that reason not to have reached the necessary standard (*Shine v General Guarantee Corp* (1988)). The two leaks in the Roadster are less easy to decide upon. On the one hand, one is to expect minor defects in a secondhand car (*Bartlett v Sydney Marcus* (1965)). On the other hand, it could be said that the oil leak which requires a new engine for it to be remedied is actually a major defect. As regards the newly discovered water leak in the Roadster, much will depend upon its extent and the ease with which it can be repaired. Therefore, it is submitted that in the case of both cars, Consultants plc has a valid claim under s 14(2), but whether that extends to the boot leak in the case of the Roadster will depend upon the seriousness of the latter.

Fitness for purpose

Consultants plc's claim in respect of the defects discussed above might equally be made under s 14(3). Conrad told Daley of a particular purpose for which Consultants plc wanted the cars, namely, the purpose of being driven by the company's executives. The defects already being relied upon under s 14(2) render the cars not reasonably fit for that purpose. Consultants plc may have no claim under s 14(3) in respect of defects of which it was aware (for example, the Speedster's leaky boot) if Consultants plc placed no reliance upon Daley's skill and judgment in respect of them. It will still have a claim in relation to the other defect (*Cammell Laird v Manganese Bronze and Brass* (1934)).

'Good little buses'

Daley's assertion that the cars were 'good little buses' arguably implied that the cars were in good condition (*Andrews v Hopkinson* (1957)). This may have amounted to: (1) an express term, either a condition or a warranty, of the contract; and (2) a misrepresentation.

Assuming it was an express term of the contract, it is submitted that that express term was broken in the case of the Roadster by virtue of its engine oil leak necessitating a new engine. Whether the same can be said of water leaks in the boots is more problematic. Much will depend upon the seriousness of those leaks and the ease with which they can be repaired.

A claim for misrepresentation can succeed only if Conrad relied upon Daley's statement. Did his pre-purchase examination of the cars indicate a lack of such reliance? Presumably not, because the statement appears to have been made *after* those examinations. Did Conrad's subsequently going for test drives indicate that he was not relying on Daley's statement? It seems not, since Daley's statement referred to the cars' reliability (that is, presumably, over a period of time) and one or two test drives could not disclose the truth or otherwise of that. It is not necessary for Consultants plc to have relied exclusively upon Daley's statement.

An untrue statement of fact by Daley which was one of the causes of Consultants plc deciding to buy will give Consultants plc a right to rescind the contract. If, however, Consultants plc wishes to claim damages for a misrepresentation, it may do so, either as an alternative to rescission (when the issue of whether to award damages is at the discretion of the judge – s 2(2) of the Misrepresentation Act 1967) or as an independent claim for damages under s 2(1). In the latter case, Daley will have a defence if he can show, on a balance of probabilities, that at the time of the contract he had reasonable grounds to believe, and did believe, the statement to be true (s 2(1) of the Misrepresentation Act 1967).

Remedies

Remedies for misrepresentation have just been discussed. For any breach of contract, there is a right to claim damages. Consultants plc has also purported to reject the cars and required the return of the price for each. Assuming that there was breach of the implied term in either s 14(2) or s 14(3), Consultants plc undoubtedly had a right of rejection, since both of those terms are implied *conditions*. The same is not necessarily true of the express term encompassed by the words 'They are good little buses; you can rely upon them'. Assuming that this amounted to an express term of the contract, it would have to be decided if the parties intended it to be a condition, that is, a term any breach of which would give Consultants plc the right to reject the goods and regard the contract as repudiated. The tendency of the courts is not to regard as a condition any express term (other than one as to the time of delivery), unless the parties have very clearly indicated it

(*Cehave v Bremer, The Hansa Nord* (1976)). Thus, the test of whether Consultants plc had any right of rejection/repudiation for breach of the express term depends upon whether the breach was sufficient to deprive Consultants plc of substantially the whole of the benefit of the contract (*Hong Kong Fir v Kawasaki Kisen* (1962)). It is submitted that neither the boot leak in the case of one car nor the boot leak and the engine oil leak in the case of the other was sufficiently serious.

Assume that Consultants plc was, because of the breach of the conditions in s 14, within its rights in rejecting the cars and demanding the return of the price. It will nevertheless have lost that right if, by the time it rejected the cars, it had already 'accepted' them within the meaning of s 35. Consultants plc rejected the Speedster just over two weeks after taking delivery. After a similar period of time, the buyer in *Bernstein v Pamson Motors* (1987) was held to have accepted the car. Even under the law as it then stood, that decision was controversial. Since then, however, s 35 has been amended so that, in determining what is a reasonable length of time, it is relevant to ask whether the buyer has had a reasonable opportunity to examine the goods for the purpose of ascertaining whether they comply with the contract. It is thus arguable that Consultants plc had not, in just over two weeks, had the Speedster long enough to have examined it for that purpose. If it had not, then it was entitled to act as it did in rejecting it. Similarly, Consultants plc arguably had not had the car long enough that it could be said to have affirmed the contract – and thus was entitled to rescind the contract (and reject the car) for misrepresentation.

Whatever may be a reasonable period of time for the buyer to examine the goods to see if they conform to the contract, there may be added to that period of time a further reasonable period. This may, for example, be a period during which the buyer investigates any apparent non-compliance (*Truk v Tokmakidis* (2000)) or a period during which the seller repairs the goods under an arrangement with the buyer (s 35(5)). So, Consultants plc clearly had not lost its right to reject the Roadster. Indeed, Consultants had taken delivery of the Roadster only one day before rejecting it.

Consequently, Consultants plc is entitled to the return of the Roadster's purchase price. It might also claim damages, although these are unlikely to be substantial in the case of the Roadster. In the case of the Speedster, if Consultants plc is held to have lost its right to reject the car, the damages would be more substantial. Assuming that the breach in relation to the Speedster was due to the fact that it had been an insurance 'write-off', the amount of damages would be the difference between the market value the car would have had if it had not got that particular history and the lower value it currently has.

Question 5

Suppose that in Question 4 above, the contracts between Consultants plc and Daley had each included a clause stating: 'All conditions relating to the quality or condition of any vehicle are hereby excluded except as regards any defects brought to the attention of the seller within seven days of delivery. The seller accepts no liability in respect of any statements made prior to the contract unless such statements have been put in writing. For a fixed amount equivalent to 5% of the purchase price of the vehicle, a guarantee is available to all purchasers of new and secondhand vehicles.'

Assuming that Consultants plc did not take advantage of the opportunity to take up the guarantee, advise Consultants plc as to the validity and effectiveness of such a clause.

Answer plan

Occasionally, examiners ask a question which refers back or forward to another question in the same paper. This, of course, saves the examiners from having to dream up a separate factual scenario. From your point of view, it means that, in reading through the paper and deciding which questions to tackle, you have to grasp only one factual scenario in order to see what two different questions are asking. You are of course not necessarily required to answer both the questions. In answering this one, which refers to the facts set out in Question 4, you must also use the facts of the scenario as painted in Question 4 – for example, the fact that in Question 4, Consultants plc rejected the Roadster in less than seven days (in fact, within two days) of taking delivery.

This question focuses on one thing, an exclusion clause. The method of dealing with it is, after quickly acknowledging that it was incorporated into the contract, to deal with the interpretation of the clause and then the effect of the Unfair Contract Terms Act 1977 and of the Unfair Terms in Consumer Contracts Regulations 1999.

Answer

Like any exclusion clause, the clause in this case will not have any effect unless it satisfies each of the following requirements:

- it was incorporated into the contract;

- as a matter of interpretation, the wording of the clause is effective to exclude liability which otherwise the seller would incur;
- the clause is not rendered invalid by either the Unfair Contract Terms Act 1977 or the Unfair Terms in Consumer Contracts Regulations 1999.

Clearly, in the present case, the first of these requirements is satisfied.

Interpretation of the clause

As regards the second requirement, the first half of the clause would clearly exclude liability for breach of the implied condition as to satisfactory quality in s 14 of the Sale of Goods Act 1979. The words of the clause are clear and there is no longer any presumption (at common law) that the clear words of a clause are not to be given effect, and that is so even if they clearly purport to exclude what used to be referred to as a fundamental breach of contract (*Photo Productions v Securicor Transport* (1980)). Does it also exclude liability for the condition of fitness of purpose? The *contra proferentem* rule of construction which the courts use in construing exclusion clauses requires that, where a clause is truly ambiguous, the meaning which gives the clause the lesser effect is adopted. This is the rule as applied over the years in such cases as *Wallis and Wells v Pratt and Haynes* (1911) and *Andrews v Singer* (1934). Nothing in the *Photo Productions* case does away with the *contra proferentem* rule in cases of true ambiguity. Referring to the wording of the clause, the condition as to fitness is excluded if it relates to the 'quality or condition' of a vehicle. Clearly, on the facts of the problem given, it is the quality which is in issue and, undoubtedly, the quality of a car can affect its fitness for a particular purpose. However, the fitness for purpose condition implied by s 14(3) is not confined to matters of quality or condition. A car can be of excellent quality and in excellent condition and still not be fit for a particular purpose for which the buyer has indicated he wants it. For example, a buyer may have stated that he wants a car fit for carrying exceptionally heavy loads in the boot. If the clause in issue here were held to exclude the condition as to fitness for purpose, it would rule it out in the latter example as well as where the unfitness is caused by defects in quality or condition. Applying the *contra proferentem* rule, therefore, it seems likely that a court would hold that the fitness for purpose condition was not excluded.

It appears then that the first sentence of the clause, as a matter of interpretation, does exclude liability for breach of the condition as to satisfactory quality, but may well not do so as regards the condition of fitness for purpose. However, even in relation to the former, the liability is excluded only as regards defects not brought to Daley's attention within seven days of delivery. Thus, it appears that in relation to the Roadster car, even liability for breach of the satisfactory quality condition is not excluded, since it was only one day after taking delivery of the Roadster that Conrad rejected the cars.

Let us turn to the matter of Daley's possible liability in respect of the pre-contract statement about the cars being 'good little buses'. The latter part of the clause would appear to exclude that liability, since there is no indication that Daley's statement was put into writing. There are, however, a couple of arguments which might prevent such a conclusion. First, it is possible that Daley's words might give rise to liability not just for a misrepresentation, but also for breach of an express term of the contract (*Andrews v Hopkinson* (1957)). It might be argued that the clause was intended to exclude liability for the former but not for the latter. The clause refers to statements made 'prior to the contract'. It does not refer to statements which are part of the contract itself, which an express term – even one not reduced to writing – would undoubtedly be. The point is clearly an arguable one, since it could alternatively be said that the intention of the clause is to exclude all liability in respect of pre-contract statements, including terms of the contract itself, unless those terms are in writing.

Unfair Contract Terms Act 1977

Assuming that the clause is effective at common law to exclude at least some possible liabilities, is it robbed of that effect by the Unfair Contract Terms Act (UCTA) 1977? This Act applies differently to different heads of liability. Section 6 deals with the clause insofar as it purports to exclude liability for breach of the implied conditions in s 14 of the Sale of Goods Act 1979. If Consultants plc dealt as a consumer in buying the cars, neither of those implied terms can be excluded. Did Consultants plc deal as a consumer? It seems that all the requirements (set out in s 12 of UCTA 1977) for an affirmative answer are satisfied except possibly one, namely, that Consultants plc did not make the contract in the course of a business. It may appear that since the cars were wanted for the company's executives to drive, the purchase must have been in the course of Consultants plc's business. If, as seems likely, Consultants plc were not car dealers, the purchases would seem to have been incidental to whatever Consultants plc's business was. In *R and B Customs Brokers v UDT* (1988), it was held that a purchase which is incidental to the buyer's business is not made 'in the course of a business' unless the buyer regularly makes that sort of purchase. In that case, the Court of Appeal followed the reasoning of the House of Lords in *Davies v Sumner* (1984), a case dealing with a similar phrase in a statute imposing criminal liability. The decision in *R and B Customs Brokers v UDT* to apply that reasoning in interpreting a statute concerned with civil liability is now highly questionable in the light of *Stephenson v Rogers* (1999), where the Court of

Appeal rejected that approach in interpreting the same phrase ('in the course of a business') in s 14 of the Sale of Goods Act 1979. It thus seems very likely that, if the matter were to be litigated, the court today would therefore decide that Consultants plc bought the cars in the course of a business and did not deal as a consumer – and that is so irrespective of whether it had any previous practice of buying cars.

If Consultants plc did not deal as a consumer in buying the cars, the exclusion clause will be held not to exclude liability for the implied terms as to satisfactory quality or fitness for purpose except insofar as Daley is able to show that the clause satisfies the requirement of reasonableness set out in s 11 of UCTA, to which the guidelines in Sched 2 to UCTA are relevant. One particular matter from those guidelines would seem to be relevant, namely, the opportunity to take out the guarantee, since the guidelines require consideration to be given to any alternative means where the customer's requirements could have been met. That would require a consideration, of course, of whether the charge of 5% of the purchase price was prohibitive so as to put off customers taking the guarantee, and a consideration also of the extent of the cover which the guarantee offered. Would it, for example, cover not only remediable defects, but also circumstances such as that one of the cars had previously been treated as an insurance 'write-off'? If not, then the guarantee would hardly have been an adequate means of Consultants plc covering itself. A further matter relevant from the guidelines is the condition attached to the first sentence of the clause. Was it likely to be practicable for Consultants plc to bring any defects to Daley's attention within seven days? It is submitted that it was not. It is true that after a relatively short time the buyer is taken to have accepted the goods and thereby loses his right to reject them. However, the clause would also remove the right to damages in the case of defects not notified within the seven days. In a different context, a notification period of three days was held to be an unreasonable condition in *Green v Cade* (1978). Seven days seems little better.

Let us turn to the effect of UCTA on the clause insofar as it purports to exclude liability for misrepresentation and possibly for breach of unwritten express terms of the contract. The clause is again subject to the requirement of reasonableness. This is provided for by s 8 of UCTA (amending s 3 of the Misrepresentation Act 1967) in the case of misrepresentation and by s 3 of UCTA in respect of the exclusion of breach of an express term of the contract. The latter section will apply, since it appears that the clause in question is one of Daley's standard terms, being identical in both contracts. The requirement of reasonableness is the same as it was in the case of the purported exclusion of the implied terms as to satisfactory quality and fitness for purpose. Technically, neither s 3 nor s 8 of UCTA refers to the guidelines in Sched 2. However, there is little doubt that similar considerations will be applied and, in one sense, the second sentence of the clause is more draconian than the first because it does not even allow liability for defects notified within seven days. The court is very likely to consider the clause as a whole in deciding whether it satisfies the requirement of reasonableness.

In any case where that requirement is under consideration, account needs to be taken of the factor, highlighted in the cases, that a clause which does not merely limit liability but purports totally to exclude it is much less likely to satisfy the requirement of reasonableness (compare *Mitchell v Finney Lock Seeds* (1983) and *Ailsa Craig Fishing v Malvern Fishing* (1983)). It has already been said that perhaps the clause in Consultants plc's case will, on its wording, be held not to exclude liability for the condition as to fitness for purpose or for breach of an express term of the contract. Even so, in relation to those liabilities which it does purport to exclude, its exclusion of liability is complete. This fact strengthens the argument that the clause fails to satisfy the requirement of reasonableness.

Unfair Terms in Consumer Contracts Regulations 1999

These Regulations are capable of rendering an exclusion clause of no effect. However, they have no application to the contracts in this case, because, in making the contracts, the buyer, Consultants plc, was not acting for purposes outside its trade, business or profession. Whereas the Unfair Contract Terms Act 1977 applies differently according to whether or not the buyer is dealing as a consumer, the Regulations have no application at all to contracts which are not consumer contracts.

It is no consolation to Consultants plc that in 2002, the Law Commission issued a Consultation Paper in which it was proposed to extend the 1999 Regulations to cover business-to-business contracts as well as business-to-consumer ones. That proposal is not yet the law.

Conclusion

In conclusion, whatever interpretation is held to be the correct construction of the clause, it seems very likely that the clause will not satisfy the requirement of reasonableness in the Unfair Contract Terms Act. It will therefore be of no effect.

Question 6

Abraham is a well known dealer in antique vases. On 1 February, he went into China Galore and asked the shop assistant if they had anything special. He was shown a vase described by the shop assistant as a 'Shing' vase and, after examining it behind a glass case, Abraham agreed to buy it for £3,000 and took the vase with him. Abraham was very pleased with the purchase because he had a customer who would pay handsomely for such a vase.

On 12 February, Abraham left the vase with his customer to see if he would be interested in buying it for £3,800. The vase was returned two days later because it emerged that it was not genuine and that it was worth less than £300. A week later, during a dinner party, Abraham discovered that water leaked from the vase which he was using to display a bunch of flowers.

Abraham contacted China Galore immediately, demanding his money back, and he was told that it was not the shop's policy to make refunds in any circumstances.

Advise Abraham.

Answer plan

The central issue in advising Abraham is whether he is better off arguing that the pre-contractual statement that the vase was a 'Shing' vase had become part of the contract or suing for misrepresentation. The main points that need to be considered are as follows:

- China Galore's policy about not refunding money (was this part of the contract anyway?);
- description: s 13 of the Sale of Goods Act 1979;
- satisfactory quality: s 14(2);
- fitness for purpose: s 14(3);
- misrepresentation, common law and the Misrepresentation Act 1967;
- when a buyer loses the right to reject goods (acceptance/affirmation);
- remedies.

Answer

Abraham has bought a vase which he now wishes to return and has been told that he is not entitled to a refund of the purchase price. It is clear that any attempt to restrict or limit liability is subject to the strict requirements of incorporation. China Galore's policy of refusing refunds in any circumstances cannot be effective to prevent Abraham from pursuing the matter against them if a term to that effect has not been incorporated into their contract. We are not told what the express terms and conditions were under the contract, or whether reasonable notice of the policy had been given before or at the time of the contract. Indeed, if there was such a notice displayed, perhaps in the shop, then such a term will be incorporated within their contract even if Abraham did not read it. Assuming that there was no such notice, China Galore is not entitled to rely on a policy which has not been disclosed to Abraham, and the question of whether or not the policy is reasonable is not in issue. If there were such a notice, it would probably be ineffective by virtue of the Unfair Contract Terms Act 1977, and might well attract criminal liability under the Consumer Transactions (Restrictions on Statements) Order 1976.

It is clear that Abraham was not dealing as a consumer. Thus, the amendments to the law made by the Sale and Supply of Goods Regulations 2002 do not apply, and the new rights as to repair and replacement do not fall to be discussed in this answer. Whether Abraham has the right to return the vase will depend on finding a breach of a term of the contract or an actionable misrepresentation. There are four possible grounds here:

- description;
- satisfactory quality;
- fitness for purpose;
- misrepresentation.

Description

The relevant description in this case is that it was a 'Shing' vase. Section 13 of the Sale of Goods Act 1979 states that where goods are sold by reference to a description, it is an implied term that the goods should correspond with the description. In considering whether the sale is one by description, the court will have regard to *Harlingdon and Leinster v Christopher Hull Fine Art Ltd* (1990), that is, whether the seller in making the description has held himself out as having special knowledge and whether the buyer has relied on that description. In that case, a painting was sold described by art dealers, who were not experts in German art, as one by the German painter Gabriele Munter. The buyer who did not make further inquiries, but was an expert in

German art, bought the painting for £6,000. It later transpired that the painting was a fake, worth less than £100, and the buyer rejected the painting on the ground that it did not comply with its description. The Court of Appeal held that the sale was not one by description since the description was not influential in the sale.

Applying the *Harlingdon* case to the question, although we are told that Abraham is a well known dealer in antique vases, we are not told whether China Galore, with its name, was a known expert in this type of vase. Only if it was within the reasonable contemplation of the parties that Abraham would rely upon the description 'Shing' could there be a sale by description. If China Galore was, unlike the art dealers in *Harlingdon*, knowledgeable in 'Shing' vases, or held itself out to be, Abraham would be entitled to reject the vase and claim damages.

We are told that Abraham examined the vase before agreeing to buy it. A sale of goods is not, however, prevented from being a sale by description solely because the buyer himself selects the goods (s 13(3) and *Beale v Taylor* (1967)).

Satisfactory quality

China Galore clearly sells in the course of business so the implied term in s 14(2) applies. The goods will not be of satisfactory quality if they do not meet the standard a reasonable person would regard as satisfactory, taking account of the price, any description and all other relevant circumstances (s 14(2A)). One relevant aspect of their quality is their fitness for all the purposes for which goods of the kind in question are commonly supplied. The issue which needs to be looked at here is whether the vase was fit for the purposes for which it might commonly be supplied. Abraham paid £3,000 for the vase. It is reasonable to assume that most people paying this high price for a vase will be buying it as an investment or for its resale value. Thus, the vase should be of satisfactory quality as an investment, but what of the fact that the vase is only worth £300? The Court of Appeal considered this point in the *Harlingdon* case, and Nourse LJ's view was that the purpose or purposes for which goods of this kind are commonly bought are the 'aesthetic appreciation of the owner or anyone else he permits to enjoy the experience'. Thus, even if there was a defect in the quality of the vase, it was not one which made it 'unsaleable'. The question of whether goods are reasonably fit for resale cannot depend on whether they can or cannot be resold without making a loss. The test is an objective one, not dependent on the purpose for which Abraham himself required the vase. It seems, therefore, that since most people would have bought the vase for its aesthetic appreciation, the fact that it was not a 'Shing' vase did not make the vase unfit for aesthetic appreciation which, despite its value being so much lower than the price, did not mean that the goods were of unsatisfactory quality.

We are told that Abraham subsequently discovers that the vase leaks when he uses it to display a bunch of flowers. Can Abraham claim that this rendered the vase of unsatisfactory quality? Before the 1994 amendments to s 14, there was authority that the term as to merchantable quality did not require that the goods were reasonably fit for all the purposes for which goods of that description were commonly supplied, and that it was sufficient if they were fit for one of those purposes (*Aswan v Lupdine* (1987)). Now, however, s 14(2B) provides that one aspect of the quality of the goods is their fitness for all the purposes for which goods of that kind are commonly supplied. Certainly, vases are commonly supplied for use as display containers holding fresh flowers and water. It is difficult to know if that is one of the purposes for which 'Shing' vases are commonly supplied. If it is, then the fact that the vase leaks suggests that it is not of satisfactory quality. If such vases are, however, commonly supplied for only one purpose, aesthetic appreciation (without containing fresh flowers), then the fact that it leaks will not make it of unsatisfactory quality.

Fitness for purpose

Section 14(3) provides that where goods are required for a particular purpose which has been made known to the seller, there is an implied term that the goods should be reasonably fit for that purpose. This will not apply if Abraham did not rely or it was unreasonable for Abraham to rely on China Galore's skill and judgment in supplying the goods. In relation to the problem, two questions therefore need to be asked. First, did Abraham make known to China Galore the exact purpose for which the vase would be required? Secondly, if so, was it reasonable for him to rely on China Galore's skill and judgment? The answer to the first question seems likely to be 'yes', since Abraham is a well known dealer and it is therefore reasonable to assume that if China Galore is aware of this, it would also know that Abraham would have bought the vase for resale as an antique item. The answer to the second question, however, is likely to be 'no', because, as was discussed in relation to 'description' (above), as between the parties Abraham was the expert in 'Shing' vases and it would be unreasonable for him to rely on China Galore's skill and judgment. It seems, therefore, that China Galore is not liable under s 14(3).

Misrepresentation

The false statement that the vase was a 'Shing' vase may amount to an actionable misrepresentation, entitling Abraham to rescind the contract and claim damages. The requirements of an actionable misrepresentation are that there was a statement of an existing fact by one party which induced the other party to enter the contract. It must be a statement of fact and not opinion, although an opinion which is not honestly held at the time or is based on facts which the maker of the statement ought to have known may be actionable.

It is clear from this question that the shop assistant did describe the vase as a 'Shing' vase. Abraham's reliance on this description does not have to be reasonable (*Museprime Properties v Adhill* (1990)). The court held in the *Museprime Properties* case that the reasonableness of the reliance was relevant to determining whether there was actual reliance, but that the test of reliance is subjective (the more unreasonable the reliance, the less likely the court is to believe that it did actually affect the buyer's decision to enter into the contract). It is also clear that the statement does not have to be the sole reason for entering into the contract; it is sufficient that it was one reason (*Edgington v Fitzmaurice* (1885)). It may be, therefore, that Abraham has a stronger claim in misrepresentation than under the implied conditions under the Sale of Goods Act.

Once it has been established that an actionable misrepresentation has been made, the remedies will depend on whether the misrepresentation was made innocently, negligently or fraudulently. (A detailed knowledge of misrepresentation is not usually required on commercial law courses, but bear in mind that the examiner is entitled to test you on the general principles of contract law.) It is unlikely that the shop assistant will have made the statement that it was a 'Shing' vase fraudulently. Either he made it innocently (that is, in genuine ignorance of the fact that it is untrue) or negligently (that is, he had no reasonable grounds for believing that the statement was true) under s 2(1) of the Misrepresentation Act 1967.[1] If the misrepresentation was made innocently, Abraham will be entitled to rescission of the contract. If the misrepresentation was made negligently, Abraham will be entitled not only to rescission, but he may recover for all losses caused by the misrepresentation, unrestricted by the rules of remoteness (*Royscot Trust Ltd v Rogerson* (1991)). Moreover, in *East v Maurer* (1991), it was held that this included lost profits.

One final point which needs to be made is that whether Abraham decides to pursue the matter for breach of contract or for misrepresentation may depend on the fact that it was some three weeks after he bought the vase that he tried to reject the goods against China Galore. Any action for breach of contract is subject to the rules of acceptance under s 35 of the Sale of Goods Act which, *inter alia*, deems the buyer to have accepted the goods if after a lapse of reasonable time, he retains the goods without intimating to the seller that he rejects them. In *Bernstein v Pamson Motors (Golders Green) Ltd* (1987), a period of three weeks was regarded as beyond a reasonable time in which to examine a motor car. Since then, s 35 has been amended and a reasonable period now will normally include a reasonable opportunity for the buyer to examine the goods for the purpose of ascertaining whether they conform to the contract. This may well mean that the reasonable period of time before the buyer is taken to have accepted the goods will be longer than previously. Abraham has in fact had the vase over three weeks before giving notice of rejection. Furthermore, he discovered after two weeks that it was not a 'Shing' vase. Assuming that that is a breach of condition, it is arguable that keeping it a further week afterwards before rejecting it amounts to acceptance. If, however, he was using that week in order to have experts examine it to confirm whether or not it was a 'Shing' vase (although we are told nothing to suggest that he was), that would have the effect of lengthening the reasonable period of time (*Truk v Tokmakidis* (2000)). If he has accepted the goods, then his only remedy for breach of contract would be a claim for damages, the amount of which would depend greatly on whether, on the one hand, he could establish a breach of contract arising out of the description 'Shing' vase or, on the other, was able only to rely on the fact that the vase leaked.

An action in misrepresentation is not subject to the acceptance rules and a buyer is only deemed to have lost his right to rescind if he has affirmed the contract which, after three weeks, it may be held that he has done. If it were established that the misrepresentation were fraudulent, then time begins to run only from when Abraham discovered the truth. It seems that Abraham knew of the lack of authenticity of the vase around 14 February and it was only a week later that he contacted China Galore. Thus, if it was a fraudulent misrepresentation, Abraham would be able to rescind the contract. He would in any case be entitled to damages for misrepresentation, unless China Galore could show that it had reasonable grounds to believe it was a 'Shing' vase.

Note

1   It is possible, of course, to bring the action under the common law, that is, under the rule in *Hedley Byrne v Heller* (1964). Since the Misrepresentation Act 1967, however, s 2(1) is the preferable cause of action because then the burden of proof is on the defendant to show that there were reasonable grounds for believing that the statement was true.

Question 7

Joseph, in the course of his business, agreed to buy from Mary '1,000 Christmas trees, Norwegian Spruce, five feet to six feet high, fair average quality for the season, packed 50 to a pallet, delivery to Joseph's premises on 10–12 December'. The contract contained an exclusion clause which satisfied the requirement of reasonableness in the Unfair Contract Terms Act 1977 and which excluded liability for any breach of the statutory implied conditions as to satisfactory quality and fitness for purpose. On 12 December, Mary tenders delivery to Joseph.

Consider the legal position on 12 December in each of the following alternative situations:

(a) 90% of the trees are between five feet and six feet high but 5% of them are slightly less than five feet and 5% are slightly over six feet high;

(b) a number of the trees are unevenly tapered in shape and are thus not 'fair average quality for the season';

(c) the trees are packed 75 to a pallet;

(d) the delivery tendered is of 1,010 trees.

Answer plan

This question, with its exclusion clause, plainly effective to exclude the implied conditions as to satisfactory quality and fitness for purpose, is clearly concentrated on the implied condition as to description and to the (often) related issues that arise in relation to delivery of the wrong contract quantity or of contract goods mixed with non-contract goods. A simple approach here is to deal with each numbered part of the question in turn, taking care to refer back where necessary to an answer already given rather than become repetitive where issues are the same in relation to the different parts of the question.

Answer

(a)

The fact that 10% of the trees are outside the definition of five feet to six feet high could cause the seller to be in breach of the condition, implied by s 13 of the Sale of Goods Act 1979, that the goods must correspond with their description. So far as we are informed, the shortness or extra length does not render the trees of any less quality or likely to be less fit for any purpose for which Joseph had indicated to Mary that he wanted them. It seems clear that the description 'five feet to six feet high' was part of the contract description and thus any failure to comply would be a breach of the condition in s 13. We are not told how short of five feet or how much in excess of six feet the non-conforming trees measured, except that we are told that the deviation was 'slight'. Mary might seek to invoke the maxim *de minimis non curat lex* and thus argue that any deviation was so small that it ought to be ignored. However, the measurements of five feet to six feet, given in the contract description, are precise measurements and it has been held by the House of Lords that a contract requirement on the seller to supply staves 'half an inch thick' was exactly that and that supplying staves up to nine-sixteenths of an inch thick was a breach of the implied condition implied by s 13 (*Arcos v Ronaasen* (1933)). If the seller had wished for a margin, he should have stipulated for it in his contract. In the present case, that reasoning can be taken further by the observation that there *was* a margin stipulated for in the contract, that is, anything from five to six feet high. Thus, it seems that Mary is in breach of the condition in s 13.

Normally, a breach of condition entitles the buyer to reject the goods. In the case of a breach of the conditions in ss 13–15 of the Sale of Goods Act, however, this is subject to an exception which applies where (like Joseph) the buyer is not dealing as a consumer. This exception means that Joseph will not be entitled to reject the goods if the breach was so slight that it would be unreasonable for him to reject them (s 15A). Although we are told that some of the trees were 'slightly' over or under the contract height, we are not given enough facts to know if s 15A does apply – and it is for Mary, the seller, to show that it does. If it does not apply, then Joseph has a whole range of options open to him. First, he could waive his right to reject the goods (which would leave him in exactly the same position as if s 15A does apply) and simply claim damages for his loss, if any, arising from the fact that some of the trees were too short and some too long. If he suffered no damage or loss because of that, then he would be entitled only to nominal damages. Secondly, he could reject the whole consignment and, assuming that Mary is unable to supply a complete consignment of complying trees by the end of the contractual delivery deadline (12 December), he could claim damages which would be assessed on the difference between what he was contracted to pay Mary and the market price (if higher) on 12 December of 1,000 trees matching the contract description (s 51). Thirdly, Joseph could accept those trees which did conform to the contract description and reject some or all of the 10% which did not (s 35A). In this scenario, he must pay for those he accepts *pro rata* at the contract rate. He will also be able to claim damages in relation to the 10% he rejects, the damages being the difference between the contract price for the number of rejected trees and, if higher, the market price on 12 December for that number of trees conforming to the contract description.

(b)

Given the facts that (i) Joseph was not dealing as a consumer, and (ii) the exclusion clause satisfies the requirement of reasonableness, the implied conditions as to satisfactory quality and fitness for purpose cannot be relied upon by Joseph. Unless there is some special statutory provision relating to Christmas trees or to trees, there are no other implied conditions as to quality (s 14(1)). That leaves two possible causes of action available to Joseph. The first is that Mary is in breach of the condition as to description, in that the trees do not conform to the contract requirement that they be 'fair average quality for the season'. However, it seems unlikely that the court would regard those words as part of the contract 'description' (*Ashington Piggeries v Hill* (1972)). This is because the contract description does not normally include quality requirements but is confined to those elements in the contractual requirements which help to 'identify' the goods. The result of this, combined with the exclusion clause, is that reliance on the implied conditions as to description and quality is ruled out. This means that Joseph is thrown back on his other possible cause of action, namely, a claim for breach of an *express* term of the contract, that is, a term that the trees be fair average quality for the season. This term is unlikely, however, to be regarded by the court as a condition of the contract since the parties have not, it appears, indicated that it was their intention that any breach of the term would entitle Joseph to regard the contract as repudiated. That being so, the term is only a warranty (or intermediate term) of the contract and Joseph could not regard the contract as repudiated by a breach of that term unless the breach deprived Joseph of 'substantially the whole benefit' of the contract (*Hong Kong Fir v Kawasaki Kisen* (1962); *Cehave v Bremer* (1976)). We are neither told of the severity of the poor shape of the trees nor of the number affected. If more than half are affected and they are severely misshapen and if, as a result, Joseph cannot sell them without damaging his own commercial reputation, then the court would very likely be prepared to regard the breach as a repudiatory one. If the breach is sufficiently severe to amount to a repudiatory breach, then Joseph is entitled to accept those which conform to the contract and to reject some or all of those which do not. Whether Joseph refuses to accept all or just some of the goods, the risk for him is that the court may subsequently hold that the breach did not deprive him of substantially the whole benefit of the contract. In that case, then, Joseph would himself be in breach of contract for refusing to take delivery and would be liable to Mary for non-acceptance of the goods. The measure of damages would be the difference between the contract price for the number of trees rejected and the market price, if lower, on 12 December. Joseph should therefore be advised to consider accepting the trees and reselling them for whatever he can get. He would in those circumstances be able to claim damages for breach of the express term that the trees be fair average quality for the season. His measure of damages would, *prima facie*, be the difference in the value to him of the trees actually delivered and the higher value they would have had if they had been fair average quality for the season (s 53(3)).

(c)

Even if the fact that the trees are packed 75 instead of 50 to a pallet renders them of unsatisfactory quality or unfit for their purpose, Joseph will be unable to rely upon the implied conditions in s 14 of the Sale of Goods Act, for the reasons just given in relation to the contract requirement that the trees be fair average quality for the season. Again, therefore, Joseph has two possible causes of action. The first is for breach of an express term of the contract and the second is for breach of the implied condition as to description. As regards the former, again, it seems unlikely that the court would construe the express term as a condition of the contract and therefore, again, any right of Joseph to regard the contract as repudiated (and, hence, to reject the goods) must depend upon whether the breach (the trees being packed 75 instead of 50 to a pallet) deprives Joseph of substantially the whole benefit of the contract. Unless there are some unusual facts which are not disclosed by the words of the problem as set, it seems unlikely that Joseph has suffered such a breach. Thus, Joseph's only right is to claim damages for breach of the express term, on the same basis as just explained in relation to the requirement that the trees be fair average quality for the season. That is so, unless he can claim that Mary is in breach of the condition as to description in s 13. Such a claim depends upon the requirement 'packed 50 to a pallet' being accepted by the court as being part of the contract 'description'. In *Re Moore and Landauer* (1921), a somewhat similar requirement was accepted by the Court of Appeal as being part of the contract description. This has the result that any deviation (even if quite a small one) from the requirement is a breach of condition and entitles the buyer to reject the goods. In *Re Moore and Landauer*, the buyer was held entitled to reject a consignment of tinned pears because although the correct contract quantity had been delivered, some of them were packed in cases of 24 tins instead of (as the contract required) in cases of 30 tins. That decision has, however, since been doubted in the House of Lords (*Reardon Smith Line v Hansen Tangen* (1976)). It is clear now that the courts are unlikely to find that an express term of the contract comprises part of the contract description unless it helps to 'identify' the goods. This means that the court is highly unlikely to regard the requirement that the trees be packed 50 to a pallet as anything other than a warranty (or intermediate term) of the contract. Furthermore, s 35A has been added to the Sale of Goods Act 1979 by the Sale and Supply of Goods Act 1994 with the result that, even if there has been a breach of condition, Joseph has no right to reject the goods if the breach was so slight that it would be unreasonable for him to reject them. Joseph therefore should be advised not to reject the trees but to accept them and to claim damages for any loss as a result of the trees being packed 75 to a pallet.

(d)

This question seems no more than a straightforward example of the seller tendering more than the contract quantity. However, it must also inevitably be that the trees are not all 'packed 50 to a pallet', since 1,010 is not divisible by 50! For a discussion of that aspect of the matter, see the answer to (c) above. Leaving that issue aside, there remains the matter of the extra quantity. The normal rules on over-supply are as follows. First, Joseph can reject all the goods for breach of the condition to supply 1,000 trees (s 30(2)). Secondly, he can accept the contract quantity and reject the surplus 10 (s 30(2)). Thirdly, he could accept the lot and pay for the extra *pro rata* at the contract rate (s 30(3)). However, the operation of s 30 is subject to any custom and practice between the parties and to any usage of the trade (s 30(5)). Even if there is no such relevant custom, practice or usage, the court may well regard the over-supply of 10 trees (that is, a mere 1% of the contract quantity) as *de minimis*. In that case, Joseph has suffered no breach and will be required to pay nothing for the extra 10 trees.

Question 8

(a) The law on disclaimers in relation to trade descriptions offences is in a mess.

Discuss.

(b) When, in April, Lounger booked his mobile home holiday with Montrose Travel Ltd, he had looked at one of their brochures (which had been distributed the preceding December) which showed a picture of a mobile home with a barbecue set standing next to it and which stated that all Montrose mobile homes had air conditioning and that the holidays were available from 1 May to 30 September each year. On his holiday (in June), Lounger enjoyed the use of a Montrose mobile home which did not, however, have a barbecue set or any air conditioning.

Consider the liability, if any, of Montrose under the Trade Descriptions Act 1968.

Answer plan

As always with the (a) and (b) type of question where no weighting is indicated for each part, it is wise to try to keep the answer to each part of roughly equal length.

Part (a)

This requires both an explanation of the law of disclaimers and also some critique of it. The order of treatment chosen here is largely a chronological one, which happens to coincide no doubt with the sequence of the lecture notes which many students would have on the topic and also allows critical comments on the way that the law has developed.

Part (b)

There is only one section involved (s 14), although there are possibly two false statements. With s 14, there are three basic questions which will always need to be addressed, namely: (i) was there a false statement about accommodation, services or facilities?; (ii) did the defendant have any *mens rea*?; (iii) can the defendant raise a defence under s 24? The present problem raises two further sub-issues which are: first, the issue of whether the statement related only to the future; and, secondly, the issue of the liability of a corporate body. Apart from the latter which is woven into the answers to the other questions, the order in which these issues are addressed is set out at the start of the answer. It is often a good policy to tell the examiner briefly at the start of an answer the issues with which you are going to deal.

Answer

(a)

The Trade Descriptions Act 1968 created three principal offences (ss 1, 11 and 14) which were, with the exception of s 14, *prima facie* strict liability offences. It also created certain specific defences (see ss 24 and 25). Under this scheme, the burden of proof of the offences falls upon the prosecution, but the burden of proof of one of the defences (on a balance of probabilities) is placed by ss 24 and 25 upon the defendant. Nothing is said in any of the sections about a defence of disclaimer.

After the Act was passed, one of the commonest complaints of persons having committed offences under the Act (s 1) was in relation to 'clocking', that is, the turning back of the mileometer (or odometer). It was, and still is, well known within the car trade (and outside it) that any secondhand car might well have a misleading mileometer reading. In the early days after the Act was passed, a car dealer who had sold a secondhand car with a false mileage reading on the odometer would be charged with an offence contrary to s 1(1)(b) and would then seek to rely upon the defence in s 24(1) that: (i) the offence was due to the default of another person (an earlier owner who must have done the 'clocking'); and (ii) he, the car dealer, had taken all reasonable precautions and exercised all due diligence to avoid the commission of the offence. Alternatively, the car dealer would rely upon the s 24(3) defence, but this also required him to prove that he could not with reasonable diligence have discovered that the car did not conform to the stated mileage. Whichever of these sections the car dealer relied upon, he could not succeed unless he could show that the condition of the car was generally consistent with the mileage stated on the mileometer and/or that he had taken reasonable steps to confirm the accuracy of the mileage with the previous owner(s) (see *Naish v Gore* (1971)). The burden of proof was upon the defendant.

Subsequently, the courts developed the 'defence' of disclaimer which was definitively approved in *Norman v Bennett* (1974). This was done by some determined judicial construction of the words of s 1 of the Act. Thus, it was held that if the disclaimer was sufficiently strong as to neutralise the description, then the description was not 'applied'; the disclaimer had to be as 'bold, precise and compelling' as the false description itself. Thus, if a sufficiently bold, precise and compelling disclaimer was displayed, the defendant was not guilty. This 'defence' of a disclaimer is not a defence in the same sense as the defences in ss 24 and 25. An assertion by the defendant that he used a disclaimer is not an admission of the s 1 offence coupled with the plea of a defence. Rather, it is an assertion that the s 1 offence was not committed. Thus, once the defendant raises the disclaimer issue, the burden of proof rests upon the Crown, who must prove beyond all reasonable doubt that the disclaimer was not used or else that it was not sufficiently precise, bold and compelling. Thus, the defendant no longer has to show that he took all reasonable steps such as checking the condition of the car against the stated mileage or endeavouring to make enquiries of the previous owners. It has now been held that where a car dealer knows that an odometer greatly understates the actual mileage, it is not sufficient (thus, it is no defence) that he displays a *pro forma* disclaimer which fails to make clear the extent of the difference between the true mileage and the recorded mileage: *Farrand v Lazarus* (2002). This is a welcome piece of common sense in limiting the scope of the disclaimer 'defence'. It might, with luck, lead to the car dealers abandoning the use of disclaimers in favour of the simple practice of just covering up the mileage reading – which, if there were no disclaimer defence, no doubt they would do, at least in those cases where they were not pretty sure of the accuracy of the odometer mileage reading. Sensible as the decision in *Farrand* was, it does, actually and as a matter of logic, undermine the whole basis of the defence set out in *Norman v Bennett*. According to *Norman v Bennett*, the disclaimer is effective if it is sufficiently bold, precise and compelling as to neutralise the effect of the false odometer reading. How can the disclaimer's effect (presumably upon the reasonable consumer seeing it) depend upon the knowledge of the defendant? How can it be said to neutralise the false odometer reading when the defendant is ignorant of the true mileage and not when he knows it?

The disclaimer defence also creates a further absurdity. Thus, if the car dealer does make all the checks he possibly can in order to verify that the reading is accurate and has every possible reason to believe it accurate, he still may be unable to rely upon the defence in s 24 unless he has displayed a disclaimer. This is because displaying a disclaimer is so easy and if he has not done so, he may be held not to have taken *all* reasonable precautions to avoid committing the offence (*Simmons v Potter* (1975) – although compare *Ealing LBC v Taylor* (1995)). Thus, the honest car dealer has little incentive to do any checking at all, but every incentive to leave the mileage reading visible and simply put up a disclaimer.

A further refinement of the law is that the disclaimer defence, although available to someone charged under s 1(1)(b), is not available to someone charged under s 1(1)(a) (*R v Southwood* (1987)). This achieves an element of obvious justice, so that the car dealer who does the clocking himself is disabled from avoiding liability by displaying a disclaimer. It is difficult, however, to reconcile that with the original judicial justification of the disclaimer defence, namely, that a sufficiently bold, precise and compelling disclaimer means that a false trade description is not 'applied'. The s 1(1)(a) offence is committed by someone who 'applies' a false trade description. This logical flaw in the law was considered by the court in *R v Shrewsbury Crown Court ex p Venables* (1994) and neatly side-stepped by the decision, which on its unusual facts disposed of the case. The decision was that a person who altered an odometer not in the course of a trade or business, but who later sold the vehicle in the course of a trade or business was *prima facie* guilty of an offence under s 1(1)(b) and not s 1(1)(a), and therefore could rely upon a disclaimer. There are two further observations about the present state of the law. First, the disclaimer defence, although developed in the context of mileometer readings, is in principle available to anyone charged under s 1(1)(b). Secondly, it has never been approved in the House of Lords and therefore could be swept away if that House had occasion to undertake a review of the position.

(b)

Montrose may be liable under s 14. In advising Montrose, five matters must be addressed. First, was a false statement made about any services, accommodation or facilities? If so, was it a statement of fact or was it merely a promise as to the future? Thirdly, did Montrose have the necessary *mens rea*? Fourthly, did Montrose have a defence? Fifthly, may Montrose be required to pay compensation?

There were two errors, apparently, in the brochure which Lounger saw. One was the statement that all Montrose mobile homes had air conditioning and the other the statement (implied by the picture) that they all had a barbecue set. That a statement can be implied by a picture in a brochure is clear (see, for example, *Wings v Ellis* (1985)), although it must be a question of fact whether the fact that the barbecue set was in the picture did imply that all Montrose mobile homes would have one.

In relation to both the possible errors in the brochure, Montrose may have a good line of argument based on the notion that the statements were statements about the future and therefore, arguably, were not statements of fact. Much, however, turns upon the proper construction of the statements in the brochure. The brochure is to be interpreted in the way that an ordinary reader might understand it, rather than in the way that a person with a trained legal mind would construe it (*R v Sunair Holidays* (1973); *British Airways Board v Taylor* (1976)). It is submitted that an ordinary person would understand the statement that all Montrose mobile homes had air conditioning as not just a promise about the future, but as a statement of fact about the present. Such a person would also understand that it was company policy that all its mobile homes had air conditioning. Now, that also is a statement of present fact. It may be (perhaps it is less likely) that the same would be understood about the mobile homes all having barbecues. Such statements were made in the brochure, but were continued to be made (or alternatively were made again) each time the brochure was read (*Wings v Ellis*). Thus, even if the brochure statements were true when the brochure was put out in December, an offence will *prima facie* have been committed if they were untrue when the brochure was read by Lounger in April.

Did Montrose Travel Ltd have the necessary *mens rea*? It did, provided that one of its controlling spirits (that is, a director) had the necessary *mens rea* (*Tesco Supermarkets v Nattrass* (1971)). It has to be proved that at the relevant time, such a person either: (a) knew that the statement was false; or (b) was reckless. If the case for the prosecution is that the brochure was false when read by Lounger in April, then the relevant time is April (*Wings v Ellis*). If, in fact, the directors had by then discovered that the brochure had contained false information and had done their best to recall all the brochures, then they will have had the necessary knowledge to be guilty. If they did not have such knowledge, they may have been reckless. It will not necessarily be a defence that no director looked at the brochure. The recklessness concept requires that the defendant has positively considered (more than in a mere passing fashion) whether the brochure contained any falsehoods (*MFI Warehouses v Nattrass* (1973)).

Montrose may wish to rely upon a defence, for example, under s 24. This requires it to satisfy the burden of proof. If perhaps it discovered that the brochure was inaccurate (for example, through no fault of its own but because of that of some contractor) and had done its utmost to recall all copies, they might seek to rely upon the defence of 'default of another'. It would, in addition, need to establish that it had taken all reasonable precautions and exercised all due diligence to avoid the commission of the offence. The fault could be the default of one of their own staff (other than a director) since such a member of staff would come within the definition of 'another person' (*Tesco v Nattrass*). The second requirement would require proof that they had given that employee clear instructions (so as to avoid the commission of the offence) and adequate supervision.

If Montrose Travel Ltd is guilty of the offence in s 14, it is in principle liable to have a compensation order made against it in favour of Lounger, under s 130 of the Powers of Criminal Courts (Sentencing) Act 2000. If the magistrates do not make such an order, they are required to give reasons why not. Even if Montrose has already been convicted in respect of the same brochure previously, it will not be abuse of the court's process for another prosecution to be launched, the purpose being to secure a compensation order in favour of Lounger (*R v Thomson Holidays* (1974)).

Question 9

Last December, Sarah bought a new dishwasher from Dishwashers Ltd. At the time, Dishwashers Ltd was advertising a special pre-Christmas offer under the terms of which anyone buying a dishwasher in December would be entitled to receive free from the dishwasher manufacturers, Wishdashers Ltd, a complete 34 piece dinner service of Regal Oulton pottery. In addition, Dishwashers Ltd was itself offering to give to anyone buying a dishwasher between 1 and 22 December a free Christmas turkey, to be delivered by Dishwashers Ltd on Christmas Eve. The deal, which on 21 December Sarah made with Dishwashers, included it giving her a reduction of £50 off the price of a dishwasher in return for her trading in her old dishwasher and included the arrangement with the sellers, Dishwashers Ltd, that everything would be delivered on Christmas Eve, and that Dishwashers Ltd would install and plumb in the new dishwasher. This was duly done. After that, Sarah and her family suffered in the following ways. First, despite proper cooking, the turkey, dished up by Sarah on Christmas Day, gave both Sarah and her husband, Daniel, food poisoning. Secondly, the Regal Oulton has suffered and the glaze on those pieces which have been washed up by hand has crazed all over, and the pieces which have been cleaned in the dishwasher have simply cracked right across and broken. It is the case also, however, that some of Sarah's other crockery has cracked and broken in the dishwasher. Thirdly, the dishwasher has flooded the kitchen because, it appears, the exit pipe is not properly plumbed in. For their part, Dishwashers Ltd have complained to Sarah that her old machine is not in working order.

Advise Sarah and Daniel.

What difference, if any, would it make to your answer if Sarah had paid for her dishwasher using her credit card?

Answer plan

This question raises issues of implied terms in relation both to goods (for example, satisfactory quality) and to services (for example, exercise of due care and skill). There are also issues of possible liability in negligence and for product liability under the Consumer Protection Act 1987, as well as (in the rider) under s 75 of the Consumer Credit Act 1974. The order of treatment adopted in the answer here is to take in turn each item which seems to have caused a problem and then to conclude with the rider.

Answer

Food poisoning

First, advice will be offered to Daniel in relation to his food poisoning. Daniel, it appears, did not have any contract with anyone whereby he may claim in respect of his food poisoning. Nor was any contract made purporting to benefit him, or expressly giving him the right to enforce it, under the terms of the Contracts (Rights of Third Parties) Act 1999. Thus, his claim will have to be in negligence or under the Consumer Protection Act 1987. We do not know why the turkey gave him food poisoning. However, we are told that Sarah cooked it properly. So, it would appear that the turkey was in some way defective within the meaning of the Consumer Protection Act 1987. Prior to 4 December 2000, there could be no liability in respect of agricultural produce under that Act unless it had undergone an industrial process giving it 'essential characteristics'. We are not told by the question how the turkey may have been processed before delivery to the customer. If it had been processed into being 'oven ready', that is, plucked and gutted and graded, that would, it is submitted, qualify as a process giving it essential characteristics, these being that it is 'oven ready'. If that is the case, then there can be liability under the 1987 Act, but prior to 4 December 2000, that liability would attach not to the producer (for example, the farmer), but only to whoever put the turkey through the plucking, gutting and grading process. This was so even if the defect in the turkey was attributable to the farmer and not to the industrial processor. The Consumer Protection Act has been amended so that, from 4 December 2000, the producer (that is, the farmer) can be liable in respect of unprocessed agricultural produce. This does not in any way, however, remove the liability (just explained) of the industrial processor. Thus, both the farmer and the industrial processor may be liable. It may be that Daniel cannot identify who the industrial processor and the farmer were. In that case, Daniel is entitled to ask Dishwashers Ltd who they were and, unless Dishwashers Ltd tells him who they were or alternatively who supplied the turkey to them, Dishwashers can itself be liable. Liability under Pt I of the 1987 Act is strict and certainly covers personal injury which is what Daniel has suffered.

Sarah's ability to make a claim will be the same as Daniel's, except that Sarah may well have an alternative or additional route to recover damages. This is because she was the purchaser of the dishwasher and thus she acquired the turkey under the terms of a contract. It was not, however, a contract of sale of goods. This is because although, no doubt, the contract relating to the dishwasher was a contract of sale of goods, the contract for the acquisition of the turkey was not one for which there was a money consideration and without a money consideration, the contract is not one of sale of goods (see s 1(2) of the Sale of Goods Act). So what was the consideration given by Sarah for the supply of the turkey? The answer is that she entered the contract to buy the dishwasher. The terms of the offer of Dishwashers Ltd were, in effect, 'Buy a dishwasher from us during the period 1–22 December and we will supply a free turkey'. That being so, the turkey was not given as part of the contract to supply the dishwasher but was a separate collateral contract, made by Sarah entering a contract to buy the dishwasher. Her doing that was, at the same time, her acceptance of Dishwashers' offer to supply a free turkey and also her providing the consideration for that supply. She made what is sometimes referred to as a unilateral contract. The analysis just given is the same as that adopted in *Esso Petroleum v Commissioners for Customs and Excise* (1976). Thus, the implied terms of the contract relating to the turkey are not those of the Sale of Goods Act, but are those of the Supply of Goods and Services Act 1982 (s 4). By this section, Sarah has a claim in respect of the turkey not being of satisfactory quality or fit for its purpose and that is a claim she has against Dishwashers Ltd.

The crockery

Now, we turn to the matter of the Regal Oulton. Here, it seems that the person with whom Sarah had a contract for the supply to her of the Regal Oulton pottery was Wishdashers Ltd. Insofar as Dishwashers made the offer, it may be argued that it was doing so as agents of Wishdashers Ltd. If that was the case, then Sarah had a collateral contract with Wishdashers Ltd, the terms of which were that it was offering to supply the crockery to her if she would enter a contract with Dishwashers Ltd to buy a dishwasher. For a similar analysis, albeit in a different context, see *Shanklin Pier v Detel Products* (1951). On this analysis, Sarah accepted Wishdashers' offer by making the contract with Dishwashers Ltd to buy the dishwasher from it. In that contract also, there were terms implied by the Supply of Goods and Services Act 1982 (s 4) as to satisfactory quality and fitness for purpose. It is not, however, absolutely clear that those implied terms were broken. This is because we cannot be sure that it was the crockery which was defective and not the dishwasher. True, we are told that some of Sarah's other crockery has also become cracked and broken in the dishwasher. This might suggest that Sarah's other crockery is not suitable for putting in a dishwasher and that the Regal Oulton is likewise unsuited, in which case, Wishdashers is liable for supplying the crockery which was thus defective. Alternatively, it might suggest that, although all the crockery is suitable for putting into a dishwasher, there is something defective about the dishwasher which causes crockery to crack and break. If that is the case, Sarah's claim is against Dishwashers Ltd for selling a dishwasher which is not of satisfactory quality. Her claim would in that event be under the Sale of Goods Act 1979 (s 14), since her purchase of the dishwasher was a contract of sale of goods. This is so even though part of the purchase price was settled by means of a trade-in of her old machine (*Dawson v Dutfield* (1936)).

If it is the case that the dishwasher was defective and thus was not of satisfactory quality, Sarah has the right to reject the dishwasher and reclaim the price provided that she has not had it long enough that a reasonable time has elapsed so that she will be deemed to have accepted it (s 35 of the Sale of Goods Act). In any case, she will have a claim for damages which will include the consequential loss of the damage to the crockery. If the Regal Oulton crockery was not of satisfactory quality, then again Sarah will be entitled to reject the crockery and recover the purchase price and/or claim damages. Let us consider the situation where the facts of this problem have arisen after the European Directive on Certain Aspects of Sale of Goods and Guarantees was implemented (on 31 March 2003) by the Sale and Supply of Goods Regulations 2002. In that case, Sarah has additional rights if an item purchased is not of satisfactory quality or not reasonably fit for its purpose. She is in principle entitled to claim a remedy of repair or of replacement of the item, unless such a claim would be disproportionate. If such a claim would be disproportionate or, alternatively, if such a claim is made and not complied with within a reasonable time, then Sarah is entitled to a reduction in the price or to rescind the contract. It appears that these additional rights may not be that useful to Sarah. If it was the dishwasher which was defective, then we have seen that, even without them, she has the right to reject it and get her money back (unless she has had it long enough that she can be said to have 'accepted' it) and she is entitled to recover damages for the loss of/damage to the crockery. The additional rights might be useful to her, however, if she has 'accepted' the dishwasher and thus lost her right to reject it. In that situation, she could ask for it to be repaired or replaced and, if it is not, then she is entitled to rescind the contract and get her money back (less a deduction for the value of any use she has had out of it). In any case, she would retain the right to claim damages for the consequential loss or damage to the crockery.

Let us now turn to the problem of the crazing of the glaze on the Regal Oulton. This clearly gives her a claim, if at all, under the Supply of Goods and Services Act 1982 (s 4). It may be, however, that she has no valid claim. It is true that the crockery must be of satisfactory quality. However, that does not require it to be of the very best quality; it only has to be of a standard that a reasonable person would regard as satisfactory – and that rather depends upon the circumstances. If, in fact, it was described as normally costing a very high price and if it was described as of high quality, then those would be circumstances telling in Sarah's favour and tending to show that the crockery was not of satisfactory quality. Otherwise, it might be difficult to show that crockery given away 'free' with another item was to be expected of a particularly high quality.

Kitchen floods

There now falls to be considered the flooding of Sarah's kitchen. This, we are told, is due to defective plumbing in of the dishwasher. Again, this involves a consideration of the Supply of Goods and Services Act 1982 – this time because, although we are dealing with a contract of sale of goods (the dishwasher), there is also an element of service with it. It is within Pt II of the 1982 Act and, by s 13, there is an implied term that the service will be carried out with reasonable care and skill where it is done, as it was here, in the course of a business. It appears that this implied term was broken; otherwise, the exit pipe would be well enough plumbed in. Thus, Sarah has a claim for damages for breach of that implied term by Dishwashers Ltd. The measure of damages would be the value of the damage to her property (for example, the carpet) plus the cost of having the machine's exit properly plumbed in. Failing such a claim, Sarah would have a claim in the tort of negligence against whoever did the plumbing in and/or his employer.

Defective traded-in machine

Finally, there is the fact that the traded-in machine does not work. If Sarah had stated that it did work, then Dishwashers Ltd may have a claim against her for misrepresentation or breach of an express term of the contract. If, however, she said no such thing, there is no implied condition about the quality of the traded-in machine. The implied conditions as to satisfactory quality and fitness for purpose in s 14 of the Sale of Goods Act do not apply unless the goods are 'sold' in the course of a business. There is nothing in the problem set to suggest that Sarah was selling in the course of a business. Indeed, the whole scenario suggests exactly the opposite.

The rider

The fact that Sarah paid by credit card would make no difference to the advice given above. It might, however, enable additional advice to be given. If the credit card were not a mere charge card and, thus, was one which was regulated by the Consumer Credit Act 1974, then the additional advice would be that Sarah would be able to bring any claim for breach of contract which she has against Dishwashers Ltd also or alternatively against the credit card issuer. At least, that would be so, provided the following condition was satisfied, namely, that the cash price of the dishwasher exceeded £100. This £100 minimum relates not to the size of the claim that Sarah might make but to the amount of the cash price of the dishwasher. This joint and several liability exists by virtue of s 75 of the Consumer Credit Act 1974, but would apply only to Sarah's claim in respect of the defective dishwasher and/or defective plumbing in. It would not apply to her claim in respect of the food poisoning from the turkey, because s 75 applies to a 'transaction financed by' the credit card agreement and her acquisition of the turkey was not so financed, because the consideration for the turkey was Sarah entering a contract to buy the dishwasher.

CHAPTER 3

PASSING OF PROPERTY AND RISK

Introduction

This chapter covers the passing of property and risk. It incorporates the topic of retention of title clauses, and also deals with perishing goods.

Checklist

The following topics should be prepared in advance of tackling the questions:

- the provisions in ss 16–19 of the Sale of Goods Act 1979 on the passing of property and the case law thereon;
- the provisions in s 20 of the Sale of Goods Act 1979 on the passing of risk and the case law thereon;
- the rules in ss 20A and 20B applicable where the buyer has paid for unascertained goods out of an identified bulk;
- retention of title (*Romalpa*) clauses;
- the rules in ss 6 and 7 of the Sale of Goods Act 1979 on the perishing of specific goods and the analogous common law rules on the perishing of unascertained goods out of a specific bulk;
- the law on the doctrine of frustration and how it interrelates with the item just mentioned.

Question 10

Jones plc makes industrial fabric which it commonly sells to other companies. Its sales are usually made on trade credit terms, with about 50% of its sales being to regular customers while the rest are to 'one-off' customers. Jones plc's accountant has suggested that it ought to consider incorporating a retention of title clause into its standard terms of sale. Advise Jones plc on this issue, including advice as to the extent to which it could enforce such a clause without registering a charge.

Answer plan

The question invites an explanation of the purpose of retention of title clauses and a discussion of the effects and effectiveness of them. You should approach the question as follows:

- explain the purpose of retention of title clauses;
- deal with the passing of risk;
- state the requirements for an effective clause;
- explore the limits on effectiveness without being registered where:
  - (a) the buyer sub-sells the goods (and can the seller take an interest in the proceeds of the sub-sales?);
  - (b) the buyer pays for the goods (and what if he only makes part-payment or if the buyer owes other money to Jones plc?);
  - (c) the goods lose their identity.

Answer

The reason that the company's accountant has made this suggestion is to enable Jones plc to protect itself against the risk of one of its customers becoming insolvent and hence going into liquidation before the customer has paid Jones plc for the fabric supplied. Without a retention of title clause or some other form of security, Jones plc would in that event be a mere unsecured creditor of the insolvent buying company and would be lucky to get more than a small proportion of the debt owed to it. The purpose of a retention of title clause would be to put Jones plc in a stronger position in the event of the buyer going into liquidation – that is, if the goods had not been paid for, to enable Jones plc to retake possession of the goods (Jones plc's goods) and to do so irrespective of how many other creditors the insolvent buyer might have.

Passing of risk

Before dealing with the effectiveness of a retention of title clause to protect Jones plc, a warning should be given about the passing of risk. A retention of title clause, when it works, will result in title (that is, ownership, or what the Sale of Goods Act terms 'property') being retained by Jones plc (that is, not passing to Jones plc's buyer) for some considerable time after delivery. However, by s 20(1) of the Sale of Goods Act 1979, the goods will, unless the contrary is agreed, remain at the seller's risk until the property in them passes to the buyer. Thus, Jones plc would be well advised, when including a retention of title clause in its conditions of sale, either to include also a clause stating that the goods will be at the buyer's risk from the moment of delivery, or else to see that Jones plc is covered by its own insurance for loss or damage caused after delivery by accident, act of God or act of a third party.

Effectiveness without being registered

By a properly drafted retention of title clause, Jones plc can ensure that it retains property in the goods supplied until one of three events occurs. As soon as the first of these events occurs, property will pass (that is, Jones plc will lose title to the goods). Those three events are: first, that the goods are sold by the buyer and property passes under that contract to the buyer's sub-buyer; secondly, that the buyer pays Jones plc; thirdly, that the goods, although still unsold by the buyer, lose their identity on becoming incorporated in something else. The point is that, until one of these events occurs, Jones plc will have *retained* title to the goods and will be able, on the buyer going into liquidation, to retake the goods, thereby enforcing its rights of ownership. Such a right does not have to be registered as a charge, because the requirement (in s 365 of the Companies Act 1985) to register applies only to charges *created* by the buying company. Thus, both the Court of Appeal (in *Clough Mill v Martin* (1985)) and the House of Lords (in *Armour v Thyssen* (1990)) have held that retention of title clauses are enforceable without being registered. Attention will now be paid to each in turn of the three possibilities which will cause Jones plc to lose ownership in the goods even where there is a retention of title clause.

Buyer sells the goods

Jones plc may think that it would be wise to retain title until the goods have been paid for and to ensure that if they have not been paid for, Jones plc still retains title even if the buyer sells the goods. This, however, would be unrealistic. It is very likely that Jones plc's buyer needs to be able to sell the goods in order to maintain its own cash flow and thereby to be able to settle its debts, including those owed to Jones plc. On the other hand, if that buyer were unable to pass on good title to a sub-buyer to whom it sold the goods, it would be very unlikely to be able to find willing sub-buyers. In any case, even if the retention of title clause were to purport to retain title for unpaid goods even after they had been sold on to a sub-buyer, there is always the risk that the sub-buyer, if unaware of the retention of title clause, would claim nevertheless to obtain title by virtue of one of the exceptions to the principle *nemo dat quod non habet* – in particular, the one in s 25(1) of the Sale of Goods Act 1979. Therefore, a sensibly drafted retention of title clause will authorise the buyer to sub-sell the goods (see the *Romalpa* case) so that the buyer in sub-selling the goods will, vis à vis the sub-buyer, be selling as a principal and, vis à vis Jones plc, be selling as an agent of Jones plc. Technically, of course, Jones plc would not lose ownership and the sub-buyer would not acquire ownership until, according to the terms of the sub-sale, property passes from the buyer to the sub-buyer.

If then, as seems inevitable, Jones plc is not to retain ownership after the time when property is to pass to the sub-buyer, is there any way that Jones plc can continue to protect itself against the subsequent insolvency of the buyer? The answer, confirmed by the decision in the *Romalpa* case, is that an appropriately worded clause *may* give Jones plc an interest in the proceeds of sale received by the buyer from the sub-buyer. For such a result to be achieved, the clause will need to make it clear that in having possession of and sub-selling the goods, the buyer is agent of, bailee of, fiduciary of, and selling for the account of the seller. Then, if the buyer has kept any such proceeds of sale in a separate account, Jones will, in priority to the buyer's other creditors, be able to take those proceeds of sale to satisfy the outstanding debt due to Jones plc. If the proceeds have been mixed by the buyer with other monies, then Jones plc would be able to trace according to the equitable principles of tracing (*Re Hallett's Estate* (1880)). It is important that the clause complies with the requirements set out above. Even then, there is uncertainty surrounding clauses aimed at securing to the seller (here, Jones plc) an interest in the proceeds of sub-sales by the buyer. Some of this uncertainty was exposed in *Pfeiffer GmbH v Arbuthnot Factors* (1988), where the clause authorised the buyer to sub-sell and required the buyer to pass on to the seller all the buyer's rights under those sub-sales contracts, requiring this to be done up to the amount of the buyer's indebtedness to the seller. It was held in the High Court that this was a charge created by the buyer and was void because it was not registered under the Companies Act. There were two significant distinctions between the clause here and that in *Romalpa*. First, the clause providing that the buyer in sub-selling was doing so for the account of the seller was expressly limited to the amount of the outstanding debts owed by the buyer to the seller. Secondly, it failed expressly to state that the buyer was, in selling the goods, a fiduciary of the seller. One possibly significant uncertainty in all of this is that in *Romalpa*, the one case where a seller has successfully claimed an interest in the proceeds of sub-sales, the decision rested on a concession made by counsel for the buyer's receiver, namely, a concession that the relationship of seller and buyer was that of bailor and bailee. Advice to Jones plc is therefore to include in the contractual retention of title provisions a clause which deals with the proceeds of sub-sales and satisfies the requirements indicated above, but to recognise the uncertainty over its legal effect, if not registered as a charge created by the buyer.

Buyer pays Jones plc

For those customers of Jones plc that are 'one-off' customers, the clause need retain title only until the purchase price has been fully paid. The effects of such a clause were set out in *Clough Mill v Martin* (1985) (partly *ratio* and partly *obiter*). If the buyer goes into liquidation before paying for the goods, then Jones plc can retake the goods. Jones plc can then resell the goods itself, since they are its property. If Jones plc sells them for more than the original price that the buyer had agreed to pay, then Jones plc will make a profit which it would not have made if the buyer had paid for the goods before going into liquidation; Jones plc will be entitled to retain that profit. If Jones plc is able to resell the goods only for a lower figure than the buyer had agreed to pay, then Jones plc will have a claim for damages against the buyer for the consequent loss; however, Jones plc will be unlikely to recover much of that loss, in respect of which it will be merely an unsecured creditor of the insolvent buyer. If, at the time when the buyer had gone into liquidation, the buyer had paid *part* of the purchase price to Jones plc, and if Jones plc, having repossessed the goods, is able to sell them for the same price that the buyer had agreed to pay, Jones plc will be under a duty to refund the buyer's part-payment. If, however, Jones plc has been able to resell the goods only at a lower figure than the buyer had agreed to pay, then Jones plc will be able to deduct that loss from the amount of any refund.

For Jones plc's regular customers, the clause should, in the interests of Jones plc, be an all liabilities clause; it should retain title until the buyer has satisfied all his liabilities to Jones plc, whether arising under this or any other contract. That such a clause can be effective was confirmed by the House of Lords in the Scottish case of *Armour v Thyssen* (1990), and it is not thought that the law is any different in this respect in England. Indeed, the reasoning in that case would seem also to legitimise a clause which retains title to Jones plc until all debts owed to Jones plc by the buyer *or by any subsidiary or associated company of the buyer* have been paid.

Goods lose their identity

It has been established in various cases that a retention of title clause will cease to be effective once the goods have lost their identity by becoming incorporated in something else. This usually occurs in the buyer's manufacturing process, for example, resin becoming incorporated in chipboard (see *Borden v Scottish Timber Products Ltd* (1981)), or pieces of leather becoming incorporated into handbags made by the buyer (see *Re Peachdart Ltd* (1984)). It seems that Jones plc cannot retain title to the fabric once that fabric has been used in the manufacture of other products, such as curtains, bedspreads, furniture, etc. It seems unlikely that the fabric (unlike the engines in *Hendy Lennox v Grahame Puttick Ltd* (1984)) could be incorporated in something else without losing its identity. Thus, Jones plc cannot protect itself where the fabric has been incorporated in something else in the buyer's manufacturing process, without registering a charge created by the buyer over the manufactured product.

Conclusion

Jones plc would be well advised to include retention of title provisions in its contracts, which, if carefully drafted, should serve to give some security against the risk of the buyer becoming insolvent. Without being registered as a charge, those provisions should be effective in the case of unmixed goods and, possibly, the proceeds of sale of unmixed goods.

Question 11

Winefest Ltd is a wine merchant. Its stock in its warehouse a month ago was:

* 100 bottles of 1960 Chateau Orczy;
* 200 bottles of 1970 Chateau Pimpernel which, unknown to Winefest Ltd, were the last bottles of that vintage remaining unconsumed anywhere in the world;
* 350 bottles of 1980 Chateau Chauvelin;
* assorted other wines.

In the last month, Winefest has made and received no deliveries of wine, but has made the following agreements to sell wine:

* '100 bottles of 1960 Chateau Orczy' to Oliver;
* '200 bottles of 1970 Chateau Pimpernel' to Percy;
* '300 bottles of 1980 Chateau Chauvelin, currently in Winefest's warehouse' to Charles;
* '50 bottles of 1980 Chateau Chauvelin' to Donald.

As regards payment: Oliver paid Winefest when he made the contract; Percy agreed to pay upon collecting the goods from Winefest's warehouse; Charles and Donald each agreed to pay upon delivery by Winefest to their respective premises.

Yesterday, Winefest despatched to Donald 50 bottles of 1980 Chateau Chauvelin. Unfortunately, the lorry (Winefest's own) crashed en route and all the wine on board was lost. Last night, a fire destroyed Winefest's warehouse and its contents.

Advise Oliver, Percy, Charles and Donald.

Answer plan

This question is plainly concerned with the issue of whether risk had passed from the seller to the buyer. However, the answer must not be confined to that, because it is important to know whether the contracts are still binding and, if not, what the position is.

Answer

Each of the buyers will be advised as to whether the risk in the goods had passed to him and, if not, whether the contract is still binding.

We are not told if the contracts contained any provision stating when risk was to pass to the buyer or when property was to pass. It will be assumed that there was no such provision. In any case, even if there were a provision that property was to pass to the buyer at a particular stage, that provision could not, in the case of a contract for the sale of unascertained goods, come into effect until those goods were ascertained (s 16 of the Sale of Goods Act 1979).

In the absence of contrary agreement, and subject to a couple of provisos, risk passes with property (s 20). Subject to the rule in s 16 just mentioned, property passes when the parties intend it to (s 17) and, unless a different intention appears, property passes according to the rules in s 18. The application of these rules depends upon whether the contract in question was for specific goods or unascertained goods.

Specific or unascertained goods?

The time for determining this issue is at the time the contract is made. If the contract is for goods which are 'identified and agreed upon' at the time the contract is made, then it is one for the sale of specific goods (s 61(1)). The agreement which Oliver has is not one for specific goods, since, even if the parties had expected that Oliver's contract would be fulfilled from Winefest's stock, there was apparently no contractual agreement to that effect, but simply an obligation on Winefest to deliver '100 bottles of 1960 Chateau Orczy'. Thus, if Winefest chose to keep for itself the 100 bottles in its stock at the time of the contract or if it chose to supply them to another customer, it could still comply with its contractual commitments to Oliver by getting hold of 100 other bottles of 1960 Chateau Orczy and supplying those to Oliver. That makes it a contract for the sale of unascertained goods, since the contract did not identify the 100 bottles in Winefest's stock as the contractual bottles (*Re London Wine Shippers* (1986)).

Similarly, the contract with Percy did not identify the 200 bottles of 1970 Chateau Pimpernel in Winefest's stock as being the contractual bottles. Had it been possible to do so, Winefest could have bought a further 200 bottles and used those to fulfil its contract with Percy. It is submitted that it is irrelevant that it would in fact have been impossible to buy more such bottles. It may be argued that a contract to buy 'a painting of the Mona Lisa by Leonardo da Vinci' is no different from a contract to buy 'the painting of the Mona Lisa by Leonardo da Vinci', since there is only one such painting. However, in the present case, Winefest was unaware that the bottles in its warehouse were the only ones in existence and, in those circumstances, it cannot be said that the 1970 Chateau Pimpernel bottles were 'identified and agreed upon at the time the contract was made' as being the contractual goods, since, so far as the parties were concerned, the contract allowed other goods to be supplied which corresponded with the contract description. Thus, Percy's contract also was for the sale of unascertained goods.

The contract with Charles did identify Winefest's stock as the source from which Charles's bottles must come. However, it did not identify which of the 350 bottles in its stock were to be supplied to Charles. Thus, Charles's contract was also a contract for the sale of unascertained goods (*Re Wait* (1927)).

Donald's contract, apparently, did not even require his bottles to be supplied from Winefest's current stock. So, for the same reasons as applied to Oliver's contract, Donald's was a contract for the sale of unascertained goods.

Section 20A

This section provides for the buyer to obtain an undivided share of goods in unascertained goods from an identified bulk. There is, however, no question of s 20A applying to any of the goods in this problem. There is only one lot of goods which are to come from a bulk which is identified by the parties, either in the contract or subsequently. Those are the 300 bottles that Charles has agreed to buy. Section 20A does not apply to these goods, because it comes into operation only when the buyer pays for the goods and Charles is not due to pay until delivery occurs. It follows that the passing of ownership and risk will be determined by reference to anything the parties may have agreed and, failing that, by reference to ss 16–19.

Passing of property

It may be that, in the case of Oliver, the parties intended property to pass at an early stage, since Oliver paid for the goods at the time of making the contract. However, nothing was done to ascertain which bottles were to be supplied to Oliver. Therefore, no property ever passed to Oliver, since no property can pass in goods until they are ascertained (s 16).

Where, after the making of the contract, goods become ascertained, property will not pass (unless a contrary intention appears) until goods are unconditionally appropriated to the contract by one party with the assent of the other (r 5 of s 18). In the case of Percy, so far as we are told, nothing was done to appropriate the goods to the contract. Therefore, there being nothing to indicate a contrary intention on the part of the parties, property never passed to Percy.

If, contrary to the opinion advanced above, the sale to Percy was in fact a sale of specific goods, then, assuming that the contract was an 'unconditional' one and that the wine was in a deliverable state, property will have passed to Percy at the time the contract was made. At least, that is so according to r 1 of s 18, which states that it is immaterial that payment or delivery or both are postponed. However, the application of that rule coupled with the rule in s 20 would mean that risk had passed to Percy even though the goods were still in Winefest's warehouse. That would be an unsatisfactory result to achieve unless the parties had very clearly indicated it to be their intention, as it would be quite likely that Winefest was covered by insurance for the loss of or damage to its goods on its premises, and quite unlikely that a buyer would expect to have to take out insurance cover for goods of which he had yet to take delivery and for which he had yet to make payment. Maybe it was for that sort of consideration that Diplock LJ said in *Ward v Bignall* (1967) that in the case of specific goods, very little is needed to give rise to the inference that the parties intended property only to pass upon payment or delivery. If the court found the parties' intention by that means, then r 1 of s 18 would not apply, since the s 18 rules apply only where the intention of the parties is not apparent. Therefore, it is submitted that even if the sale to Percy were of specific goods, the property was intended to pass only upon delivery and payment and that therefore no property in the wine passed to Percy.

It could be that, in the case of Charles, his 300 bottles became ascertained by exhaustion (see *Karlshamns Olje Fabriker v Eastport Navigation Corp, The Elafi* (1982)). This is because the contract requires his bottles to be supplied from the 350 in stock and as soon as the 50 are despatched to Donald, Charles's have become ascertained as being the remaining 300. However, although no property can pass before the goods become ascertained, it does not follow that the parties intended that property should pass as soon as the goods became ascertained. Unless the intention of the parties appears otherwise, the property has not passed unless there is unconditional appropriation of the goods to the contract. It might be argued that Winefest made the unconditional appropriation by despatching the 50 bottles to Donald, since Winefest was thereby effectively committing itself to delivering the remaining 300 to Charles. In that case, however, it would seem that Winefest was unconditionally appropriating the 50 bottles to Donald. But was it really? Certainly, it would have been had it consigned the 50 bottles to an independent carrier to deliver to Donald (see r 5(2) of s 18). Is this still the case when it sends its own lorry? If this was an unconditional appropriation of the 50 bottles to Donald, then it is submitted that there was an unconditional appropriation of the remaining 300 to Charles. In that case, it seems likely that we can infer that Charles impliedly assented in advance to that appropriation (as is possible; see *Aldridge v Johnson* (1857)), since he must have assumed that Winefest was free to dispose of all but 300 of its stock of 1980 Chateau Chauvelin. It is arguable, however, that consigning the goods to Donald on Winefest's own lorry did not amount to an unconditional appropriation and that such an appropriation would occur only upon delivery by Winefest's lorry to Donald. If the lorry had been recalled, for example, by Winefest calling the driver via a mobile telephone in the lorry's cab, then Winefest would still have 350 bottles from which to select Charles's. Thus, the despatch of 50 bottles in Winefest's own lorry did not, it is argued, demonstrate an intention to attach those 50 irrevocably to Donald's contract, or the remaining 300 irrevocably to Charles's. It is submitted that, therefore, property did not pass to either Charles or Donald. Even if the despatch to Donald did amount to an unconditional appropriation, it would still be the case that no property would have passed to Donald (as opposed to Charles), since there is nothing from which to infer Donald's assent given in advance to such an appropriation and thus his assent would only be given upon delivery to him, which never occurred because of the lorry crash.

Passing of risk

It has been argued that no property passed to any of the buyers in the problem. It follows that no risk passed to them either (s 20) unless it could be that delivery was delayed for any of their faults (s 20(2)). It is possible that delivery to Percy was delayed through his fault, depending upon whether he has taken more than the agreed (or else a reasonable) time in coming to collect his wine. If he did, then the 200 bottles of Chateau Pimpernel were at Percy's risk, since their loss in the fire is certainly something that might not have happened if he had collected them earlier (s 20(2)).

Risk not having passed (except possibly to Percy), Winefest is not excused from having to deliver to Oliver and to Donald wine which corresponds to the descriptions in their respective contracts. Nothing has rendered their contracts impossible to perform, because they were contracts for the sale of purely generic goods. If Winefest does not carry out those contracts, it will be liable to the buyers for non-delivery.

On the other hand, both Percy's and Charles's contracts have become impossible for Winefest to carry out; Percy's because there is no more of that wine left in the world and Charles's because the contract provided for the goods to come from a particular source and that source is now void (*Howell v Coupland* (1876)). The contracts being for unascertained goods, s 7 will not apply, but the contracts are frustrated at common law, assuming the frustration was not self-induced, that is, that the fire was not Winefest's fault. That being so, Winefest is not liable for non-delivery and nor are Charles and Percy liable to pay the price. Even if (that is, in Percy's case) the contract had been for the sale of specific goods, the result would have been the same (that is, provided that risk had not passed) by virtue of s 7.

If risk had passed to Percy, that is, if delivery was delayed because he was contractually late in collecting, then Percy's contract will not be avoided or frustrated, but instead he will be liable for the price.

Question 12

(a) 'The rules in the Sale of Goods Act 1979 relating to the passing of risk do not always place the risk upon the party who should sensibly bear it.'

Discuss this statement.

(b) Ahmed had 400 sacks of jute lying in X's warehouse. He contracted to sell to Henry '300 sacks of Ahmed's jute now lying in X's warehouse'. On receiving a cheque for the purchase price, Ahmed gave Henry the invoice and written delivery authority. Today, a month later, when Henry has gone to collect the jute, it has been discovered that, since the contract was made, 200 of Ahmed's sacks have been stolen. Henry has been offered delivery of the remaining 200 sacks and seeks your advice.

Advise Henry.

Answer plan

Many law examiners do not indicate how many marks are allocated to each half of the question. The fact that this is poor examination setting is no help to the examinee. The only safe guide to adopt in such a case is that either the (a) and (b) parts carry equal marks, or else there will not be a very great disparity between the marks allocated to each part. It is certainly unreasonable to assume that, because the question in (a) is shorter, the answer should be.

The answer to (a) is to some extent a matter of taste. There is certainly no right answer. One could mount a good case for the rules being sensible. The approach taken in this model answer is to attack the rules on the basis that if you can come up with some plausible criticisms of the area of law under scrutiny, it is usually easier to attack the state of the law than it is to defend it.

Part (b) is a typical problem on the passing of risk. The most common cause of students throwing away marks on problems on this topic is a failure to do any more than consider who bears the risk, that is, a failure to spell out the consequences, such as a possible frustration of the contract and whether the buyer still has to pay the price. The plan adopted in (b) is to consider on whom the loss of the theft falls, and then to consider the possible consequences of it falling on Ahmed or Henry.

Answer

(a)

Apart from the addition of ss 20A and 20B in 1995, the rules referred to in the question have remained virtually unchanged since the first Sale of Goods Act was passed in 1893. That Act was itself a codifying Act which simply sought to put into statutory form rules that had been arrived at by judges deciding individual cases. Thus, they do not result from a considered comprehensive approach to the whole range of issues that ought to bear upon a piece of legislation. They do, however, reflect the basic 'freedom of contract' philosophy which imbued the decisions in commercial cases by 19th century judges. This accounts for the opening words of s 20 ('unless otherwise agreed') which allow the parties to determine the rules within their own contract. To that extent, the comment in the question is certainly unjustified, since it is surely sensible to have risk borne by the party who it has been agreed in the contract should bear it.

Where the matter is more debatable is in those cases where the contract is silent as to who bears the risk. In this situation, apart from two exceptions specifically catered for in sub-ss (2) and (3), the basic approach adopted is to tie the passing of risk to the passing of property. This approach is flawed because the passing of property is significant for other purposes as well as for determining the passing of risk – those other purposes including the seller's right to maintain an action for the price (see s 49) and the right of the relevant trustee in bankruptcy to take the goods in the event of one or other of them becoming bankrupt. The rules on the passing of property are themselves subject to the freedom of contract principle which allows the parties to agree when they intend property to pass. In that case, the rules on the passing of risk and the passing of property are not lacking in sense, since the parties can presumably remember to cater for the one when making a specific provision for the other. It would certainly be quite absurd of the parties to include a retention of title clause whereby the seller retains title (that is, property) long after delivery to the seller without also including a clause stating that the risk passes with delivery.

It is where the parties do not remember or think to include express provisions on these matters that the rules in s 20 (on the passing of risk) and the related rules in ss 16–19 (on the passing of property) appear particularly flawed. The plain fact is that it would be logical (apart from the clear justice of the exceptions in s 20(2) and (3)) to link the passing of risk with physical delivery of the goods, unless the parties have expressly agreed otherwise. There are two very sound reasons for this. First, it is obvious that in the vast majority of cases, it is the person in possession who has the greatest ability to take care of the goods to see that they are not stolen, burnt, damaged, etc. If he has to bear the risk of any loss, then he has the consequent incentive to exercise that care. The second reason is that it is likely to be much easier to secure insurance cover for goods on your own premises or otherwise within your own possession. Of course, it is possible to secure insurance cover when they are elsewhere. One does wonder, however, how many businesses fail to insure goods of which they are not in possession but for which they are bearing the risk. It may be objected that the notion of insuring goods where, although the risk of loss or damage is borne by the insured, the property in the goods is with someone else, would raise problems of whether the insured had in law an insurable interest. If that is a problem, then the law on insurable interest needs changing. Not only do the rules in ss 16–20 not tie the passing of risk and of property to the transfer of possession of the goods, they expressly recognise that the passing of property and/or risk can occur independently of whether delivery has occurred – see the wording of r 1 of s 18 and s 20. There is undoubtedly something inconsistent about saying, as s 20 does in its principal rule in sub-s (1), that it is immaterial whether delivery has been made or not and then saying in an exception to that rule that where delivery is delayed due to the fault of one of the parties, any loss which might not have occurred but for the delay is to be borne by the party at fault.

There is, however, a further difficulty which would more commonly arise if the rule tying the passing of risk to the passing of property in the absence of contrary agreement were abolished. This is the absurdity since if, whilst the risk is with one party and the property is with the other, the goods are destroyed or damaged by the negligence of a third party, the party who suffers the loss is unable to maintain an action for damages against the culprit (*Leigh and Sillavan v Aliakmon Shipping Co* (1984)).

Finally, it must be acknowledged that the somewhat complicated rules relating to the sale of a specified quantity of unascertained goods out of a specific bulk were a sensible amendment to the law. They are stated in ss 20A and 20B which were introduced in 1995. They were designed to deal with the situation where the buyer has paid for the goods and where they are still unseparated from the identified bulk at the time when the bulk is damaged or lost in whole or in part. Now, unless the parties have agreed something to the contrary, the buyer will no longer be a mere unsecured creditor in the event of the seller's insolvency. So far as risk is concerned, the seller's proportion of the bulk will be assumed to have perished or been damaged first, but if the loss or damage goes beyond that, each buyer will have to bear the risk of loss or damage to his share of the bulk.

(b)

The question requires us to establish, if possible, at whose risk the goods were when 200 sacks were stolen. Much depends upon whether they were stolen before or after Henry paid for the goods (that is, gave over his cheque to Ahmed). If they were stolen after that point, then ss 20A and 20B are relevant. These sections apply where there is a sale of a specified quantity (here, 200 sacks) out of a bulk which is identified in the contract (here, Ahmed's jute lying in X's warehouse). Their effect is that, upon payment of the price, the buyer (Henry) acquires property in an undivided share of the bulk. From that point onwards, there is a possibility that loss of or damage to the bulk will to some extent fall upon Henry. Where only some of the bulk is lost or damaged, then that loss is taken first of all to have fallen on that share of the bulk retained by the seller, Ahmed. The problem does not state that there is any other buyer to whom Ahmed has agreed to sell any of the bulk. It appears therefore that after Henry paid the price of his 300 sacks, the bulk of 400 sacks comprised 300 for Henry and 100 retained by Ahmed. The loss occasioned by the theft of 200 thus falls first on Ahmed's 100 and thereafter on Henry's 300. Thus, after the theft, there are none of Ahmed's left and only 200 sacks of Henry's left. These remaining sacks will then have become Henry's by a process of exhaustion. He is entitled to the remaining 200 sacks, but is not entitled to recover any of the purchase price he paid.

The result whereby the loss is taken to have fallen first on Ahmed's share of the bulk is challengeable by Ahmed if he can rely on s 20(2) or if it can be said that the arrangement over giving the delivery authority to Henry indicated that the parties intended risk to pass on the handing over to Henry of the delivery authority. In either of those two eventualities, Henry and Ahmed would bear the loss in the proportions of their respective interests in the bulk: 75% and 25%. As regards s 20(2), we are told that Henry went to collect the jute 'a month later', that is, presumably a month after being given the written delivery authority. It is quite possible that a month was an unreasonable delay and that therefore one could describe delivery as having been delayed through Henry's 'fault'. If so, Henry has to bear the consequences of the theft if that loss might not have occurred if he had collected the goods within a reasonable period of time (say, within a week). We are not told when the theft occurred. If it is established that it occurred before the lapse of what would have been a reasonable length of time for Henry to turn up to collect the goods, then Ahmed cannot rely on s 20(2). If it occurred after a lapse of that length of time, or if it might have done, then it is a loss which 'might' not have occurred if Henry had collected on time and s 20(2) applies. Alternatively, the arrangement over the giving of the delivery authority, and Henry thus taking on the task of collecting the goods, could well be something which a court would take as indicating the intention of the parties that risk should pass to Henry upon the handing over to him of the delivery authority (*Sterns v Vickers* (1923)). In the situation where either s 20(2) applies or else the theft occurred after the parties intended risk to pass (for example, on the handing over of the delivery note), the result is as in *Sterns v Vickers*, namely, that all 400 sacks were *pro rata* (that is, 75%) at Henry's risk. This is because he had agreed to buy 75% of the 400 sacks. In that case, he has to bear 75% of the loss of 200 sacks, that is, the loss of 150 sacks. In that case, he is entitled to take delivery of a further 150 sacks, but must pay the full contract price. In this scenario, there is no possibility that the contract has become frustrated by virtue of the theft, since the only way to make sense of the rule that Henry has to bear the risk is to make him pay for the goods, despite the fact that some of them have been stolen.

We now consider the situation if Ahmed had agreed to sell the remaining 100 sacks to another buyer (B2) who had also paid for them before the theft from X's warehouse. In that situation, both Henry and B2 would have an undivided share in the bulk in the proportions 75% and 25% respectively and they would bear the loss in those proportions. This would mean that they would suffer the loss as follows: Henry would lose 150 sacks and B2 would lose 50. This would mean that they would each be entitled to take from the remaining bulk 150 and 50 sacks respectively. In that scenario, Henry would be entitled to 150, not 200, of the remaining sacks. He would not, however, be entitled to any repayment of the price he has paid.

We now turn to the situation where the theft occurred before Henry paid Ahmed. In that situation, Henry had not at that time acquired any property or any undivided share in the goods. Thus, the risk will have at that time been with Ahmed. In that case, frustration becomes a possibility. Section 7 of the Sale of Goods Act 1979 will not apply because it refers only to contracts for the sale of specific goods. It is possible, however, for the contract to be frustrated at common law if it is a contract for the sale of unascertained goods out of a specific bulk (*Howell v Coupland* (1876)). This would certainly be the case where the whole of the bulk was lost or stolen. In that case, Ahmed would not be liable for non-delivery and Henry would not be liable to pay the price. However, the court may infer an intention on the part of the parties that, where only part of the bulk has been lost, the contract should not be regarded as frustrated, but that there was an implied term that: (a) the seller was excused from his obligation to deliver the whole contract quantity of 300 sacks; and (b) the buyer was to have the option of buying what was left at a *pro rata* proportion of the contract price (*Sainsbury v Street* (1972)). The solution adopted in this latter case would leave Henry with a choice as to whether to take the remaining 200 sacks at two-thirds of the contract price or to decline to take any at all. The solution adopted in *Sainsbury v Street* might not be quite so simple for a court to adopt in Ahmed's and Henry's case if Ahmed had in fact also made a contract to sell the other 100 sacks to someone else. In that case, the option allowed to the two buyers, Henry and the other one, would presumably be an option to take a proportion (in Henry's case, 75%) of the remaining 200 sacks and pay for them *pro rata* at the contract rate. Or could it be that, in the event of the other purchaser not wanting to take his proportion of the 200 sacks, Henry would be given the option of taking all 200? These are some of the possible difficulties in the court adopting a *Sainsbury v Street* approach and could lead the court instead simply to decide that the contract is frustrated. In the latter case, Henry would have no right to take any of the remaining 200 sacks, but might be able to negotiate a new contract with Ahmed about them.

CHAPTER 4

NEMO DAT QUOD NON HABET

Introduction

This chapter covers the *nemo dat* principle and the exceptions to it.

Checklist

The following topics should be prepared in advance of tackling the questions:

- the *nemo dat* principle;
- the following exceptions to it:
  - estoppel;
  - mercantile agents (s 2(1) of the Factors Act 1889);
  - voidable contracts;
  - seller in possession (s 8 of the Factors Act and s 24 of the Sale of Goods Act 1979);
  - buyer in possession (s 9 of the Factors Act and s 25 of the Sale of Goods Act);
  - Pt III of the Hire Purchase Act 1964;
- the law enabling an owner to sue in conversion;
- the implied condition as to title in s 12 of the Sale of Goods Act.

Question 13

John had a car on hire purchase terms from Fillip Finance. He still owed three monthly instalments on the car when four months ago he sold it to Arthur, a car dealer, who bought it for his wife to use as a runabout to do the shopping and collect the children from school. Before buying the car, Arthur had a check done by HPI, of which he was a member. HPI responded that the vehicle in question was not registered with HPI as being the subject of a credit agreement. Two months later, Arthur sold the car to another car dealer, Bert, who has since sold it to Ronald.

Advise the parties as to who owns the car now and what claims and liabilities each might have.

Answer plan

This is a problem dealing with the *nemo dat* principle and the exceptions to it. In this case, the problem is located in hire purchase and involves a consideration of the following: estoppel; Pt III of the Hire Purchase Act 1964; s 9 of the Factors Act 1889 (and s 25 of the Sale of Goods Act 1979); and the doctrine of feeding the title. The punchline at the end of the question is unusually helpful because it alerts you to the need to deal not only with who now owns the car, but also with any claims which the parties may have between themselves. Always in this type of question, these latter matters involve a consideration of who can maintain an action for conversion against whom and similarly who can make a claim against his seller under s 12 of the Sale of Goods Act.

Answer

It is assumed that, at the outset of the story told in this problem, Fillip Finance had good title to the car. First, we must try to ascertain who now has ownership. We will do so by dealing with the transactions in the problem in chronological order. John did not have good title to the car. So, the *nemo dat* principle means that he did not confer good title upon Arthur unless it can be shown that the sale to Arthur came within one of the exceptions to the *nemo dat* principle. Certainly, someone who has possession of goods under a hire purchase agreement is not a *buyer* in possession of the goods and, therefore, when he sells the goods, the buyer in possession exception (in s 9 of the Factors Act 1889 and s 25 of the Sale of Goods Act 1979) cannot operate to defeat the title of the owner (*Helby v Matthews* (1895)).

Also, when John sold the car to Arthur, there is no question of Pt III of the Hire Purchase Act 1964 applying, since Arthur was a car dealer. That is so despite the fact that he bought the car for his own (or rather for his wife's) private use (*Stevenson v Beverley Bentinck* (1976)). Another means by which it might be argued that Arthur obtained good title is by virtue of the doctrine of estoppel. That argument was used in a case involving very similar facts to this in *Moorgate Mercantile v Twitchings* (1976). It failed because an estoppel has to rest upon a representation by the person to be estopped (here, Fillip Finance), and failing to register an agreement with HPI is not the same thing as making a representation. Rather, it is the opposite; it is an absence of doing something. Nor could it be said that the finance company was in breach of any duty of care in failing to register the agreement, since it was not under any duty to join HPI in the first place. We are not told anything about the current terms of membership of HPI. If, as at the time of the *Twitchings* case, the terms of membership do not impose a duty on members to register their credit contracts, then the result has to be the same, that is, Fillip Finance cannot be liable to Arthur for failing to register and Arthur cannot raise an estoppel against Fillip Finance.

In fact, the problem does not tell us that Fillip Finance did fail to register with HPI the credit agreement it had with John. It is possible that the reason that Arthur was given the response he was given by HPI was that this was due to negligence by HPI. We are not told the terms of the agreement between Arthur and HPI. Depending upon what those terms are, HPI may well be liable to Arthur in negligence or for breach of the implied term to carry out its service with reasonable care and skill (s 13 of the Supply of Goods and Services Act 1982). Any exclusion clause in its contract purporting to exclude such liability will be subject to the requirement of reasonableness in the Unfair Contract Terms Act 1977. Of course, even if the fault did lie with HPI, and even if HPI is liable in the way just canvassed, that will not alter the question of who owns the car. It will serve only to give Arthur a claim in damages.

It seems unlikely then that any of the exceptions to the *nemo dat* principle will have served to give Arthur good title. When Arthur sold the car on to Bert, it seems very likely that John had still not completed the payments to Fillip Finance under his hire purchase agreement, since when he bought the car, John still had three monthly instalments to pay and Arthur sold the car after having it for only two months. If Arthur did not have good title, then he could not confer title upon Bert, unless some exception to the *nemo dat* principle applied. Again, Pt III of the Hire Purchase Act 1964 will not apply because Bert also was not a private purchaser. However, does the 'buyer in possession' exception apply, that is, the exception stated in s 9 of the Factors Act 1889 and in s 25 of the Sale of Goods Act 1979? Undoubtedly, Arthur was a buyer (someone who had bought or agreed to buy) who obtained possession of the goods with the consent of the seller (John). Undoubtedly, Arthur delivered the car to Bert and, presumably, Bert took it in good faith unaware of the defect in title. Despite the fact that there was a compliance with the wording of the two sections, nevertheless, they do not apply. The House of Lords has held that the two sections can defeat the title only of an owner who has entrusted the possession of his goods to a buyer (*National Mutual General Insurance Association v Jones* (1988)). Thus, a disposition by Arthur to Bert cannot by virtue of those two sections defeat the title of anyone except the seller who entrusted them to Arthur. The two sections cannot defeat the title of Fillip Finance.

Bert sold the car to Ronald. We are not told of Ronald's status. If he was a private purchaser, he may be able to take advantage of Pt III of the Hire Purchase Act 1964. This is because although Ronald did not buy the car from the hire purchase customer (John), the Act gives its protection to the first private purchaser provided that that private purchaser bought the car *bona fide* and unaware of the hire purchase agreement. It is immaterial how expensive the vehicle was and it is immaterial whether John's hire purchase agreement was a regulated agreement within the Consumer Credit Act 1974. There are no financial limits to the operation of Pt III of the Hire Purchase Act 1964.

There is a further way in which either Bert or Ronald may have acquired good title to the car. We are told that, four months before Bert sold the car to Ronald, John owed three monthly instalments on his hire purchase agreement. We are not told if John subsequently paid those off. If he did, then he will have done what is necessary for title to pass from Fillip Finance to John. If and when that happened, then title will have been fed automatically down the chain of buyers to Ronald (*Butterworth v Kingsway Motors* (1954)). For this to happen, there is no need for the buyers to have been in good faith and, equally, it is immaterial if any or all of them were car dealers. If it did not, then we are left wondering whether Ronald was a private purchaser or not.

Consequences

If Ronald was not a private purchaser, he will not have obtained good title unless John has paid off his hire purchase instalments. If Ronald did not get good title, Fillip Finance is entitled to succeed against Ronald in an action in conversion. The measure of damages, however, would not be the value of the goods at the date of conversion (which is the usual measure of damages for conversion), but would be the lower of two amounts which are:

(a) the value of the car at the date of conversion (that is, when Ronald bought it or refused to hand it over to Fillip Finance);

(b) the outstanding balance of the hire purchase price owed by John to Fillip Finance.

This is the rule in *Wickham Holdings v Brooke House Motors* (1967), confirmed in *Chubb Cash Ltd v John Crilley & Son* (1983).

If Ronald is liable to Fillip Finance in the way just described, then he will have a claim for his losses against Bert under s 12 of the Sale of Goods Act and Bert will, in turn, have such a claim against Arthur and Arthur will have such a claim against John, although one guesses that the latter claim may not be worth much if John has no means of paying.

If Ronald was a private purchaser who obtained good title by virtue of the 1964 Act, then Fillip Finance would have no valid claim against Ronald, but would be entitled to succeed in conversion against either Bert or Arthur. Indeed, even in the scenario just considered, that is, that Ronald was not protected by the 1964 Act, Fillip Finance would not be required to bring proceedings against Ronald; the finance company could choose instead to sue Arthur and/or Bert. They have each committed conversion by selling Fillip Finance's car. Conversion is a tort of strict liability and it is no defence to either of those dealers that, in selling Fillip Finance's car, they were unaware of Fillip Finance's interest in it. The measure of damages would again be calculated according to the rule in *Wickham Holdings v Brook House Motors*.

There is one further matter which is relevant if Ronald does not have good title. It is that he is then entitled to reject the car and demand the whole of his purchase price back from Bert, who is entitled to do the same to Arthur, who is entitled to do the same to John (although, again, John may not have the means to make the refund). The ability to reject the car depends upon the ruling in *Rowland v Divall* (1923) which, in the case of a breach of the condition as to title in s 12, regards the buyer as having suffered a total failure of consideration.

Question 14

Fred left his car for repair at George's Garage, carelessly leaving the car's registration document in the (unlocked) glove compartment. Whilst the car was at George's Garage, George telephoned Fred and informed him that another customer had seen the car and wished to buy it for £5,000. Fred said that he had not intended to sell the car, but that if George were to receive an offer in excess of £6,500, he would be interested. Without again contacting Fred, George sold the car for £6,000 to Jim, handing over the registration document and the ignition key.

Consider the legal position.

Answer plan

This question requires an understanding of the *nemo dat quod non habet* rule and the exceptions to it. It requires a knowledge of the estoppel exception and a detailed knowledge of the case law on s 2(1) of the Factors Act 1889. Sometimes, examiners allow you in the examination to refer to the statutory provisions. Without a knowledge of the case law, those provisions will take you only so far. Indeed, the question requires consideration of some possible distinctions between the facts of the problem set and those of a couple of cases.

The sensible layout of an answer is very straightforward indeed. It is to consider first who now owns the car (no definite answer, however, can be given to that). That involves considering the two relevant exceptions to the *nemo dat* principle. Many candidates answering this type of question are content to leave it there. The question does, however, ask you to consider the legal position and that must also involve setting out the rights of the parties vis à vis each other in the light of the conclusion (or different possible conclusions) you come to as to who now owns the car. It is often important in questions such as this to consider possible claims in conversion and claims under s 12 of the Sale of Goods Act 1979.

Answer

It is necessary first to establish who now owns the car, and then to advise the parties as to the legal position flowing from that.

Title

The first issue is who owns the car now? Fred, we are told, owned it to start with and since he has never agreed to sell it, he is still the owner unless one of the exceptions to the *nemo dat* principle applies. The *nemo dat* principle states that someone who lacks title to goods (for example, George) cannot transfer that title. Only if one of the exceptions to that principle applies will George have conferred good title upon Jim. Two such possible exceptions present themselves for discussion: estoppel and the mercantile agent exception. The first of these can be quickly dismissed, since it is now clearly established that the mere act of the owner of letting someone have possession of his goods is insufficient to enable an estoppel to be raised against him. The position is still the same even if the owner (here, Fred) has parted not only with possession of the goods (here, a car), but also the ignition key and the registration book; the registration book is not a document of title (*Central Newbury Car Auctions v Unity Finance* (1957)).

Does the mercantile agent exception apply? There are a number of requirements, each of which must be complied with before this exception, in s 2(1) of the Factors Act 1889, will apply. First, George must have been a mercantile agent, that is, someone having, in the customary course of his business as an agent, authority to sell. On the given facts, it seems likely that George as a car dealer had such customary authority, including the customary authority to sell the goods in his own name (*Rolls Razor v Cox* (1967)). Secondly, George must with the consent of the owner (Fred) have had possession of the goods (or documents of title) at the time of the sale to

Jim, which he clearly did, since he had possession of the car. George must have also been at that time in possession of the car in his (George's) capacity as mercantile agent. There is some ambiguity about this in the question, since originally Fred left his car with George for repair and therefore not with a view to George selling it, or seeking offers for it. However, after George's telephone call, Fred could be said to have left the car with George in two different capacities, one as a repairer and one as a factor (that is, authorised to seek and/or consider offers). This is because Fred in that telephone call clearly contemplated the possibility of George receiving further offers. Section 2(1) does not require that George 'obtained' possession with the consent of the owner, merely that he was (that is, at the time of the disposition to Jim) in possession with that consent. The same presumably applies to the judicial gloss on the section which requires him to have been in possession in his capacity as a mercantile agent. Furthermore, there does not seem to be any logical reason why George should not have been in possession in two capacities at the same time.

There is, however, a problem over the registration document. It is not a document of title, but for the mercantile agent exception to operate, the seller (here, George) must be in possession of the goods, not just in his capacity as a mercantile agent, but also in such a way as to clothe the seller with apparent authority to sell; in the case of a motor vehicle, that really requires the seller to be in possession not just of the vehicle, but also of its registration document (*Pearson v Rose and Young* (1951)). This also ties in with the further requirement for the exception to apply, namely, that the seller in selling acts in the normal course of business of a mercantile agent. It was said in *Stadium Finance v Robbins* (1962) that selling a car without its registration document would not be a sale in the ordinary course of business. On the given facts, George was in possession of the registration document which, together with the ignition key, he handed over to Jim. However, it was held in *Pearson v Rose and Young* that not only must the seller be in possession of the registration book as well as the car, but also he must be in possession of the registration book (as well as of the car) *with the consent of the owner*. In that case, the seller was in possession of the registration book, but did not have the consent of the owner to that possession, since the seller had obtained possession of it by a trick he played upon the owner. This was taken one stage further in *Stadium Finance v Robbins*, where it was held that the owner accidentally leaving the document locked in the glove compartment did not amount to the seller having possession of it with the consent of the owner. The only possible distinctions between that case and the present problem are: first, that in Fred's case, the document was in an *unlocked* glove compartment; secondly, that very possibly the key to the glove compartment in Fred's car was the same as the ignition key which Fred presumably left with the car;

thirdly, that possibly (although we do not know) something was said in the telephone conversation between George and Fred which alluded to the registration document and indicated Fred's 'consent' to George's possession of it.

Subject to what has just been said about the registration book, it seems that all the requirements of the exception have been satisfied, including the requirement that Jim took the car in good faith without notice of George's lack of authority to make the sale. There is nothing in the stated facts of the problem to indicate that Jim should have been 'put on notice'; at least that is so provided the sale price of £6,000 was not so low as itself to be a cause of suspicion. If there is a substantial doubt about Jim's good faith, that could cause him a problem, since the burden of proof to show that he took in good faith is upon Jim (*Heap v Motorists Advisory Agency* (1923)).

Consequences

Assuming that all the requirements of s 2(1) of the Factors Act are satisfied, then Jim now has good title to the car. That means of course that Fred, in any action for conversion, would fail against Jim. Fred would, however, have a good claim for conversion against George. This is a tort of strict liability and since George has effectively disposed of the car to Jim, could result not in any order for the goods to be returned to Fred, but only in an award of damages. The *prima facie* measure of damages to which Fred is entitled would be the value of the car at the date of the sale to Jim. This would be a matter of evidence, but presumably Fred will try to insist that it was worth at least £6,500, since that was a figure he would have been interested in. The value, however, is not necessarily the car's value to Jim, but its market value. It is of course possible that, before selling the car, George had carried out the repairs. In that case, the cost of the repairs will need to be taken into account in one way or another, either by a set-off of their cost or by deduction of an improvement allowance by virtue of the provisions of the Torts (Interference with Goods) Act 1977. That allowance might well be less than the cost of the repairs, since it is the proportion of the value of the car (that is, at the date of the sale to Jim) which is attributable to the improvement effected by the repairs.

If Jim did not satisfy the requirements of s 2(1) of the Factors Act, he will not have acquired good title. In that case, Fred would be entitled to succeed against Jim in an action in conversion. It is assumed that the car was not unique. Therefore, the result of such an action would not be to compel Jim to return the car, but would be an award of damages (with Jim perhaps being given the option of returning the car). The damages would be calculated as in the case of the claim against George just discussed. Thus, the improvement allowance (due to the repairs by George – assuming George had effected those repairs) would be deducted. If Jim chose to return the car to Fred, Fred would be liable to pay the improvement allowance to Jim.

If Jim were to be held liable to Fred in the way just outlined, Jim would have a claim against George for breach of the condition as to title in s 12 of the Sale of Goods Act 1979. He would be entitled to the return of his purchase price, but would have to give credit for any improvement allowance received by him from Fred. The entitlement to the return of the purchase price is based upon the notion that since Jim never got title, he has suffered a total failure of consideration. Thus, according to the controversial decision in *Rowland v Divall* (1923), Jim is entitled to the return of the full purchase price (minus, if applicable, the improvement allowance) even if he has some months' use of the car before having to surrender it to Fred, for example, if it was some considerable time before the truth was discovered and the car's whereabouts traced to Jim.

Question 15

Oona is the proprietor of a jewellery shop. Adrian came into the shop, selected a diamond brooch and paid for it. Adrian explained to her that he had an appointment to play football that afternoon and asked if it would be all right to leave the brooch with Oona until after his football game. A little later that same afternoon, Barnard, who looked the very image of Christopher Dean, the famous ice dancer, came into the shop and selected the very same brooch (which by an oversight Oona had failed to remove to be kept for Adrian). Oona let Barnard pay the £300 price by cheque, which Barnard did – signing himself Christopher Dean. Subsequently, the cheque was dishonoured and Oona informed the police, who traced the brooch to Colin's shop in Croydon. It has turned out that Barnard has a stall at Bermondsey market in South London and that he sold it (for £160) early one morning to Colin, a jewellery dealer, who considered at the time that he had a real bargain.

Advise Oona.

Answer plan

The question deals with certain 'exceptions' to the *nemo dat* rule, namely, the position where a seller sells goods which the seller has already sold to an earlier buyer; when a buyer misrepresents (or a seller is mistaken as to) the buyer's identity; and the rule (in s 25 of the Sale of Goods Act 1979) dealing with a buyer in possession who sells the goods. Also expected is the knowledge that the exception relating to market overt has been abolished. It is logical to deal with the transactions in chronological order. In that way, the passing of title can be traced through those transactions. As always in this sort of examination question, certain key facts are not given, with the result that the examinee cannot always be sure if an exception does or does not apply. This requires, as the answer progresses, copious use of the expressions 'if' or 'assuming that'.

Answer

It will be assumed that Oona was at the outset the owner of the brooch, since there is nothing in the question to suggest otherwise. Therefore, each of the transactions (the sales to Adrian and to Barnard and the sale by Barnard to Colin) must be examined to see if it operated to pass title.

Oona's sale to Barnard

The sale by Oona to Barnard appears to have been affected by fraud on the part of Barnard, who passed himself off as being Christopher Dean. Whether or not he said anything to that effect, he certainly made a representation of it by signing himself as Christopher Dean. The effect of this was either to render the contract between himself and Oona void or to render it voidable. In one case on somewhat similar facts (*Ingram v Little* (1961)), it was held that the contract was void. That, however, is now generally regarded as a case on its own special facts. The law presumes that as the parties were dealing face to face, Oona intended to deal with the person there in the shop, albeit that she was mistaken as to that person's identity (*Lewis v Averay* (1972)). This is not a situation, like that in *Shogun v Hudson* (2001), where the parties were not face to face but contracted via an intermediary. Thus, there was an agreement between Oona and Barnard which, however, was a voidable contract. This was the result achieved in a case on remarkably similar facts, involving a sale of a ring by a jeweller (*Phillips v Brooks* (1919)). Thus, assuming for the moment that Oona had title, good title passed to Barnard, unless and until such time as Oona avoided the contract. In circumstances like those in the present case, it is impractical to suppose that the seller (Oona) can contact the buyer (Barnard) in order to avoid (set aside) the contract, since Oona does not actually know who Barnard was. If, however, the seller, when she realises the fraud, does her best to avoid the contract, for example, by informing the police, that will be regarded as avoiding the contract (*Car and Universal*

Finance v Caldwell (1965)). This is what Oona did. Such avoiding of the contract operates to rescind it and thus to cause the title to revert to the seller (Oona). However, it will not have that effect if, as in *Phillips v Brooks*, the rogue buyer (Barnard) has already sold the goods to a purchaser who was ignorant of the fraud and who bought in good faith. We are not told whether Barnard sold the brooch to Colin before or after Oona informed the police of the fraud upon herself. If it was afterwards, then Oona's informing of the police will have operated to rescind her contract with Barnard and to cause title to the brooch to revert to Oona. If Barnard sold the brooch to Colin before Oona informed the police, then, since Barnard had title at that time, Colin will have received title and, assuming that he was ignorant of the fraud and a purchaser in good faith, his title will be unassailable by Oona. The fact that the price which Colin paid was low would not seem to prevent him having been a purchaser in good faith. Indeed, one would expect prices in a street market to be significantly less than in, say, a Hatton Garden jewellers.

Oona a seller in possession

The position relating to the sale by Oona to Barnard is complicated by the fact that the brooch in fact belongs to Adrian. If the transaction between Oona and Barnard was not avoided before Barnard sold the brooch on to Colin, the question arises as to whether that transaction operated to transfer title from Oona who did not have title, that is, so as to defeat the title of Adrian. Oona was a seller (she had sold to Adrian) and she continued in possession of the goods with the consent of the buyer (Adrian). In those circumstances, if she sold and delivered the goods to another person who received them in good faith and without notice of the previous sale to Adrian, that transaction has the same effect as if Oona had been expressly authorised by Adrian to make it (s 24 of the Sale of Goods Act and s 8 of the Factors Act 1889). Thus, it would operate to transfer Adrian's title to the innocent buyer. The question then arises as to whether Barnard was 'in good faith'. In one sense, he very clearly was not acting in good faith because he was himself fraudulent. Section 24 is clearly intended not to allow someone who takes in bad faith to benefit from the section. The difficulty is that if the absence of good faith prevents the sale from Oona to Barnard transferring title to Barnard, it is not Barnard who suffers but the person (Colin) to whom Barnard sold. The requirement of good faith may possibly simply relate to the matter of the previous sale (in this case, to Adrian). It may mean that the buyer is not acting in good faith – and s 24 does not operate – if the buyer (even though he may not have 'notice' of the previous sale) has reason to suspect that there is a previous sale. If that is what it means, then Barnard was (in that limited sense) presumably acting in good faith (that is, without the slightest suspicion of any earlier sale of the brooch by Oona). In that case, if the sale by Barnard to Colin took place before Oona informed the police, Barnard (and, through Barnard, Colin) will have secured good title by virtue of s 24. In that case, Adrian will have lost title.

Barnard's sale to Colin

It is necessary now to consider the position if the sale by Barnard to Colin occurred after Oona informed the police. In those circumstances, Barnard was selling something to which he did not have title and, according to the *nemo dat quod non habet* principle, he will not have conferred title upon Colin. However, there is one exception to that principle which might have relevance. This is the possibility of Colin relying upon s 25 of the Sale of Goods Act. First, however, it must be pointed out that the exception which used to exist in relation to any sale in market overt no longer exists, since s 22 of the Sale of Goods Act was repealed in 1995. Thus, the fact that it was in Bermondsey market that Barnard sold the brooch is of no significance.

Section 25

It is possible that Colin can claim good title by virtue of this section which is virtually identical in its wording to s 9 of the Factors Act 1889. Assuming, as has been argued above, that the sale by Oona to Barnard was a voidable (and not a void) contract, then Barnard was someone who had 'bought or agreed to buy'. He was in possession of the brooch with the consent of the seller (Oona) and he delivered the brooch under a sale to Colin. That all being so, the conditions of s 25 were all satisfied, apart from the requirement that Colin received the brooch in good faith. It would seem that Colin's belief that he had a good bargain would not cast doubt on his *bona fides* unless the price (of £160) was so low that it ought to have put him on notice. Once the conditions of the section are satisfied, the sale and delivery of the brooch by Barnard to Colin has the same effect as if Barnard were a mercantile agent in possession of the goods with the consent of Oona. This wording of s 25 taken literally means that even if all the conditions of s 25 were satisfied, Colin will have obtained good title only if the conditions for the passing of title by a mercantile agent (that is, under s 2(1) of the Factors Act 1889) were also satisfied. This means that s 25 will operate to pass good title only if the buyer in possession (here, Barnard) sells the goods in the normal course of business of a mercantile agent – that is, even if he was not in fact a mercantile agent. This seems to have been the approach adopted by the Court of Appeal in *Newtons of Wembley v Williams* (1965), where the buyer in possession sold the goods (a car) in a street market where mercantile agents commonly sold cars.

It was held in that case that s 25 did operate to pass good title in circumstances (such as those in the present problem) where the buyer in possession had acquired the goods under a contract which was voidable for his own fraud, and which had in fact been avoided before the sale by the buyer.

However, s 25 is probably of no use to Colin unless he can use it to defeat the title of Adrian as well as that of Oona, since we have seen that Adrian appears to have obtained good title prior to Oona's agreeing to sell the brooch to Barnard. We are here dealing with the situation where it is after Oona contacted the police that Barnard sold the brooch to Colin. In that situation, s 25 is of no use to Colin, because s 25 can be relied on to defeat the title only of the seller (Oona) who entrusted the goods to the buyer (Barnard) who has then sold them on to the innocent purchaser (Colin) (*National Mutual General Insurance Association v Jones* (1988)).

Thus, Oona is advised that Adrian obtained title by virtue of having bought the brooch from her. If Oona informed the police and thus avoided her contract with Barnard before he sold the brooch to Colin, then Adrian still has that title. The sale to Colin will not operate to transfer title to Colin because: (a) the market overt exception to the *nemo dat* rule had been abolished; and (b) s 25 cannot operate to transfer to the buyer (Colin) any title other than that of the person (Oona) who entrusted goods to the seller (Barnard). It will not operate to defeat Adrian's title. In those circumstances, Adrian could then demand return of the brooch from Colin and, failing its return, would be entitled to succeed in an action against Colin in conversion. If Oona did not inform the police before Barnard sold the brooch to Colin, then (subject to the correct interpretation of the expression 'in good faith' in s 24) Colin will have obtained good title by virtue of having bought from someone (Barnard) who obtained good title by virtue of s 24 of the Sale of Goods Act. In those circumstances, Oona will be liable in conversion to Adrian for having sold his brooch.

CHAPTER 5

PERFORMANCE AND REMEDIES

Introduction

This chapter deals with remedies for breach of a contract of sale of goods, including coverage of the measure of damages.

Checklist

The following topics should be prepared in advance of tackling the questions:

- the provisions in ss 11(4), 35 and 35A of the Sale of Goods Act 1979 on acceptance and rejection;
- the measure of damages and rules thereon in ss 50 and 51 of the Sale of Goods Act 1979;
- the effect of an anticipatory breach;
- severable contracts and s 30 of the Sale of Goods Act 1979.

Question 16

On 1 January, Rex had 2,000 widgets in stock. On that date, Bonzo contracted with Rex to buy 1,000 widgets from Rex's current stock for £1,000, delivery to take place at Bonzo's premises on 1 February. On 25 January, when the market price of widgets had dropped to 50 pence per widget, Bonzo sent a fax to Rex informing him that Bonzo no longer wanted the widgets. On 26 January, the market price of widgets began to rise and thereafter it fluctuated, so that on the succeeding days it was as follows: 26 January, 60 pence per widget; 27 January, 65 pence; 28 January, 70 pence; 29 January, 60 pence; 30 January, 80 pence; 31 January, 85 pence; 1 February, 90 pence. On 27 January, Bonzo telephoned Rex stating that after all, he did need the widgets. Rex stated, however, that he could not supply them because he had already sold and delivered his whole stock of widgets to Fido.

Advise Bonzo in each of the following alternative situations:

(a) that Rex sold and delivered his stock of widgets to Fido on 24 January;

(b) that Rex sold and delivered his stock of widgets to Fido on 26 January.

Answer plan

With a question such as this, where there is a single problem but a sub-set of questions, it cannot be assumed that the length of answer for each question is necessarily to be the same. Indeed, here some of the same principles require discussion in each of the two different scenarios. The whole question is concerned with repudiation of the contract and the consequent measure of damages. Given that the two scenarios are clearly alternatives, it makes sense to take them separately.

Answer

This question is concerned with anticipatory repudiation, who is liable to whom and for how much.

(a)

Let us first take scenario (a) (Rex selling to Fido on 24 January). This must have been a repudiatory (and anticipatory) breach by Rex of his contract with Bonzo, since it was an act which was totally repugnant to and inconsistent with Rex's continuing ability to perform his contract with Bonzo. It seems, however, that Bonzo did not accept that repudiation as ending the contract, since it seems that Bonzo was unaware of it. This seems clear from the fact that the next day Bonzo sent a fax stating that he no longer wanted the widgets. Thus, that fax appears itself to have been a repudiatory breach by Bonzo. For the moment, it will be treated as such in this answer. The question then arises as to whether Rex accepted Bonzo's breach as terminating the contract. It is arguable that he did, since he informed Bonzo two days later on the telephone that he could not (that is, was not going to) supply the widgets.

In those circumstances, Rex is entitled to claim damages for the anticipatory breach by Bonzo. The damages claimable are for non-acceptance of the goods, and the *prima facie* measure of damages is the difference between the contract price (£1 per widget) and the (lower) market price on the date when, under the contract, delivery was due to take place (90 pence) (s 50(3)). That is still the relevant measure of damages, even where the buyer's non-acceptance takes the form of an anticipatory breach which has been accepted by the seller as putting an end to the contract (*Tai Hing Cotton Mill v Kamsing Knitting Factory* (1978)). Thus, the *prima facie* measure of damages available to Rex is 1,000 x 10 pence, which is £100.

This *prima facie* measure of damages is based upon an assumption that the seller waits until the contractual date for delivery under the contract and then goes out into the market and sells on that day. Even if that is not what the seller has in fact done, the measure of damages is nevertheless based on the assumption that it is. Thus, if the seller chooses to sell in the market either earlier or later than the contractual date for delivery, that fact will normally make no difference to the measure of damages (*Pagnan v Corbisa* (1970)). However, in the present case, the seller, Rex, had already sold the goods, that is, before the repudiation by Bonzo, and in doing so had disabled himself from being able to perform the contract with Bonzo. In those circumstances, the *prima facie* measure of damages can be reduced. We are not told the price at which Rex sold the widgets to Fido. Given that on 25 January, the market price was 50 pence per widget, it would seem likely that Rex sold at about that price. In those circumstances, the question arises as to by how much, if at all, the measure of damages should be reduced. By selling to Fido on 24 January, Rex actually increased his own losses, since he sold at a much lower figure than he would have done if he had held on until the contractual delivery date under his contract with Bonzo. So, at first sight, this would seem to be far from a case for *decreasing* the *prima facie* measure of damages. The fact, however, is that Rex, by virtue of his having sold the widgets to Fido, had already (that is, before Bonzo's repudiation) disabled himself from fulfilling his contract to Bonzo. Thus, Bonzo's later repudiation did not cause Rex any loss at all. According to this analysis, Rex is entitled only to nominal damages (see *The Mihalis Angelos* (1971) and *Gill and Duffus v Berger & Co* (1984)).

There is a possible different analysis of the above facts which would, however, produce a not dissimilar result. This analysis rests upon the principle that if a party to a contract relies upon a bad reason for treating the contract at an end when in fact there was available to him a valid reason, his treatment of the contract as at an end will not be regarded as wrongful (see *The Mihalis Angelos* (1971) and *Glencore Grain Rotterdam BV v Lebanese Organisation for International Commerce* (1997)). Applying this principle, Bonzo's fax indicating that he did not want the widgets was not a wrongful repudiation of the contract, but was a rightful one because of Rex's repudiation in selling the stock elsewhere. That Rex's act in selling his stock elsewhere did amount to a repudiation of his contract with Bonzo cannot really be doubted, given that the contract with Bonzo required Rex to deliver not just any widgets but 1,000 widgets from Bonzo's current stock. Thus, Bonzo is entitled to maintain an action against Rex for non-delivery of the widgets. Bonzo's subsequent change of mind and request on 27 January to reinstate delivery do not alter that position, since his request was declined by Rex. The measure of damages to which Bonzo is entitled is *prima facie* the difference between the contract price and the market price, if higher, on the day when delivery was due to occur (s 51(3) and *Tai Hing Cotton Mill v Kamsing Knitting Factory*). According to this rule, however, Bonzo has suffered no loss since the market price on 1 February (the day when delivery ought to have taken place) was 90 pence per widget, which is less than the contract price of £1. Thus, Bonzo is entitled to only nominal damages.

(b)

In this scenario, there is no doubt that Bonzo committed a wrongful repudiation by his fax on 25 January, since at that time Rex had not resold the goods. Taking it that Rex by his response on the telephone to Bonzo on 27 January accepted Bonzo's repudiation as putting an end to the contract, the question again arises as to the measure of damages. Again, the *prima facie* measure is the difference between the contract price and the market price on the day due for delivery (s 50(3) and *Tai Hing Cotton Mill v Kamsing Knitting Factory*). So, again, this will produce a figure of 1,000 x 10 pence, that is, £100. However, in this case, Rex has himself sold the widgets elsewhere prior to the contractual date (1 February) for delivery. It must be determined what effect, if any, that has on the *prima facie* measure of damages. Normally, the fact that the seller chooses to sell at an earlier or later time than the contractual date will make no difference (*Pagnan v Corbisa*). That principle is subject to the principle that the innocent party (here, Rex) who accepts the other party's wrongful repudiation as putting an end to the contract becomes under a duty to take reasonable steps to mitigate his loss. With the benefit of hindsight, we can say that Rex's sale on 26 January was mistaken, because it left him with a larger loss than if he had waited until 1 February to resell. In *Hoffberger v Ascot International Bloodstock Bureau* (1976), in very different circumstances from those in the present problem, the seller was held entitled to recover, as part of the damages awarded, the extra loss which his reasonable attempt to minimise his loss had in fact caused. If Rex's sale on 26 January can be described as a reasonable attempt to mitigate his loss – albeit one which as events turned out increased that loss – then the court may, in its discretion, award a measure of damages fixed by reference to some date other than the contractual date for delivery (*Johnson v Agnew* (1979)). That date would clearly then be the date (26 January) when Rex sold the widgets to Fido. This would result in a higher measure of damages which would be the difference between the contract price (£1) and the market price on 26 January (60 pence), namely, 1,000 x 40 pence, which is £400. It is difficult to know whether the sale on 26 January *was* a reasonable attempt to mitigate damages. Clearly, if the price (60 pence) of widgets on 26 January appeared to be the 'top' of a brief strengthening of market confidence, then it would be plausible to describe the sale as a reasonable attempt to mitigate. But how does a market 'appear'? How, at any one time, can a seller predict whether the market will continue to rise or is about to turn?

There is one important fact which we do not know, namely, the price at which Rex sold to Fido. We know that the market price on the date in question (26 January) was 60 pence. If in fact the sale to Fido was at a higher price than that (for example, 70 pence), then that would lend some support to the suggestion that the sale was Rex taking a good and sensible opportunity to minimise his loss. Of course, in such a case, if the court did exercise its discretion not to apply the *prima facie* rule, it obviously would fix the measure of damages not by reference to the market price (60 pence) on 26 January, but by reference to the higher price actually obtained by Rex on his sale to Fido. Leaving aside the possibility that Rex sold at above the market price on 26 January, our conclusion is that Rex is entitled to damages and that either he will receive £100 damages (that is, according to the *prima facie* measure set out in s 50(3) of the Sale of Goods Act 1979) or £400 (that is, if in its discretion the court considers Rex's sale to Fido on 26 January a reasonable attempt to mitigate his loss).

Question 17

Victor agreed to sell to Phillip 900 mahogany desks. The contract required delivery to be made in three equal instalments on 20 January, 25 January and 30 January. It also contained the clause 'This entire contract is governed by English law'.

On 20 January, Victor delivered 280 mahogany desks, mistakenly including 20 teak desks in the consignment. Today is 25 January and Victor has delivered 295 mahogany desks.

Phillip has now found a cheaper supplier and wishes to return all the desks delivered so far and to cancel delivery of the third consignment.

Advise Phillip.

What difference, if any, would it have made to your advice if today is 3 February and Victor has only just delivered the second consignment?

Answer plan

There are two particular issues in the question which, on the facts given, it is impossible to determine for sure. These are 'has Phillip accepted the first consignment within the meaning of s 35 of the Sale of Goods Act 1979?' and 'is the contract severable or entire?'. Because of this, it is important not just to point these things out, but also to identify the position in the different possible eventualities. Thus, it is essential to use that wonderful word 'if' which is so often useful to examinees in law examinations.

As the question gives a story of two defective deliveries, the structure adopted for the answer here is to deal with them each in turn and then, at the end, to deal with the rider to the question.

Answer

It is proposed to deal initially with the effect of the defective first delivery five days ago and then with the effect of today's defective delivery.

The first delivery

When Victor delivered the first consignment, he was in breach of contract in one or both of two respects. First, 20 of the desks were not mahogany and therefore did not comply with what must have been part of the contract description. That put Victor in breach of the condition implied by s 13 of the Sale of Goods Act 1979. Secondly, one can say that Victor delivered too small a quantity of the contract goods (that is, mahogany desks). Either way, there has been a breach of condition, giving the buyer the right to reject the goods (see s 30(1) of the 1979 Act) and this, we are told, is what Phillip wishes to do. There are, however, two problems with that. First, it is not clear whether the contract is a severable one. If it is, the defective first delivery may not give Phillip the right to reject the later two consignments. Secondly, it is possible that Phillip may have lost his right to reject the goods because he may be held to have 'accepted' the first defective delivery.

To take the second of these issues first, a buyer who accepts the goods or part of them is precluded from rejecting the goods (s 11(4) of the Sale of Goods Act 1979). Section 35 of the 1979 Act states three things which will amount to acceptance. The problem simply gives us no information on the first two; we are therefore unable to state whether Phillip has either intimated to Victor his acceptance of the goods or else done any act inconsistent with rejecting them. As to the third thing (s 35(4)) listed in s 35, it is debatable whether a lapse of a reasonable length of time has occurred. Phillip has had the desks for five days. It is true that a reasonable period of time will not have elapsed if Phillip has not had the goods long enough to have been able to examine them to see if they conform with the contract. However, it must have been fairly obvious almost immediately upon delivery that: (a) 20 of the desks were missing; and (b) 20 of those which were delivered were teak and not mahogany. It is arguable in those circumstances that five days is more than a reasonable period of time in which to reject. Certainly, three weeks was held to be more than a reasonable period of time in the first instance decision (on the very different facts of a defective motor car) in *Bernstein v Pamson Motors* (1987). We are not told what were the provisions of the contract regarding the time of payment. If a period of, say, one month was allowed for Phillip to pay, then it may be that a reasonable period of time would be held to last at least until the deadline for payment (*Truk v Tokmakidis* (2000)).

Since s 35 was amended, there is now a right of partial rejection which would allow Phillip to reject the desks which do not conform to the contract and to accept the rest (the other 260). However, it is clear from the facts that Phillip would prefer to reject the lot. Thus, assuming that Phillip has not 'accepted' the first consignment, he will have the right to reject that consignment (the whole of it). Whether that gives him the right to reject the later consignments also depends upon whether the contract is an entire contract or is a severable one. If it is not severable, then the breach of condition entitles Phillip to reject all consignments. The test of whether a contract is severable is one of construction (interpretation) of the contract, that is, one is trying to discover from the words of the contract what was the intention of the parties. Was it their intention that a breach in relation to one consignment should entitle the purchaser to reject all? If not, then the contract is severable – see generally *Jackson v Rotax Motor and Cycle Co* (1910). The fact that the desks were to be delivered in instalments is some evidence that the contract was severable. We are not told, however, whether under the contract, the consignments were each to be separately paid for. If they were, then that would be strong evidence that the contract was severable. It may be argued that the parties had themselves clearly labelled the contract as not being severable but as being entire, because of the clause in the contract which read that the 'entire' contract was governed by English law. It is submitted, however, that this clause is nothing more than a choice of law clause and that the word 'entire', in the particular context of that clause, does not bear upon whether the contract was severable, but merely means that all of the contract, as opposed to part of it, was to be governed by English law.

If Phillip has not 'accepted' the first consignment and if the contract is not severable, then he is entitled to reject all the goods, including the later two consignments. If he has not 'accepted' the first consignment and the contract is severable, then he may still be able to regard the whole contract as repudiated and thus be able to reject the two later consignments. Whether the whole contract is repudiated depends upon the following two factors: (a) the ratio that the breach bore quantitatively to the whole contract; and (b) the likelihood of the breach being repeated in later instalments (*Maple Flock Co v Universal Furniture Products* (1934)). This is not so easy to determine. At the time that the breach occurs, one cannot tell anything about the second of these factors. As to the first, it could be said that the breach is fairly small in relation to the whole contract. First, it relates to only one consignment out of the three and, within that consignment, it affects only a small proportion of the total quantity of the desks.

Thus, based on the first defective delivery, one's advice to Phillip would be cautious since: (a) he may have 'accepted' the goods; (b) the contract may be severable; and if it is, the *Maple Flock* test may not be satisfied so as to allow him to regard the whole contract as repudiated.

The second delivery

The breach in relation to the second delivery is simply a delivery of too small a quantity. The missing five desks would appear too much for the courts to be prepared to ignore the breach on the *de minimis non curat lex* principle. Thus, it is a breach of condition.

If the contract was not severable and Phillip has not 'accepted' the first consignment, then he is entitled to reject all three consignments because of the breaches of condition in relation to the first two consignments. If the contract was not severable and Phillip has 'accepted' the first consignment, then the position is clouded by the fact that the effect of s 11(4) and the new s 35A is not entirely clear. Section 35 introduced the concept of partial rejection, allowing the buyer to reject some or all of the non-conforming goods, provided he accepted all of the conforming goods. One thing which does seem clear is that ss 11(4) and 35A do not allow the buyer to reject any goods (whether conforming or not) which he has actually accepted. Thus, if the contract is not severable and Phillip has 'accepted' the first consignment, he cannot now reject any of the first consignment (though he may claim damages in respect of the breaches relating to the first consignment). As regards the second consignment, he is entitled to reject any non-conforming goods, but not conforming goods. However, there are no non-conforming goods, since the only breach relating to the second consignment is a shortfall in the number of desks. Section 30(1) entitles the buyer to reject all the goods if a quantity less than the contract quantity is tendered. The buyer appears, however, to be precluded from exercising this right by his acceptance of the first consignment. This is the effect of s 11(4) in the case of a non-severable agreement. Although s 11(4) is subject to s 35A, the latter is of no help to the buyer in this instance. Section 35A(1) applies only where it is non-conforming goods which are being rejected. Section 35A(2) also appears to be of no help, since it applies only where the buyer has a right to reject an instalment, and that is the very issue which we have to determine (that is, does the buyer have a right to reject the second instalment?). If this seems an odd result, it is explicable on the basis that the agreement is not severable. In the case of a non-severable agreement, acceptance by the buyer of any conforming goods precludes rejection of any goods. Perhaps this makes it more likely that the courts will regard contracts for delivery in instalments as severable contracts.

If the contract was severable, then Phillip would certainly be entitled to reject the second consignment because of the breach of condition in relation to that consignment, and that is so even if he had 'accepted' the first consignment; s 11(4) does not apply to severable contracts. In the event that the contract was severable, then the *Maple Flock* test again needs to be applied to determine whether Phillip is entitled to reject the third instalment as well. This time, however, it seems much more likely that the test is satisfied. This is because on two out of the three instalments, Victor has made a non-conforming delivery. Thus, the ratio that the breach(es) bear quantitatively to the whole contract is much higher and would also seem to suggest a higher probability that he will repeat this with the third and last delivery. On that interpretation, Phillip is entitled, even if the contract is severable, to regard the whole contract as repudiated and thus to reject the third consignment as well as the second. Whether that entitles him also to reject the first consignment is debatable. Although on its wording s 11(4) does not apply to severable contracts, it would seem unlikely that the law is such as to allow rejection of any goods which have actually been accepted. Of course, if Phillip has not 'accepted' the first instalment, then the breaches relating to the first two instalments entitle him, for the reasons just given, to regard the whole contract as repudiated, to reject all the goods delivered under the first two instalments and to refuse to accept the third.

The rider

Would it have made any difference if the second delivery had been made only on 3 February? This would affect the consideration of two issues discussed above. First, the time lapse between the first delivery and today would be longer (that is, from 20 January to 3 February) and that would increase the likelihood that Phillip would be held to have accepted the first consignment and thus be precluded from rejecting that consignment or, if the contract was not severable, any of the consignments. Secondly, it would increase the seriousness of the breach in relation to the second consignment, which would suggest that there is a greater degree of breach as compared with the contract as a whole, for there would be no doubt that the breach in relation to the second consignment did indeed affect the whole of that consignment. Thus, if the contract is severable, it would be much more likely that by the time the second delivery has come, several days late and with five desks short, Victor has committed a breach entitling Phillip to regard the contract as repudiated and therefore to reject the third consignment immediately.

CHAPTER 6

MAKING AND CANCELLING A CREDIT AGREEMENT

Introduction

This chapter deals with the common law and statutory provisions relating to the making of a credit agreement, including coverage of the triangular scenario involving a customer, a garage and a finance company.

Checklist

The following topics should be prepared in advance of tackling the questions:

- definition of 'credit';
- effects of unlicensed trading;
- ss 60–65 of the Consumer Credit Act 1974 on the documentation formalities;
- ss 67–74 of the Consumer Credit Act on cancellation;
- the Consumer Protection (Cancellation of Contracts Concluded away from Business Premises) Regulations 1987;
- s 56 on the agency of the dealer and the position at common law.

Question 18

On Monday, about three weeks ago, John visited Sellapup's garage where he test drove a secondhand Webb's Wonderful car. Sellapup told him 'It has done 40,000 miles'. John, who had an old car to give in part-exchange, asked for hire purchase terms. Sellapup produced one of Fleece You Finance Ltd's hire purchase proposal forms. John and Sellapup agreed upon the following terms:

- £8,000 cash price for the Webb's Wonderful;
- 30 monthly instalments of £250 each;
- a total hire purchase price of £10,000;
- an initial payment of £500;
- a part-exchange allowance of £2,000.

Sellapup completed the proposal form accordingly and John signed it. John left the initial payment with Sellapup, who informed him that he would be able to take delivery of the Webb's Wonderful (and at the same time leave his old one) when Fleece You Finance Ltd had confirmed its acceptance.

On Friday last, John telephoned Sellapup and informed him that he now wanted to back out of the whole deal. That same day, John learned two things: Sellapup has become bankrupt, and the Webb's Wonderful has in fact done over 80,000 miles. The very next day, Saturday last, John received from Fleece You Finance Ltd its acceptance of his proposal together with a copy of the fully executed agreement; this had been posted to John the day before, Friday. Since then, John has not taken delivery of the Webb's Wonderful and still has his old car.

Advise John.

Answer plan

The agreement in this case does not appear to be cancellable. Thus, the issues are:

- did John's telephone call to Sellapup work to revoke his offer (that is, his offer to enter the hire purchase agreement with Fleece You Finance Ltd)? This involves discussing whether notice to Sellapup was sufficient and whether the revocation came before acceptance;
- if John's revocation was effective, what are the consequences?;
- if the revocation was not effective, what remedies, if any, has John got against Fleece You Finance Ltd in respect of the misrepresentation?

Answer

The agreement in this case appears to be a regulated consumer credit agreement, since John is an individual and the amount of credit is clearly within the £25,000 limit. The amount of credit in this agreement is £5,500, being £8,000 (the cash price) minus £2,000 (the part-exchange allowance) and the initial payment (£500). Clearly, from his telephone message to Sellapup, it can be seen that John wishes to back out of the whole deal. Advice will therefore be given to him on whether he can and, if he can, the consequences of doing so. Advice will also be given to him on any remedies he may have for Sellapup's false statement that the car had covered only 40,000 miles and, briefly, on his rights under s 99 of the Consumer Credit Act 1974.

Withdrawal

The hire purchase agreement in this case is not a cancellable one within s 67 of the Consumer Credit Act since, although there were (at Sellapup's garage) antecedent negotiations including oral representations, John signed the agreement (it appears) at Sellapup's garage and therefore the requirement that he sign it away from certain business premises is not satisfied. Nor is the agreement cancellable under the Consumer Protection (Cancellation of Contracts Concluded away from Business Premises) Regulations 1987, since it was not made during or following a visit by a trader to anybody's home or to John's place of work. Thus, John's chances of getting out of the agreement depend upon: (a) whether his telephone message to Sellapup was effective to withdraw his offer to enter the hire purchase agreement; or, failing that, (b) whether he can rescind the agreement because of the misrepresentation made to him of the car's mileage. The latter possibility will be discussed later. Failing either of those possibilities, John could exercise his statutory right of termination under s 99 of the Consumer Credit Act.

Sellapup was an agent of Fleece You Finance Ltd for the purpose of receiving notice of cancellation. That is so at common law (*Financings v Stimson* (1962)), a rule confirmed in the case of a regulated agreement by s 57(3). Thus, the telephone conversation on Friday in which John informed Sellapup that he wanted to back out of the deal will have the same effect as if that conversation was between John and Fleece You Finance Ltd. Section 57(2) and (3) makes it clear that the agency rule just mentioned applies equally to oral as to written notice, which 'however expressed' indicates John's intention to withdraw from the agreement. However, it is important to see if John's withdrawal came in time. He was able to withdraw only from a 'prospective agreement'. This brings into play the operation of the rules of the law of contract in order to discover whether, at the time of John's telephone call to Sellapup, the hire purchase agreement had already been made or was still only a prospective agreement. We are informed that on that same day (Friday), Fleece You Finance Ltd posted to John its acceptance of his offer. Presumably, it was reasonable to expect the post to be used as the medium of communication and, assuming that the acceptance letter was properly stamped and addressed (as seems likely, since John got the letter the following day), then the rule in *Henthorn v Fraser* (1892) applies; thus, Fleece You Finance Ltd's acceptance took effect upon posting. The result is, therefore, that John's position depends upon the relative timings, on Friday last, of the posting by Fleece You Finance Ltd of its acceptance and of John's withdrawal, that is, his telephone call to Sellapup. If the acceptance was posted first, then the contract between John and Fleece You Finance Ltd was made. In that case, John is not, on the facts given in the question, able to back out of it, other than by virtue of Sellapup's misrepresentation or by exercising his statutory right of termination under s 99 of the Consumer Credit Act 1974. If John's withdrawal occurred before the acceptance was posted, then John no longer has an option; he will effectively have withdrawn from the prospective agreement.

Assuming that John's withdrawal came in time, his withdrawal, although it in fact came *before* the acceptance, nevertheless has the effect laid down in s 57. The effect is as if the agreement had been a cancellable one within s 59, had been made and then had been cancelled. This in turn has the effect of applying ss 69–73 to the agreement. According to s 69, the agreement is cancelled and, on the facts of the problem set, there are not many complications, since John still has his old car and has not taken delivery of the new one. That is now the position which John is entitled to maintain. John has, however, parted with the £500 initial payment which he paid to Sellapup. That sum is now repayable to John (s 70(1)). Primarily, that sum is repayable by the person (Sellapup) to whom John made it, which is unfortunate for John because Sellapup is bankrupt. If the agreement had been one which fell within s 12(b), that is, within s 11(1)(b), John could have claimed the return of the money from Fleece You Finance Ltd which would have been liable to John for it, jointly and severally liable with Sellapup, by virtue of s 70(3). However, John's hire purchase agreement falls within ss 12(a) and 11(1)(a), and that rule in s 70(3) therefore does not apply to it.

However, it may be that John can recover the £500 from Fleece You Finance Ltd on a different basis, namely, on the ground that it is money had and received on a total failure of consideration. Presumably, one could say that a prospective agreement which is deemed to have been made and then immediately cancelled reveals a total failure of consideration. Even so, to succeed with such a claim, John would need to show that the money had been *received* by Fleece You Finance Ltd. If, when Fleece You Finance Ltd accepted John's offer, it also accepted Sellapup's offer to sell the car to Fleece You Ltd and if, in doing so, Fleece You Finance Ltd sent to Sellapup a cheque in payment of the cash price, £8,000, and if that cheque was in fact only for £7,500, that is, because Sellapup had been paid £500 by John, then it would be said that Fleece You Finance Ltd had received the £500, that is, by deducting it from the sum paid to Sellapup (see *Branwhite v Worcester Works Finance* (1969)). Certainly, that would be the case if the cheque to Sellapup had been cashed. If Fleece You Finance Ltd has not received the £500 in the way just discussed, then it can still be said to have received it, if it can be established that Sellapup was, when he received it, Fleece You Finance's agent. At common law, unless there was something expressly done or said to make Sellapup its agent, Sellapup would not be regarded as such (*Branwhite v Worcester Works Finance*). However, it is very likely that by virtue of s 56(2) of the Consumer Credit Act, Sellapup is to be treated as having been its agent. Undoubtedly, the negotiations between Sellapup and John were antecedent negotiations within s 56(1)(b). There is an argument that perhaps s 56(1)(b) and 56(2) does not apply to a prospective agreement unless and until it is made.[1] However that may be, John can here rely on the fact that the agreement was made and then cancelled, that is, by virtue of the deeming provisions of s 57. Thus, John has good grounds for saying that Fleece You Finance Ltd has received the £500 and therefore is liable to return it to him.

Misrepresentation

Now consider the position if John's withdrawal came *after* Fleece You Finance Ltd's acceptance was posted. The hire purchase agreement would in that case be effectively made. John would, however, have a claim against Fleece You Finance Ltd in respect of the claim made by its agent (see s 56), Sellapup, that the car had covered 40,000 miles. John would be entitled to rescind the agreement for misrepresentation.

Arguably, he did just that when he telephoned Sellapup telling him that he was backing out of the agreement. The difficulty with that is that Sellapup would not have been Fleece You Finance Ltd's agent for receiving that notice. Section 56(2) would not apply as that only applies to 'antecedent' negotiations and presumably, once the agreement is made, those have come to an end. Section 102, which expressly makes the person who was the negotiator in antecedent negotiations agent of the creditor for the purpose of receiving notice of rescission, would not apply either; this is because 'notice' according to s 189(1) is confined to 'notice in writing'. So, whether John can rescind the contract depends upon whether he has by some other means already communicated to Fleece You Finance Ltd his intention to rescind and, if not, whether he is still within a reasonable period of the making of the agreement, since the equitable remedy of rescission depends upon no unreasonable delay and, unless the misrepresentation can be proved to be a fraudulent one, time runs from the time of the making of the agreement (*Leaf v International Galleries* (1950)). It is likely that John is still in time, since the agreement was only made on Saturday last. Irrespective of any claim to rescind the contract, John can claim damages under s 2(2) of the Misrepresentation Act 1967, unless Fleece You Finance Ltd can prove that there were reasonable grounds to believe and that up to the time the contract was made, it (or perhaps, rather, Sellapup) believed that the car had only done 40,000 miles. The damages will be assessed as in the tort of deceit (*Royscot Trust v Rogerson* (1991)), although if John succeeds in rescinding the contract, it is difficult to see what damage he will have suffered.

It is just possible that as an alternative to, or in addition to, a claim for misrepresentation, John could make a claim for damages (and to reject the goods and repudiate the contract) for breach of the condition as to description, which is implied by s 9 of the Supply of Goods (Implied Terms) Act 1973 (that is, the equivalent in a hire purchase agreement to s 13 of the Sale of Goods Act 1979). For this, however, he would have to assert that the goods were bailed (that is, contracted for) by description and that that description included the statement that the car had covered 40,000 miles. Unless that statement was repeated in writing in the agreement, it might be difficult to show that it was part of the contractual description.

If John's withdrawal did not occur before Fleece You Finance Ltd posted its acceptance, and if he has lost his right to rescind for misrepresentation (for example, through lapse of time), then he does have a statutory right to terminate the agreement under s 99 of the Consumer Credit Act. The consequences of exercising such a right are set out in s 100 and would be costly, making it a very unattractive option for him. It should, however, be an unnecessary one, since on the facts given, even if John's withdrawal was too late to be an effective withdrawal from the prospective agreement, he should still be able to rescind the agreement for misrepresentation.

Note

1   For a discussion of whether s 56 operates only in the case of agreements that have actually been made, see an article by AP Dobson, 'Consumer credit – finance company's liability for dealer's default' [1975] JBL 208, p 212.

Question 19

Layback Ltd sells psychiatrists' couches. Layback Ltd has arrangements with Money Ltd whereby Money Ltd provides finance to psychiatrists wishing to have a psychiatrist's couch from Layback Ltd. Recently, Sandra, one of Layback's saleswomen, visited Lunar who runs his psychiatrist's practice from home, and she persuaded Lunar to have a new psychiatrist's couch, agreeing to take in part-exchange (at an agreed allowance of £500) Lunar's old couch (which had collapsed that day). Lunar completed and signed a proposal form of Money Ltd's, proposing to take the new couch on instalment terms of a £500 initial payment (stated in the agreement to be the part-exchange allowance) and 40 monthly instalments of £100 each. Five days ago, Money Ltd decided to accept Lunar's proposal and posted to him a copy of the executed agreement. Four days ago, Layback Ltd delivered the new couch to Lunar and took away his old one. Three days ago,

Layback Ltd went into liquidation. Today, Lunar has received a request from Money Ltd for the £500 initial payment. Lunar wants to back out of the agreement.

Advise Lunar in each of the following circumstances:

• his agreement with Money Ltd is a hire purchase agreement;

• his agreement with Money Ltd is a simple hire agreement.

Answer plan

The agreement will be a regulated agreement and either: (i) a regulated consumer credit agreement; or (ii) a regulated consumer hire agreement. Lunar wishes to back out of the agreement and therefore there are two obvious areas for the answer to explore: first, have the formalities/documentation requirements been complied with?; secondly, can Lunar cancel the agreement? The issues will be dealt with in that order, taking them first in relation to the possibility that the agreement was a hire purchase agreement.

Answer

Is the agreement regulated? If it is a hire purchase agreement, it is a regulated consumer credit agreement, since Lunar is an individual and the total purchase price is only £4,500 (that is, 40 x £100 plus £500) and, therefore, the amount of credit cannot possibly exceed the limit of £25,000. If the agreement is a simple hire agreement, then it is a regulated consumer hire agreement, since Lunar is an individual and the agreement is capable of lasting more than three months and does not require payments totalling more than £25,000.

Documentation

Lunar wishes to back out of the agreement. It is possible that if the formalities/documentation requirements of the Consumer Credit Act 1974 were not complied with, the agreement will not be enforceable against Lunar, which would come to much the same result as Lunar wants, since he could not then be sued for the instalments. The question does not indicate whether the documentation provisions have been complied with. It does not indicate whether the form which he signed complied with the requirements of ss 60 and 61 and the relevant regulations. The question does make it clear that Lunar signed the completed form as required by s 61 and it does make it clear that Lunar was sent, as he was supposed to be, a copy of the executed agreement. This copy was also sent within the time required by s 63(2), since it was sent 'within the seven days following the making of the agreement'. The agreement was *made* when Lunar's offer was accepted. That occurred, by virtue of the postal rule (*Henthorn v Fraser* (1892)), when the executed agreement was put in the post to Lunar, which is still only five days ago. The question does not state whether Lunar was given a copy of the unexecuted agreement which he should have been given on the occasion when he signed the agreement. If he was not, then that was an infringement of the requirement in s 62(1) of the Consumer Credit Act. That particular infringement would not necessarily, however, prevent the court granting Money Ltd an enforcement order under s 127, since the court has a discretion nevertheless to grant such an order, after having regard to the degree of culpability for the infringement and the prejudice, if any, caused to Lunar by it and the court's powers under ss 127, 135 and 136.

If the agreement is a cancellable one within s 67 of the Act, then there are additional documentation requirements which require that each copy of the agreement given to Lunar under ss 62 and 63 should contain a notice of his cancellation rights. If the agreement was a cancellable one (which is shortly to be considered) and if this requirement was not complied with (that is, the copy of the executed agreement did not contain that notice), then the agreement is totally unenforceable against Lunar. This is because in those circumstances, the court is not able to grant Money Ltd an enforcement order (s 127(5)). That would actually prevent Money Ltd being entitled to recover the goods, even if Lunar failed to make any further payments (s 65(2)).

Cancellation

Assuming that the documentation requirements have been complied with, or else that the court has a discretion, which it may exercise, to grant an enforcement order, it becomes important to know if the agreement is cancellable. It appears to be cancellable within the definition in s 67, since the two basic requirements seem to have been satisfied. First, Lunar signed the agreement away from any of the *relevant* business premises – the fact that he, Lunar, carried on business at those premises being irrelevant. Secondly, the antecedent negotiations included oral representations made in Lunar's presence. There were antecedent negotiations, that is, within s 56(1)(b), conducted by Layback, through its saleswoman, Sandra.

At least, that is so where the agreement was a hire purchase agreement. If, however, the agreement was a simple hire agreement and thus a consumer hire agreement, it would not be cancellable. This is because any negotiations conducted by Sandra and thus by Layback would not then fall within the definition of antecedent negotiations (see *Moorgate Mercantile Leasing Ltd v Gell and Ugolini* (1988) and *Lloyds Bowmaker Leasing Ltd v MacDonald* (1993)).

So, provided that the agreement made by Lunar was a consumer credit agreement, it will have been a cancellable one within s 67; Lunar is still within the cancellation period. We are not told when he *received* the copy of the executed agreement. We are only told that it was posted to him five days ago. He has until the end of the fifth day following the day he received it in which to cancel the agreement. It will be sufficient if, within that period, he *posts* his cancellation notice (which, however worded, makes clear his intention to withdraw from the agreement). That is so, even if it never arrives (s 69(7)).

Assuming that the agreement is a hire purchase agreement and therefore cancellable, and that Lunar cancels it, what will be the post cancellation position? Broadly, the effect of cancellation of a hire purchase agreement is to make any further obligations under the agreement ineffective, to entitle the debtor to recover any money already paid and to require him to return any goods received. These will now be dealt with separately. Subject to what will shortly be said about goods supplied to meet an emergency, Lunar will be expected to return the new couch (s 72). This does not require Lunar to transport the couch, but simply to hand it over at his own premises after service on him of a written request. He is under a duty to take reasonable care of the couch for 21 days after he serves his cancellation notice. Lunar has been asked for the £500 initial payment. However, he has already parted company with his old couch which was taken in part-exchange as representing the £500. After cancellation, Lunar is entitled to have the couch taken in part-exchange returned to him in substantially the same condition. If that does not happen, then he is entitled to the part-exchange allowance and is entitled to claim it back from Money Ltd, which is jointly and severally liable with Layback Ltd for it (s 73).

There is, however, one possible qualification to what has been said about the consequences of cancellation. This arises from the fact that we are told that Lunar's previous (that is, traded-in) couch had collapsed on the day he agreed to have the new one. It could therefore be that the new one was supplied to meet an emergency. If so, then Lunar is not required to return the new couch and Lunar will remain under an obligation to pay for the new couch (ss 72(9) and 69(2)). This presumably means that he is liable to pay the cash price of it, since the agreement will be cancelled so far as it relates to credit.

Simple hire agreement

It has been seen that if the agreement Lunar made was a simple hire agreement, it will not be cancellable within s 67. Given that Lunar wishes to back out of it, it is necessary to see if it is cancellable within the Consumer Protection (Cancellation of Contracts Concluded away from Business Premises) Regulations 1987. For these Regulations to apply, there has to have been an unsolicited visit by a trader to Lunar's home or his place of work, which, assuming Sandra's visit was unsolicited, did occur. Even so, however, the Regulations do not apply unless the customer makes the agreement for purposes outside his business (and business here includes a trade or profession). The agreement therefore is not cancellable.

Given that Lunar wants to back out of the agreement, he could attempt to negotiate with Money Ltd the terms of an agreed cancelling. There is, in the case of regulated consumer hire agreements, no equivalent to the rebate which is available for early settlement of a consumer credit agreement. There is one provision, s 132, which could help in the event of Lunar returning the couch to Money Ltd, that is, assuming that somehow he could get it to take possession of the couch. Money Ltd might take possession of it if Lunar failed to make any more payments, thereby leading Money Ltd to terminate the agreement. There is no compulsion upon Money Ltd to terminate it. If it did, it would first need to serve a default notice. In the event that Money Ltd recovered possession of the couch, s 132 would enable Lunar to apply to the court for an order relieving him of some of the payments to which he is committed under the agreement. However, there is no guarantee that the court would look kindly upon Lunar and, in the one reported case to come to court so far (a Scottish court) on s 132, the court was not noticeably anxious to exercise its power under the section (*Automotive Financial Services v Henderson* (1993)).

Question 20

Tuition fees at Newtown University have, until now, been payable by students at the time they enrol on their courses in October. For courses lasting more than one year, annual fees have been payable at the start of the academic year, again in October. The University has for some time run an instalment payment system for those students who would prefer to stagger their payments during the academic session, the arrangement usually being that the student pays one-third of the fee each term. Until now, those students using this system have paid the same amount in total as they would have paid if they had paid in full for the whole session. There has been one exception, however, whereby certain students from overseas paying a high level of fees (£4,000 to £5,000) have been allowed a reduction of £500 if they paid the fee in full in October. The University is considering introducing a new instalment payment scheme for students who do not wish to pay in October. This scheme will be different from the previous one in two principal respects. It will involve students paying a higher fee than if they paid in full in October and will involve a total number of seven payments, namely, 40% as an initial payment in October and the balance in six further equal monthly instalments payable from November to April of the academic year.

Advise the University on the legal implications of its proposed new scheme.

Answer plan

The question really requires an examination of whether the proposed instalment agreement with students will be a regulated agreement. That in turn requires a discussion of whether 'credit' will be provided and, if so, whether the proposed agreement will be or could be an exempt agreement. It is not enough, however, to tell the University to adjust the repayment pattern so as to make the proposed new arrangement an exempt agreement. It needs to be advised of the implications if it does not. Thus, the answer must in broad terms deal with the documentation, licensing and advertising implications of the scheme as currently proposed by the University.

Answer

There are three significant issues. First, in making one of these agreements with the student, will the University have to comply with the copies and documentation requirements of the Consumer Credit Act 1974? Secondly, will the University have to be licensed under the Consumer Credit Act? Thirdly, in publicising the scheme to students, will the University have to comply with the advertising requirements of the Act (including avoiding sending circulars about it to someone who is a minor, that is, under 18)?

The principal key to each of these questions is: will one of the new 'instalment' agreements between the University and a student be a 'regulated agreement' within the meaning of s 8 of the Consumer Credit Act? Clearly, most of the requirements of the definition are satisfied. First, the student will be an 'individual' and, secondly, any credit provided under such an agreement will not exceed £25,000. That leaves two further matters to be considered in order to determine whether such an agreement will be a regulated one. Will it involve the provision of credit? If so, will it be exempt?

Credit

If the proposed agreement does not provide 'credit', it will not be regulated and each of the three issues outlined at the start of this answer will be answered totally in the negative.

By virtue of s 9(1), 'credit' includes a cash loan and any other form of financial accommodation. The expression 'financial accommodation' is vague, which leads to difficulty in ascertaining what is and what is not 'credit'. Credit has, for example, been described as encompassing an element of 'have now, pay later'. This would perhaps leave the University's proposed agreement as not involving 'credit', since the student under the proposed scheme will be paying *ahead* of the tuition he is getting. This is because, at the start of term one, he will have paid over one-third of the fee; at the start of term two, he will have paid over two-thirds of the fee; and, at the start of term three, will have paid all the fee. 'Credit' has also been described by commentators as encompassing any 'deferment of a debt'. This thought also gels with the approach taken by the House of Lords in *Dimond v Lovell* (2000), to be returned to shortly.

On the one hand, the debt would normally fall due in October and therefore the proposed agreement would 'defer' some of it. On the other hand, one could say that, because of the agreement, there is no debt until the various payments become due. The latter thought would equate the situation to one where building work is to be done and the landowner agrees to make six stage payments, for example, one on completion of the foundations and five more on completion of each of the five floors; this is generally thought not to be an agreement providing the landowner with 'credit'. One difference between this situation and the University's proposed instalment scheme is that a student using the scheme will have a direct comparison with any student who is not on the scheme and who therefore pays in full in October. A student on the scheme could claim he had got a 'debt deferred' by comparison with students not on the scheme who were having to pay an immediate debt. The comparison with a student who is not on the scheme would seem to be the correct approach. In *Dimond v Lovell* (2000), the House of Lords held that where an obligation to make a payment is deferred to a time later than it would otherwise be payable, that normally denotes that 'credit' is provided. In the light of that decision, it seems highly likely that the proposed instalment scheme will indeed amount to an agreement under which credit is provided.

Exempt agreements

Certain consumer credit agreements are exempt (by virtue of s 16 of the Act and regulations made thereunder) and therefore are not regulated by the Consumer Credit Act. There are two such possible exemptions that require consideration in the present problem.

The first deals with certain low cost credit agreements, where the rate of APR does not exceed a certain variable figure (1% above the highest of the base rates charged by the main British clearing banks). The problem does not state the rate of the charge for credit which the University proposes to charge (the APR). In any case, this 'low cost' exemption will not apply to the University's instalment scheme, because the exemption is limited to 'debtor-creditor' agreements and does not apply to 'debtor-creditor-supplier' agreements. The University's instalment scheme, if it is a credit agreement at all, will be a 'debtor-creditor-supplier' agreement, since the creditor and the supplier (that is, of the tuition) are one and the same person, namely, the University. Nor is it possible, even if the APR were sufficiently low, to see any way in which the University could alter the terms of the proposed scheme to take advantage of this exemption.

The second possible exemption applies to 'fixed-sum' 'debtor-creditor-supplier' agreements where the debtor is to repay the credit in no more than four instalments within a 12 month period. The University's proposed agreement would be 'fixed-sum', that is, not 'running account', since it will be a once-only credit and it will be possible to tell at the outset the amount of credit provided to the student (the debtor). This will still be the case, even if the student takes advantage of the scheme in subsequent years, since in each year he will have an agreement for 'fixed-sum' credit. So far as this exemption is concerned, the problem with the University's proposed scheme is that it involves too many instalments. The University would be well advised to consider altering the scheme to one where the student pays an initial payment and a further *four* instalments. That would cause the proposed agreement to fall within this exemption. That in turn would prevent the agreement from being regulated by the Consumer Credit Act. The University would be well advised also to consider whether the agreements previously operated, including those for certain overseas students paying high fees, fall within this exemption.

Documentation and copies requirements

If the agreement is a regulated one, the University will need to ensure that the requirements of ss 60 to 64 (and the regulations made thereunder) are complied with. These set out detailed requirements as to the contents and signing of the agreement and the giving to students of a copy (or copies) of it. If these requirements are not met, the University would need to obtain an enforcement order (under s 65) in order to enforce the agreement against the student. Depending upon: (i) the extent of the infringement; (ii) the culpability of the University for it; and (iii) the degree of prejudice caused to the student, the University may well be totally unable to obtain such an order (s 127). The student, on the other hand, would still be able to enforce the agreement against the University, for example, in the case of a failure to provide tuition or examination results, etc.

Licensing

If the University makes regulated agreements, then it almost certainly should be licensed as a 'consumer credit business' (s 21). These licences are issued by the Office of Fair Trading only to someone who is 'a fit and proper person'. There are two particular consequences of unlicensed trading. First, it is a criminal offence (s 39(1)). Secondly, a regulated agreement made by the University while unlicensed will be unenforceable against the debtor, unless the University were to obtain a validating order from the Director General of Fair Trading (OFT), which is a matter within the Director General's discretion (s 40). There is one argument which would, if successful, alter the above. It might, however, be unwise of the University to rely upon it, since it is as yet untested in the courts. It is that the University is not carrying on a 'business' at all, and therefore does not need a licence to carry on a 'consumer credit business' (see the definition of the latter in s 189(1)). 'Business' includes a trade or profession (s 189(1)). It is thus arguable as to whether the University carries on a 'business'.

If, however, the University does not make regulated agreements, then there is no doubt about the position. It is that no licence under the Act is required. Thus, if the only consumer credit agreements made by it are exempt agreements, no licence is required.

Advertising

If the University goes ahead with its instalment scheme as proposed, and assuming that 'credit' is being provided, then the University will have to comply with the requirements of the Consumer Credit Act (and regulations) in relation to the advertising of the scheme. The concept of 'advertisement' is wide and would include pieces of paper sent or handed to students and would also include any information about the scheme in a University newsletter, etc. The regulations are complex and include a requirement about the giving of information about the APR, which must be calculated as laid down in the relevant regulations.

However, if the advertisements are issued by someone who is not carrying on a 'consumer credit business' (see the explanation above under 'Licensing'), or if the only agreements advertised are ones which are exempt within the exemption relating to agreements where the credit is repayable in no more than four instalments, then any advertisement escapes control and the University will not need to comply with the advertising requirements of the Act. Thus, if the University alters its scheme to make its agreements exempt as suggested earlier, it will on two counts avoid the advertising control of the Act.

Circulars to minors

Even if the agreements which the University proposes to make are exempt, the University should beware of committing the offence in s 50 of the Consumer Credit Act 1974 which prohibits anyone 'with a view to financial gain, sending to a minor' any document 'inviting him to obtain services on credit' or to apply for information or advice on obtaining credit. This offence is committed only if the document is 'sent', so would not catch the handing over of the document. Of course, the prohibition in s 50 would not apply if the new instalment scheme does not involve 'credit'. However, because of the uncertainty on that score mentioned earlier, the following advice is given. The University should, relying on the decision in *Alliance and Leicester Building Society v Babbs* (1993): (a) make it clear in any document advertising the scheme, including the application form, that the scheme is not available to anyone under 18; and (b) establish a system to ensure that no application from someone under 18 is accepted. The first of these precautions should effectively prevent the document being construed by a court as an 'invitation' to a minor to apply for credit. The second will provide evidence showing that the University did not send the document to the minor 'with a view to financial gain'. On the latter point, it would be wise if the University: (a) required students to apply for the loan on an application form which requires the applicant to state whether he is over 18; and (b) instructed all staff responsible for agreeing an application not to do so in the case of someone under 18.

Other matters

If the University makes a regulated agreement with a student, then all the provisions of the Consumer Credit Act would apply, including, for example, the requirement that the University allow a rebate of charges (at least equivalent to that calculated according to the statutory formula) to a student who paid off the debt ahead of time.

Conclusion

The University would avoid having to comply with the vast majority of the requirements under the Act if it so adjusted the proposed instalment scheme as to attract the exemption mentioned.

CHAPTER 7

DEFAULT AND TERMINATION OF CREDIT AGREEMENTS

Introduction

This chapter covers the termination of hire purchase agreements as well as other regulated agreements.

Checklist

The following topics should be prepared in advance of tackling the questions:

- need for and effect of a default notice under s 87 of the Consumer Credit Act 1974;
- non-default notice under ss 76 and 98;
- time orders under s 129 of the Consumer Credit Act;
- liability of surety in relation to regulated agreements;
- protected goods provision in s 90 of the Consumer Credit Act;
- accelerated payments clauses;
- hire purchase customers' right of termination under s 99 of the Consumer Credit Act;
- claim by owner against a third party to whom a hire purchase customer has sold or bailed the goods.

Question 21

Just over five months ago, Fred traded in his old car in part-exchange for a new car which he acquired from XYZ Finance under a regulated hire purchase agreement. The hire purchase agreement showed the following details:

- a cash price of £21,000;
- a total hire purchase price of £24,000;
- a part-exchange allowance of £4,000.

Under the agreement, Fred agreed to make an initial cash payment of £2,000 and 36 monthly instalment payments of £500.

Upon trading in his old car and taking delivery of the new one, Fred paid the initial payment of £2,000 and has since paid the first three of the £500 monthly instalments. However, he is now two months in arrears with his instalments and a week ago wrote to XYZ Finance, informing it that he was temporarily out of work and unable to keep up his payments.

Advise Fred as to his legal position now that he has received a default notice which complies with the requirements of the Consumer Credit Act 1974 and states that unless he pays off his outstanding arrears within seven days, XYZ Finance will regard the agreement as terminated.

Answer plan

This question demands a consideration of the area of termination of a hire purchase agreement. The plan is to consider the following:

- has a terminating event occurred?;
- what are the consequences of termination arising from Fred's breach?;
- can Fred avoid those consequences, for example, by paying off the debt before expiry of the default notice or applying for a time order (and how in all of that does the fact that the goods are 'protected goods', if indeed that is what they are, help Fred)?;
- is it worthwhile for Fred to exercise his own right of termination?;
- is there any other way out of the mess for Fred, for example, selling the car or re-financing the debt?

Answer

The question states that the hire purchase agreement is a regulated one. No information is given about whether the formalities and documentation requirements of the Consumer Credit Act 1974 have been satisfied, and it is assumed in this answer that they have been.

The problem requires a discussion of whether the agreement has been, or can be, terminated and the possible consequences of that for Fred.

Terminating event – Fred's breach

Has a terminating event occurred? There is no doubt that Fred is in breach of his agreement by becoming in arrears. There are three alternative ways in which this could be argued to be a terminating event. The first is if it amounts to a repudiation by Fred. On the facts, that argument would be difficult to sustain, since there is no outright refusal by Fred to honour the agreement and his failure to pay two instalments, coupled with Fred's letter referring to him being *temporarily* out of work, hardly signifies a repudiation.

The second way that Fred's breach could be argued to be a terminating event is if the agreement expressly gives to XYZ Finance a right to terminate the agreement, for example, if Fred falls into arrears exceeding seven days' delay in making any payment. The third way is if the agreement expressly stipulates that prompt making of payments by Fred is 'of the essence' of the contract (see *Lombard North Central v Butterworth* (1987)).

Even if one of the last two possibilities proves to be the case, XYZ Finance would not be able to treat the agreement as terminated until the expiry of the default notice (s 87). If Fred makes good his default and pays off his arrears (together with any default interest) before the expiry of the default notice, then Fred's breach will be treated as not having occurred (s 89) and therefore XYZ Finance will have no right to treat the contract as terminated.

Consequences of termination upon Fred's breach

If Fred's breach is a terminating event, what will be the consequences of termination (that is, assuming also that Fred does not pay off his arrears before expiry of the default notice)?

If the termination arose because the agreement gave XYZ Finance a right of termination upon the debtor falling into arrears, then the consequences of that termination would be those indicated in *Financings v Baldock* (1963). These would be that Fred would lose the right to keep the car and would be liable for the arrears due up to termination; assuming that the agreement imposed upon him a requirement to take reasonable care of the vehicle, he would be liable also for any loss caused by any failure of his to take that care.

If the termination arose because the agreement made Fred's prompt payment of instalments 'of the essence', then XYZ Finance would be entitled to regard the termination as having come about as a result of a repudiation by Fred and would be able to claim not only the return of the car, but also damages assessed on a *Waragowski* (1961) basis, which would allow XYZ Finance to claim not only the arrears already fallen due, but also all the outstanding instalments minus the value of the vehicle recovered and minus a deduction to reflect the fact that XYZ Finance was getting early payment of some instalments. This deduction would be assessed on a rather rough and ready basis at common law (*Overstone v Shipway* (1962)) but, under the Consumer Credit Act, would be calculated according to the regulations (under s 95) governing the rebate for early payment.

It has been said that if termination on either basis just discussed occurred, then XYZ Finance would be entitled to recover the goods. That is in principle true and at common law, an owner is entitled simply to help himself to his own goods – at least if he can do so without trespassing (see *Bowmakers v Barnet Instruments* (1945)). However, XYZ Finance would not be able simply to help itself to the car, for example, from the street, if the car was 'protected goods' within the meaning of s 90. In this case, the goods will be protected goods if Fred has made or tendered payments totalling one-third (that is, £8,000) or more of the total price (of £24,000). Fred has actually paid a £2,000 initial cash payment, plus £4,000 trade-in-allowance plus three instalments of £500, which totals only £7,500. If he were to tender payment of one more instalment, the goods would become protected goods. In that case, XYZ Finance would have to bring court proceedings for a return order (under s 133) in order to recover the car. If Fred does not offer that further payment, the goods will not be within the definition of protected goods. It would still be the case, however, that XYZ Finance would not be entitled to trespass to recover the car (for example, if it was in a garage on Fred's premises) (see s 92). Fred could, of course, waive the protection afforded by ss 90 and 92 by giving permission to XYZ Finance to recover the goods – provided that that consent is given at the time of the repossession (s 173(3)). Even then, the consent would not be effective if Fred had not been informed of what his rights would be if he refused that consent (*Chartered Trust v Pitcher* (1987)), although it is thought that the default notice is likely to have given Fred that information. Fred would be well advised not to give that consent. The ability or otherwise of XYZ Finance to recover possession of the goods without having to bring court proceedings could well be significant, since if it recovers possession of the goods – and especially if it then subsequently sold them, it would be very difficult in any later court proceedings for the court to keep Fred's hire purchase agreement alive. If, on the other hand, XYZ Finance has to bring court proceedings to recover the car, Fred will have a meaningful option to apply under s 129 for a time order. If evidence of his means is sufficiently convincing, the court could then allow Fred extra time to pay off his arrears. Furthermore, this being a hire purchase agreement, the court would have power in making a time order to re-organise the future payment pattern in relation to instalments which have not yet fallen due: s 130(2). In the event that the car is not within the definition of protected goods and is kept on the highway, then Fred might well consider applying immediately for a time order, so as to try to pre-empt any attempt by XYZ Finance to recover the goods. As a default notice has been served on him, Fred has the right to apply for a time order under s 129 without waiting for proceedings to be commenced against him.

Fred's right of termination

A different option open to Fred, rather than to await termination taking place upon his own breach of the agreement, is to exercise the right himself to terminate the agreement under s 99, which he could do simply by serving upon XYZ Finance a written notice to that effect. The effects of him doing that are laid down in s 100. He would have to return the car and would be liable to pay the arrears which have already fallen due: £1,000.

Also, he would be liable to pay such further sums as would be required to bring his payments up to one-half of the total price. After payment of his arrears, his payments to date will be £8,500. Thus, the final sum to be paid by Fred (in addition to the £1,000 arrears) would be £3,500, which would bring the £8,500 up to £12,000 (which is the total price of £24,000). This figure of £3,500 would be reduced to such sum, if any, stipulated in the agreement as payable upon termination. Normally, an agreement will state a formula which will produce exactly the same figure as, in this case, the £3,500; if the agreement fails to stipulate any sum as payable upon termination, the figure of £3,500 is reduced to zero. Assuming that the sum of £3,500 is stipulated in the agreement, the court still has discretion under s 100 to reduce the £3,500 to such lesser figure as it considers sufficient to compensate XYZ Finance. It might do this if, for example, the value of the car when recovered by XYZ Finance proved still to be very high (that is, over £12,000).

Concluding advice

Which is the better (or least negative) option outlined above largely depends upon two things. The first is the likelihood of Fred getting back into work which will enable him to resume full payments; this would certainly make an application for a time order look an attractive option if XYZ Finance can be prevented from helping itself to the car. Failing the first, the second is the value of the car at present. If it is still of a high value, exercising the s 99 right of termination might prove quite expensive and, even if Fred sat back and let XYZ Finance terminate the agreement, it might be galling to have to return a car when he has already paid £7,500 towards it and when he would still be liable for the £1,000 arrears. Of course, if he can summon up the financial resources, he could pay off the arrears before expiry of the default notice and thus put off the problem until he is next in arrears.

Otherwise, Fred might consider a different possibility. He could ask XYZ Finance for a settlement statement, thus discovering how much is required for him to pay off the whole of the outstanding debt (that is, getting the benefit of a rebate of charges under s 95), and then he could discover how much he could sell the car for. It may be that Fred would be better off selling the car and using the proceeds to pay off the debt to XYZ Finance than if he either simply let XYZ Finance terminate the agreement or he terminated it himself under s 99. If Fred could find a willing buyer at the right price, he only has either to get that buyer to pay direct to XYZ Finance the outstanding balance owed by Fred or else himself to pass that amount on to XYZ Finance. Either way, as soon as XYZ Finance is paid off, Fred will acquire title to the goods, which title would of course be 'fed' straight on to Fred's purchaser (*Butterworth v Kingsway Motors* (1954)). If Fred cannot sell the car for a figure which would help him out of his difficulties, he could possibly make a different use of his right (under ss 94 and 95) to pay off the debt early and earn the rebate of charges for doing so. That is, he might find that his bank is willing to make him a loan agreement at a significantly lower rate of interest than the hire purchase agreement is costing him. Because Fred is out of work, his credit rating may make the bank wary of any such agreement, but the possibility of re-financing the agreement could at least be investigated.

Question 22

Harley had longed for a motorcycle which he had seen in the window of Cycles Sellers Ltd. On his 17th birthday, Harley acquired the motorcycle under the terms of a regulated hire purchase agreement which he made with Davison Finance. Davison Finance had refused to make the agreement until Harley's father, Gullible, had provided a guarantee of Harley's liabilities under the hire purchase agreement. Davison Finance also has a recourse agreement with the dealer, Cycles Sellers Ltd. The hire purchase agreement provided for an initial payment of £3,000 and 36 monthly payments of £200 each. After making the initial payment and paying one of the monthly instalments, Harley stopped making payments. Davison served a default notice upon him at a time when he was two instalments in arrears and, upon expiry of the default notice without Harley having paid off his arrears, Davison Finance terminated the agreement and repossessed the cycle, helping itself to it from outside Gullible's house where Harley had left it. That was yesterday. The motorcycle is now worth £3,000 and Harley has no assets.

Advise Davison Finance.

What difference, if any, would it make if at the time when Harley fell into arrears, he had already paid three of the monthly instalments and if the agreement which Gullible signed was expressed as an indemnity?

Answer plan

This question tells us that Harley has no assets and thus it requires us to consider any claims Davison Finance may have against Harley's father and the dealer. The fact that the agreement signed by Gullible is a guarantee means that we cannot avoid examining what claims in law Davison Finance may have against Harley. Since we are not told of the terms of the recourse agreement, it seems sensible first to consider the claim against Gullible.

Answer

Gullible's liability

Since Harley has no assets, Davison Finance will not be advised to consider any proceedings against Harley. It is nevertheless necessary to ask what is the legal liability of Harley because the liability of Gullible, if not of the dealer, may well depend upon it. The most obvious issue is that Harley was, at the time of the making of the contract, a minor. This might well make the contract unenforceable against Harley. Even if that is so, however, that particular defence will not be available to someone, here Gullible, who has guaranteed Harley's liability. If the only reason that the principal debtor is not liable is that he was a minor at the time of the contract, then that will not prevent someone who has guaranteed that liability from being liable on his guarantee (s 2 of the Minors' Contracts Act 1987). Apart from that exception, Gullible, as Harley's guarantor, cannot be liable to any greater extent than Harley.

So, ignoring the fact that Harley was a minor, what is the extent of Harley's liability? The hire purchase agreement made by Harley was, we are told, a regulated consumer credit agreement. It provided for a total hire purchase price of £10,200. At the time of the termination, Harley had paid £3,200, which is less than one-third of the total price. In those circumstances, the motorcycle was not 'protected goods' within the definition in s 90 of the Consumer Credit Act 1974. That being so, once the contract had been validly terminated, Davison Finance had a right to possession of its own goods irrespective of whether the contract stated so in express terms (*Bowmakers v Barnet Instruments* (1945)). We are told that the cycle was repossessed from outside Gullible's house. We are not told if this means that it was in the street, that is, the public highway, or in Gullible's garden. If the latter was the case, then despite the fact that Davison Finance was entitled to possession of the cycle, it was not entitled to trespass in Gullible's garden in order to retrieve it (s 92) and is liable to Gullible for breach of statutory duty (s 90(3)). There is no other sanction for the entry onto Gullible's premises (if that is what occurred) to recover possession of the cycle. It will thus have no bearing upon Gullible's liability under his guarantee, other than to afford him a counterclaim in any proceedings that Davison Finance may bring against him.

Harley's liability, and hence Gullible's, would certainly include a liability to pay off the £400 of arrears already due before the termination occurred. Beyond that, the liability depends upon the terms of the hire purchase agreement. If it provided that prompt payment of all instalments under the agreement was 'of the essence' of the agreement, then that would result in a liability for the whole outstanding balance of the hire purchase price (*Lombard North Central v Butterworth* (1987)). From that would be deducted the value of the cycle when recovered (£3,000) and any rebate due for the consequent earlier payment of the outstanding instalments.

The mathematical process is thus as follows:

1	Ascertain the total hp price	£10,200
2	Deduct from the total hp price all sums already paid	£3,200
3	That leaves the outstanding balance	£7,000
4	Divide the outstanding balance into	
	(a) arrears owing at termination	£400
	and (b) future payments owing	£6,600
5	Deduct from future payments owing, both	
	(i) value of vehicle repossessed	£3,000
	and (ii) amount of rebate for early payment	£X
6	The total due is then	
	(a) arrears owing at termination	£400
	and (b) future payments owing minus the items at 5(i) and (ii) above	£3,600 less £X

7   The total due thus is   £4,000 less £X

£X is the statutory rebate for early payment of outstanding instalments.

If, however, the contract contained no provision making prompt payment 'of the essence' of the contract, then there will be no liability beyond an obligation to pay off arrears due before termination together with damages (if any) for any failure by Harley to take reasonable care of the cycle (*Financings v Baldock* (1963)). This is because, on the facts given, there is no evidence of Harley having committed a repudiation of the contract. In this situation, there is no question of Gullible being held liable to any greater extent than Harley would be, for example, for the outstanding instalments. This is because, apart from the exception which deals with the fact that Harley was a minor, a guarantor cannot be liable to any greater extent than the debtor whose debts or obligations he has guaranteed.

Documentation

So, can Gullible be held liable to the extent indicated above? The answer is probably yes, but there are some documentation requirements which need first to be considered. The guarantee given by Gullible is 'security' within the meaning of the Consumer Credit Act (see s 189(1)). Thus, it needs to be determined (the question does not tell us) whether the necessary documentation requirements were complied with, both in the making of the hire purchase agreement between Harley and Davison Finance, and also in the making of the guarantee agreement. So far as the first of these is concerned, any defence available to Harley because of any failure to observe the documentation requirements is equally available to Gullible. This is a result of the nature of a guarantee and is reinforced by s 113 of the Consumer Credit Act. It is the case, however, that except in the most extreme infringements of the documentation requirements, the court usually has a discretion whether to grant an enforcement order even when the documentation requirements have been infringed (see s 127). There are documentation requirements which should have been observed in the making of the guarantee (see s 105), which include a requirement that Gullible receive a copy of Harley's hire purchase agreement. Again, however, the court has a discretion, under s 127, to grant an enforcement order against Gullible even if the requirements were not complied with.

There is, however, one further documentation requirement to be mentioned. It is that Gullible should have been (we are not told whether he was) served with a copy of the default notice served on Harley (s 111). If he was not, then again the court has a discretion (under s 127) nevertheless to grant an enforcement order against Gullible. It is to be observed, however, that in exercising its discretion in all the above mentioned cases, the court must take into account not only the culpability (that is, of Davison Finance) for the infringement, but also any prejudice caused by it. If there was a failure to serve Gullible with a copy of the default notice, then, unless Harley informed Gullible about Harley having received the default notice, the degree of prejudice to Gullible could have been very severe. Had he been served with the default notice, then he might well have paid off the arrears owing and thus prevented the termination of the hire purchase agreement.

Liability of Cycles Sellers

We are informed that Davison Finance has a recourse agreement with Cycles Sellers. We are not told anything of its terms. It is usual, however, for these agreements to be expressed as indemnities and definitely not as guarantees. Thus, Cycles Sellers will have taken on a primary liability and, unlike Gullible, will not automatically have available to it any defence available to Harley. Also, the recourse agreement will not be within the definition of 'security' in s 189(1), since it is virtually certain that the recourse agreement was not entered by Cycles Sellers at the request (express or implied) of Gullible. Indeed, it is highly likely that Harley and Gullible will never have known anything of the existence of the recourse agreement. Thus, the agreement is not subject to the documentation provisions, nor to s 113, discussed above in relation to Gullible. Furthermore, since the recourse agreement is not (we can be reasonably sure it is not) a guarantee, it is possible for Cycles to be liable to a greater extent than Harley himself. Thus, for example, if Harley's hire purchase agreement did not make prompt payment of the instalments 'of the essence' and therefore Harley's liability was limited to *Financings v Baldock* damages, it is nevertheless possible for Cycles Sellers to be held liable for more than that if, by the terms of its recourse agreement, it had agreed to indemnify Davison Finance against any loss the latter might suffer as a result of Harley not paying the full hire purchase price (*Goulston Discount v Clark* (1967)).

The rider

If the agreement between Gullible and Davison Finance had been written as an indemnity instead of a guarantee, that would make no difference at all to the answer above. The agreement would still have been 'security' within the meaning of the Act (s 189(1)). That being so, it would have been subject to exactly the same documentation requirements as those already referred to. Furthermore, s 113 would apply and that section has the effect of rendering an indemnity (which is security within the meaning of the Act) of exactly the same effect as a guarantee. Thus, Gullible cannot be liable to any greater extent than Harley (ignoring for this purpose that Harley was a minor).

The fact that Harley had made three instalment payments before falling into arrears would considerably alter the advice given. This is because in that case, Harley would, at the time the contract was terminated, already have paid over one-third of the hire purchase price, namely, £3,600 (the initial payment of £3,000 plus three instalments of £200 each). £3,600 is more than one-third of £10,200. Thus, the cycle was protected goods within s 90. It does not appear that Harley gave his permission to the repossession at the time the cycle was repossessed, and there is no suggestion in the facts that Harley had disposed of the cycle or had abandoned it. Thus, the repossession of the goods was an infringement of the protected goods provisions and Harley (and therefore also Gullible) are relieved of any further liability under the agreement (s 91). For the same reason, Davison Finance is liable to repay to Harley all payments he has made under the agreement.

Question 23

Explain the purpose, operation and validity of an accelerated payments clause in a credit agreement and how the provisions of the Consumer Credit Act 1974 apply to such clauses.

Answer plan

With a topic which is subject to common law rules and also statutory ones, it is often best to begin one's account of the law by dealing first with the common law and subsequently dealing with the legislation. This is the approach adopted here. It involves dealing with the purpose (which inevitably brings out the basic concept) of the operation of accelerated payments clauses, and then dealing with the effect upon the creditor before moving on to the effect upon the debtor. The material at the end which deals specifically with accelerated payments clauses in hire purchase contracts is something which you would include only if you had time, since although it is clearly relevant to the question, the question did not itself pick out hire purchase agreements for special mention.

Answer

Purpose

An accelerated payments clause is one inserted in an instalment credit agreement for the protection of the creditor. The idea is that if the debtor makes all his instalment payments as is required by the contract, then the accelerated payments clause will never come into operation. If, however, the debtor falls behind in his payments, then the creditor will be able to rely upon the accelerated payments clause, which provides that in such an event, the creditor is entitled to claim all the outstanding payments. The advantage from the creditor's point of view is that without the accelerated payments clause, the creditor would be entitled to claim only arrears, that is, those payments which had already fallen due. In the latter case, the creditor would be faced with the choice of either commencing proceedings immediately for the arrears or not commencing proceedings until more (or all) of the instalments have fallen due. Waiting for all the arrears to fall due would have some attraction, since then a single court action could be brought to recover the whole debt. The problem from the creditor's point of view is that if the debtor has fallen into arrears, that may well be indicative of a general financial problem of the debtor. Waiting until the due dates of all the future instalments have passed could well involve a serious risk that in the meantime, the debtor becomes bankrupt. An accelerated payments clause addresses this problem by providing that upon the debtor falling into arrears, the whole outstanding balance of the payments will fall due immediately. This type of accelerated payments clause is one which comes into operation upon a breach of contract by the debtor. Some accelerated payments clauses provide that they come into operation upon other events, for example, upon the debtor becoming unemployed or receiving a prison sentence. These events are not a breach of contract by the debtor, but each of them increases the risk of the debtor defaulting.

Effect upon the creditor

An accelerated payments clause will result in the creditor receiving some instalments (that is, those which had not yet fallen due) earlier than he would have done if the agreement had been carried out exactly as it should have been if the debtor had made all his payments at the normal times as set out in the contract. Thus, the accelerated payments clause brings the creditor a kind of windfall, since getting one or more instalments earlier than originally contemplated enables the creditor to use that money in the interval between when the instalment is received and when it would have been paid by the debtor in the ordinary course of events. To put the same point another way – that is, from the debtor's point of view – the original credit agreement will no doubt have included a charge for credit (that is, an interest element) and that charge will have been greater the longer the instalment period; the debtor pays interest for the length of credit which the agreement gives him. The accelerated payments clause, however, means that from the time that that clause comes into operation, the debtor no longer has credit. Thus, it is normal for an accelerated payments clause to include a provision which reduces the amount of the outstanding debt by an amount which reflects the extent to which the outstanding payments have been 'accelerated'. Indeed, if there is no such provision (or an inadequate provision), the clause will, at common law, be void as a penalty (*Wadham Stringer v Meaney* (1981)). According to this case, the issue of whether the reduction is an adequate one is judged according to whether it provides for a rebate along similar lines to the statutory rebate to which the debtor would be entitled if the agreement were regulated by the Consumer Credit Act 1974. The doctrine of penalties does not, however, apply to contract provisions which come into operation on an event other than a breach of contract. This is because the doctrine is intended to prevent the contract from penalising the party in breach to an extent which is greater than is necessary to compensate the other party for the consequences of the breach. If there is no breach, then the doctrine has no relevance (*Associated Distributors v Hall* (1938)). Thus, an accelerated payments clause which includes no rebate provision will not be void as a penalty if it is a clause which comes into operation (or can be activated by the creditor) upon some event other than a breach by the debtor.

Effect of the Consumer Credit Act

So far, the position at common law has been explained. Where the credit agreement is regulated by the Consumer Credit Act 1974, the rebate provisions in regulations made under s 95 automatically apply. These provide for a rebate of charges from the total outstanding instalments. The rebate is calculated according to a formula set out in the regulations and is given irrespective of whether the event upon which the accelerated payments clause came into operation was a breach of contract by the debtor. Consider now an accelerated payments clause which:

(a) comes into operation upon a breach by the debtor;

(b) does not on its wording provide for a reduction or rebate to take account of the acceleration of the payments; and

(c) is a regulated agreement.

Is it void at common law as a penalty with the result that the statute does not apply to it (that is, since it is void and therefore does not exist) and it is thus unenforceable? Or, does the court ignore the fact that the clause does not itself provide for a rebate, apply the statutory rebate to it and find that it is not void as a penalty since the statutory rebate provisions apply to it? It is submitted that the latter is the correct approach, that is, that the clause should be assessed on the recognition that it is contained in a regulated agreement to which, therefore, the statutory rebate provisions apply.

If a clause in a regulated agreement provided for a rebate of charges which was different from the rebate provided for by the statutory provisions, the relevant rebate would be the higher of the two, since a clause can expressly relax liabilities of the debtor, but cannot impose greater liabilities than those provided for by the statute (s 173).

Effect upon the debtor

For the debtor, the effect of an accelerated payments clause can be disastrous. The typical situation is one where the debtor has fallen into arrears with one or more instalments. Unless falling into arrears was simply an oversight, the debtor is likely to be in financial difficulties already. The operation of the accelerated payments clause is to make him immediately liable to pay not just the instalments with which he is in arrears, but also the whole outstanding balance, which may in fact be an impossibility for him. Where the Consumer Credit Act applies, there are several provisions which can alleviate this problem.

Effect of the Consumer Credit Act

First, the creditor is not able to rely upon an accelerated payments clause without first serving a default notice (under s 87) or a non-default notice (under s 76). Which of these two notices is required depends upon whether the event giving rise to the operation of the accelerated payments clause is a default of the debtor (for example, falling into arrears) or some other event which is not a default (for example, becoming unemployed). The effect of a default notice is not only to spell out what might happen and to give notice (of at least seven days), but also to give the debtor an opportunity within that time to put right his default. Thus, if he pays off the arrears before the expiry of the default notice, the accelerated payments clause cannot be relied upon by the creditor at all. There is one other effect of the default notice, namely, that it allows the debtor to apply to the court under s 129 for a time order, allowing him time to remedy the default, that is, to pay off the arrears. In the case of a non-default notice under s 76, there is clearly no opportunity for the debtor to make good his default, for the reason that there has been no default. However, the debtor can apply for a time order. In the case of hire purchase agreements or conditional sale agreements, this may be particularly useful since in relation to those agreements, a time order can relate to instalments which have not yet fallen due: s 130(2).

Suppose, however, that the non-default notice expires without the debtor applying for a time order, or a default notice expires without the debtor making good his default and without the debtor applying for a time order. In that case, the creditor can activate the accelerated payments clause. Thus, the creditor can commence proceedings for the whole outstanding debt (less the statutory rebate). If he does do that, however, the debtor can in those proceedings then apply under s 129 for a time order. Here, the time order provision can be extremely useful to the debtor and that is so irrespective of whether the agreement is a hire purchase agreement, conditional sale agreement or any other kind of regulated consumer credit agreement. This is because s 129 allows the court to make a time order which allows time for the payment of sums which have already fallen due and payable under the agreement and, thanks to the accelerated payments clause, the whole outstanding debt has fallen due. Thus, under s 129, the court has power, if it so decides, to completely undo the effect of the accelerated payments clause and to provide for the money to be repaid by the debtor in a pattern of instalments, possibly a similar pattern to the original one provided by the agreement. Of course, the court will not necessarily do this, but must have regard to means of the debtor (and of any surety).

Accelerated payments clauses in hire purchase agreements

A hire purchase agreement may contain both a termination clause and an accelerated payments clause. Typically, either can be activated by the creditor upon the debtor falling into arrears. Assuming that, in the case of a regulated agreement, a default notice has been served and expired without the debtor making good his default, either of these clauses could be used by the creditor. The default notice will have needed to make clear which he is proposing to use. There is an important difference between the two. The ultimate aim of a hire purchase agreement is in reality (even if not in law) to pass ownership of the goods to the debtor once he has paid his instalments. With a termination clause, the agreement is in effect aborted, the debtor loses his right to acquire ownership and the creditor is entitled to recover possession of the goods (albeit perhaps only after bringing court action to do so – s 90). An accelerated payments clause, on the other hand, produces the original intended result prematurely; the debtor becomes liable to pay all the instalments immediately and becomes the owner immediately, that is, sooner than he would if the agreement had run its normal course. Which clause is a creditor likely to use? He is likely to use the termination clause if the goods still retain a high value, but if the goods have suffered substantial depreciation (as often occurs, for example, with computers), there is little point in the creditor recovering those goods and he is more likely to want to rely upon an accelerated payments clause. One final point in relation to regulated hire purchase agreements is that once an accelerated payments clause has been activated, that is, the default notice has expired without the debtor making good his defect, the debtor loses his statutory right to terminate the agreement under s 99 (*Wadham Stringer v Meaney*).

Question 24

John acquired a car on hire purchase terms from Fleece You Finance. It provided for an initial payment of £2,000 and 24 monthly instalment payments of £500 each. After making the first monthly instalment payment, John fell into arrears with his next instalment. Fleece You Finance served a default notice which expired without John paying off the arrears and, thus, Fleece You Finance terminated the agreement. This was a week ago and Fleece You Finance has today discovered that John had been involved in an accident with the car which has been repaired by Menders Ltd where he took it for repair. Fleece You Finance now wish to recover possession of the car.

Advise Fleece You Finance.

(i) What difference, if any, would it make to your advice if John had made his first six monthly instalment payments before falling into arrears?

(ii) What further advice would you give upon learning that, whilst Fleece You Finance was seeking your initial advice, John visited Menders Ltd, paid the repair bill, took the car to Auctioneers Ltd who, on John's instructions, sold it in an auction to a buyer whom it has so far proved impossible to trace?

Answer plan

The issues raised are:

- did Fleece You Finance have the right to terminate the agreement?;
- if so, can it recover possession of the goods without going to court?;
- (related to the latter question) are the goods protected goods?;
- does Menders Ltd have the right to enforce its improver's lien against Fleece You Finance?;
- in relation to rider (ii), is Fleece You Finance entitled to recover the car from the purchaser at auction, that is, assuming he can be traced?;
- can Fleece You Finance maintain an action against the auctioneer?

This question is written in more or less chronological order and that is the order of the issues just identified. It makes sense to deal with them in that order, taking care to deal first with the first issue, since, if the answer to that is definitely no, many of the other issues do not arise.

Answer

First, we shall examine whether Fleece You Finance had the right to terminate the agreement as it has purported to do.

Fleece You Finance has served a default notice, which presumably asked for the arrears to be paid off. It is s 87 of the Consumer Credit Act 1974 which states the requirement for a default notice prior to the creditor being entitled to terminate the agreement. Section 87 does not, however, confer a right of termination. Fleece You Finance will have had the right to terminate the agreement if either the agreement specifically stated that in the circumstances (late payment of one instalment), it was entitled to do so, or else the agreement stated that prompt payment of sums falling due under the agreement was 'of the essence' of the agreement (*Lombard North Central v Butterworth* (1987)). Otherwise, Fleece You Finance had no such right arising merely from one late instalment (*Financings v Baldock* (1963)).

Assuming that Fleece You Finance did have the right to terminate the agreement, it appears to have satisfied the s 87 requirement. At least that is so, provided that the default notice complied with the requirements of s 88, including giving at least seven days' notice. On the assumption that it has complied with the default notice requirement, it is in principle entitled to recover possession of the car. There are, however, qualifications to that proposition. First, it cannot, otherwise than by court action, recover possession 'from the debtor' if the goods are protected goods. On the facts given, the car is not protected goods since the amount so far paid under the agreement by John comes to only £2,500, which is less than one-third of the total price of £14,000. If, to adopt the hypothesis in rider (i) in the question, John had paid six of the instalments before falling into arrears, then the goods would be within the definition of protected goods in s 90. In those circumstances, Fleece You Finance would be prohibited from helping itself to the goods either from John or from the garage to whom he had taken it for repair; the phrase in s 90 preventing recovery of the car 'from the debtor' extends to prevent recovery from the garage where John had taken it for repair (*Bentinck v Cromwell* (1971)). Helping itself to the car in contravention of s 90 would involve Fleece You Finance being liable to repay to John every payment he had made under the agreement. Even if the goods were not protected goods, there is still one other problem about Fleece You Finance being able to recover the car by helping itself; it may be unable to do so without trespassing on the garage's premises. If Fleece You Finance were to do this, then it would be liable for breach of statutory duty: s 92. All of that, however, only prevents Fleece You Finance from helping itself to the car. Fleece You Finance can still bring court proceedings to recover the car. There would possibly be two people trying to resist such proceedings.

First, John might seek to resist the proceedings by applying for a time order under s 129. Depending upon the evidence of John's means, the court might grant such an order, thereby allowing John a further chance at paying off his debt in such instalment pattern as the court decides. Secondly, even if John does not resist the proceedings, Menders Ltd, the garage, may wish to claim that it has a lien over the car for the cost of the repairs that it carried out. This is an improver's lien. Of course, John is primarily liable to pay the repair bill since it was he who incurred it. In the absence of him doing so, Menders Ltd may wish to claim that its lien is enforceable against Fleece You Finance, the lien being the right to retain possession of the goods until the repair bill is paid. The lien is likely to be enforceable in law against Fleece You Finance, and that is so even if Menders knew that John was buying the car on hire purchase terms, and it is still so even if the hire purchase agreement expressly forbade John from creating a lien (*Albermarle Supply Co v Hind* (1928)). The lien being enforceable against Fleece You Finance means that it is not entitled to recover the car without first paying off the repair bill. In those circumstances, once it had paid the bill, it would of course have a right to indemnity from John under the doctrine of subrogation. There are two circumstances where the lien would not be enforceable against Fleece You Finance. The first is if the agreement expressly forbade John from creating a lien (or expressly denied him authority to do so) and Menders Ltd knew that fact when the car was brought in for repair. The second is if, when John took the car in for repair, the agreement with Fleece You Finance had already been terminated. In that case, Fleece You Finance would be entitled to the car free of the lien and that is so even if Menders Ltd was unaware that the agreement existed or, if it knew of it, was unaware that it had been terminated (*Bowmakers v Wycombe Motors* (1946)). It seems from the wording of the question that the agreement probably had not been terminated, that is, the default notice had not expired at the time John took the car in for repair. The relevant time is the expiry of the default notice, not when it was served, because, on the wording of ss 87 and 88(2), Fleece You Finance was not entitled to terminate the agreement until that moment. It appears that John did take his car in for repair before the expiry of the default notice.

What is the position if the agreement neither made prompt payment by John 'of the essence' nor expressly conferred a right to terminate in the event of a lateness in payment? In those circumstances, Fleece You Finance would have no right to recover possession of the goods, either from John or from Menders Ltd, unless of course the agreement expressly forbade the creation of a lien. In that case, the creation of the lien might well amount to a repudiation of the contract by John, in which case, Fleece You Finance might well be entitled to terminate the agreement. Whether it could recover possession without a court action would depend upon the factors already spelt out about that. Whether it could recover the car free of the lien would depend upon whether Menders Ltd knew of the restriction in the contract.

Having already dealt with rider (i) (in relation to protected goods), attention will now be turned to rider (ii). In this scenario, should the car ever be traced, s 90 will be no restriction upon Fleece You Finance recovering the car, since it only prevents recovery 'from the debtor' and does not apply where the debtor has effectively said goodbye to the goods. There may, of course, be some other, more fundamental, restriction upon Fleece You Finance recovering possession of the goods. It may be that whoever now has possession of the car has actually acquired title to it. This is because Pt III of the Hire Purchase Act 1964 will confer Fleece You Finance's title upon the first private (that is, non-trade) purchaser, provided he bought in good faith. The auctioneers will not have been a private purchaser and, in any case, probably were not purchasers at all, but were simply agents of John in his selling the car. The person who bought the car in the auction presumably bought in good faith and thus, if he were a private (that is, non trade) purchaser, will now have good title to the car. Assuming that that is the case or, alternatively, that the car is never traced, there are two possible defendants for Fleece You Finance to consider proceeding against. First of all, John has quite clearly now done an act which is wholly repugnant to the contract. If the contract has not already been validly terminated, Fleece You Finance should consider serving another default notice and thus bringing about its termination and then proceeding against John for the outstanding balance of the price. On any view, the amount of damages to which Fleece You Finance is entitled is the outstanding balance, minus any (statutory) rebate for early payment.

Fleece You Finance should also consider bringing a claim for conversion against the auctioneers. Selling someone's car without the owner's authority is undoubtedly conversion, and it is no defence to say that you were unaware that it was their car (*Union Transport Finance v British Car Auctions* (1978)). It is an example of strict liability. To be able to bring an action in conversion, Fleece You Finance needs to be able to show that, at the time of conversion (that is, the sale of the car in the auction), it had an immediate right to possession. At common law, it undoubtedly did, since either the agreement was already terminated by virtue of the late payment (default notice and its expiry) or, if not, John's putting the car into the auction, being an act wholly repugnant to the agreement, was an act entitling Fleece You Finance immediately to terminate the agreement and thereby entitling it to immediate possession (*Union Transport Finance v British Car Auctions*). However, the latter will not be effective in Fleece You Finance's case because, however repugnant John's acts are to the agreement, they do not entitle the creditor to terminate *immediately*. First, a default notice must be served. Thus, in the present case, we can say that Fleece You Finance will be able to proceed against the auctioneers in conversion only if Fleece You Finance had an immediate right to possession. Moreover, it will have had an immediate right to possession only if (as discussed earlier) it had a right to terminate the agreement as a result of the lateness of John's payment. If it did, then, on the facts given, the default notice had already expired before the car was sold at auction, and thus it would be able to maintain an action for conversion against the auctioneers.

CHAPTER 8

CONNECTED LENDER LIABILITY

Introduction

This chapter covers the liability of the creditor for breaches of contract or misrepresentation by the dealer/supplier.

Checklist

The following topics should be prepared in advance of tackling the questions:

- definitions in the Consumer Credit Act 1974 and, in particular, that of debtor-creditor-supplier agreements;
- s 56 of the Consumer Credit Act;
- s 75 of the Consumer Credit Act.

Question 25

John and his wife, Susan, have always lived in England. John has a credit card agreement, made in 1990. Susan is a second card-holder on John's account. Two months ago, whilst on holiday in France, Susan used the card in Fashions à la Mode to pay for a two piece suit; the jacket was priced at 135 euros and the skirt at 60 euros, that is, the equivalent at the then rate of exchange of £90 and £40 respectively. The pound subsequently weakened and, by the time the transaction reached John's account a month ago, the debit amounted to a total of over £150, Susan's jacket thus costing in fact over £103 and the skirt over £46. Susan has since then contracted dermatitis from the jacket as she has proved allergic to some dressing in the collar. Also, the suit, which bore a label stating (in both English and French) that it was suitable for dry cleaning, has reacted badly to being given normal dry cleaning and both items have shrunk to half their original size.

John and Susan have learned that Fashions à la Mode has become insolvent and gone out of business. Advise Susan what remedy, if any, she might have against John's credit card company.

Answer plan

The issues raised involve s 56 and, especially, s 75 of the Consumer Credit Act 1974. The issues raised are as follows:

* is John's credit card agreement one which is regulated by the Consumer Credit Act?;
* can a second card-holder take advantage of ss 56 and 75?;
* are there 'arrangements' between the creditor and the supplier?;
* do these sections apply when the card is used abroad?;
* if they do, does English law apply?;
* if the above questions are all answered in the affirmative:
  (a) are the requirements for liability under s 75 established?; and
  (b) are the requirements for liability for misrepresentation, relying on s 56, established?

Answer

If Susan's transaction with Fashions à la Mode is governed by English law, she might be able to show that she was the victim of an actionable misrepresentation and also a breach of contract by Fashions à la Mode. Whether she can show either of those will be considered a little later. Assuming she can do so, to have a valid claim against the credit card company, Susan will need to rely upon either s 56 or s 75 of the Consumer Credit Act 1974. This requires, *inter alia*, John's credit card agreement to be a regulated consumer credit agreement. It will not be a regulated agreement if it is exempt (for example, if, like a traditional American Express card, it requires each periodic account to be settled in a single payment).

Can a second card-holder take advantage of ss 56 and 75?

The question refers to the transaction reaching 'John's' account. Thus, Susan presumably is not jointly liable with John. It would seem at first sight therefore that Susan cannot rely on either of the sections in question, since s 56 refers to negotiations with 'the debtor' being conducted by the negotiator (here, Fashions à la Mode) as agent of the creditor, and s 75 applies where 'the debtor' has a claim against the supplier. Not being jointly liable with John, Susan is not in ordinary parlance a 'debtor'. However, the definition of debtor in s 189 is of 'an individual receiving credit under a consumer credit agreement ...'. Therefore, Susan arguably is a debtor since she does not have to pay immediately for the goods purchased and that is a financial accommodation; thus, she receives 'credit' which is defined by s 9 as including a cash loan and 'any other form of financial accommodation'. This interpretation is as yet uncertain, since there is no reported case on the issue, and it is also arguable that since it is John who is going to have to pay the account, it is he (and not Susan) who receives a financial accommodation, although Susan would argue that they both received such a financial accommodation. If she is not a 'debtor' within the meaning of the Act, she will have no claim against the credit card company.

'Arrangements'

There must be 'arrangements' between the credit card company and Fashions à la Mode for there to be liability by virtue of ss 56 and 75. Neither section applies unless the credit card agreement is a 'debtor-creditor-supplier' agreement. If it is such an agreement, that will be because it falls within s 12(b) of the Act and it will not fall within s 12(b) unless it was made under pre-existing *arrangements,* or in contemplation of future *arrangements,* between the credit card company and Fashions à la Mode. Given that John's credit card company is an English one and Fashions à la Mode was a French retailer, it is quite likely that John's credit card company was not the merchant acquirer, that is, was not the person who introduced Fashions à la Mode to the VISA or other payment collection system to which they both belong. It is also quite likely that Fashions à la Mode received payment *indirectly* from John's credit card company. Some banks and credit card companies have claimed that in these circumstances, there are no 'arrangements' between the credit card company and the supplier. This, however, seems a 'try on' by the credit card companies in question, since 'arrangements' is clearly a wide word and does not require direct contractual relations between the creditor and supplier. It is submitted that there are 'arrangements' between John's credit card company and Fashions à la Mode.

Use of card abroad

Does the Consumer Credit Act apply to cards used abroad? It is submitted that the Act does apply to regulated agreements made in England (as John's appears to have been). A credit card agreement contains what amounts to a standing offer, that is, an offer to supply credit on the terms of the credit card agreement. That offer is accepted *pro tanto* each time an authorised card-holder uses the card to finance a transaction. The standing offer is made in an agreement (the credit card agreement) made in England. When accepted, even by being used abroad, the account is expected to be settled (by John) in

England and in sterling. Therefore, it is submitted that English law applies not only to the credit card agreement, but also to the individual contract (pursuant to that credit card agreement) to finance Susan's purchase. Of course, there is yet a further contract, namely, the contract made between Susan and Fashions à la Mode. That contract (being a business-to-consumer contract) is probably governed by the law of the place of habitual residence of the consumer (Sarah), namely, English law. Even if it was governed by French law, that would not prevent English law applying to the credit card agreement and to the finance contract made each time the card is used.

Section 75

Are the requirements for s 75 liability established? It has already been argued that, first, English law applies; secondly, the agreement is a debtor-creditor-supplier agreement within s 12(b); thirdly, that Susan is a 'debtor' within the meaning of the Act. Is the transaction within the financial limits in s 75(2)? It will be, provided Fashions à la Mode attached to the item in question a cash price exceeding £100. The significant figure here is not the amount subsequently debited from John's account, but the cash price attached to the item by Fashions à la Mode (that is, when Susan made her purchase). Neither the jacket nor the skirt had a cash price of over £100 attached. The only way that Susan could bring herself within s 75 is by arguing that the two piece suit was sold as a single item, which might be difficult since the skirt and jacket were separately priced. Assuming Susan's argument succeeds here, she still has to show that she has a claim against Fashions à la Mode, for s 75 does not create a new claim, but merely enables the debtor to bring a claim against the credit card company which the debtor already has a right to bring against the supplier. In an English court, if French law is not proved, it will be assumed to be the same as English law. In any case, as stated earlier, English law will apply when the buyer is a consumer habitually resident in England. According to English law, Susan would very likely have a valid claim against Fashions à la Mode, first, for breach of the conditions as to satisfactory quality and fitness for purpose in s 14 of the Sale of Goods Act 1979 and, secondly, for misrepresentation. For her dermatitis, provided that Susan did not contract this condition because she was unusually sensitive (see *Griffiths v Peter Conway* (1939) and *Slater v Fining* (1997)), she would have a valid claim under both conditions in s 14. Equally, both conditions would seem to be broken in circumstances where a description attached to the clothes stated that they were suitable for dry cleaning when they were liable to considerable shrinkage under normal dry cleaning (see the definition of satisfactory quality in s 14(6) of the Sale of Goods Act 1979). Thus, subject to the many difficulties already outlined, Susan may be able to bring that claim against John's credit card company under s 75.

Misrepresentation

It is possible, assuming, as stated above, that English law applies or that the French law on misrepresentation is not proved to be different from English law, that Susan has a claim against Fashions à la Mode for misrepresentation – that is, provided that before she bought the clothes she had read, and been influenced by, the label indicating that they were suitable for dry cleaning. If so, Susan could rely on s 75 to bring that claim against the credit card company – again, subject to the difficulties already outlined. Alternatively, Susan may be able to rely on a claim for that same misrepresentation by the credit card company, that is, via its agent, Fashions à la Mode. This would involve relying on s 56 to establish that agency. Section 56 is subject to many of the same difficulties as s 75. However, it is not subject to the requirement that the cash price attached to the item in question was over £100.

Conclusions

There are many difficulties, including uncertainty as to the law in one or two respects, in the way of Susan establishing liability on the part of the credit card company. It may be that she can succeed. Although not asked for by the question set, Susan might be well advised to consider the alternative of an action (that is, in respect of her dermatitis) for product liability under Pt I of the Consumer Protection Act 1987; this would be a claim against the manufacturer or, if the clothes were imported into the European Community, whoever imported them.

Note

Some of the issues raised in this question were discussed in an article in the Student Law Review Yearbook of 1992. Some of them were also discussed in the book *Credit, Debit and Cheque Cards* by Graham Stephenson, published by Professional Publishing in 1993. Stephenson appears not to agree with the views expressed in this answer about the position of the second authorised card-holder.

Question 26

(a) 'Section 75 of the Consumer Credit Act 1974 represents a flawed implementation of a flawed policy.'

Discuss.

(b) Betty decided to have a new kitchen installed. At Kitch Kitchens Ltd, she contracted to have the work done according to an agreed specification. She needed to borrow money to finance the new kitchen and, at Kitch Kitchens Ltd, she also signed a proposal form for a loan from Flash Finance. This was a loan of £5,000 to be paid direct to Kitch Kitchens and to be repaid by Betty by monthly instalments spread over five years. All documentation and other formalities required under the provisions of the Consumer Credit Act were observed in the making of the loan agreement. It is now three months since the new kitchen was installed and Betty has found that the new waste disposal unit is defective, the new cupboards are falling off the walls and the turbo-charged oven will never work properly, since it needs an outlet to the outside. Therefore, it must be installed immediately in front of an outside wall, and Betty's kitchen has no outside wall.

It is going to cost £3,000 for Betty to get a substitute oven and to have the other matters put right. Kitch Kitchens Ltd is insolvent and has gone into liquidation.

Advise Betty.

Answer plan

This is a typical two part question, where (a) requires some critical discussion of an area of law and (b) requires an application of those same rules of law to a specific situation. As with all such questions, it is wise to spend a roughly similar amount of time on each part. When dealing with a question, such as in (b), which demands an application of the rules in s 75, it must be established that there is legal liability on the part of the supplier and that the basic requirements for s 75 have been satisfied. Those two issues are dealt with in that order followed by the consequences for Betty.

Answer

(a)

The origin of s 75 is to be found in the Crowther Report, which laid the policy foundations for the Consumer Credit Act 1974. That report described the close business link sometimes to be found between a supplier (of goods or services) and a finance house. Those links would arise from the fact that a supplier would need to be able to offer credit to his customers. Thus, a finance company would be quite keen to have a supplier hold a stock of that finance company's proposal forms and to have the supplier suggest that a customer wanting credit should fill out the form. The arrangement often to be found between the finance company and the supplier includes the understanding that the finance company will make finance available to such of the supplier's customers who apply for it and who satisfy the finance company's usual credit-worthiness criteria. The Crowther Committee described such suppliers and finance houses as being in a 'joint venture for mutual profit'. The Committee pointed out that the existence of this link and the ready supply of credit to customers of the supplier meant that sometimes a supplier was kept in business for longer than would occur without such support. The Committee recommended that there should be 'connected lender' liability, that is, that the finance company should share liability towards the customer for breach of contract or misrepresentation by the supplier.

In all of this, there is one clear flaw in the policy and there are several others which are flaws either in the policy or else in its implementation in s 75.

The first and obvious flaw is that whilst it is no doubt beneficial for the credit customer to have the liability of his supplier towards him effectively guaranteed by the creditor, there is actually no reason why the credit customer should have this guarantee and the cash customer should not. Thus, the customer who has saved up for his purchase and then paid cash has no remedy for the defective goods or services once the supplier has become insolvent, but the credit customer is given such a remedy. Not only does this not encourage thrift and saving up prior to purchase, but it then positively favours the credit customer. When an unbonded travel agent becomes insolvent, it is the cash customer who is penalised and the credit customer who is saved. Yet, the latter is no more deserving than the former.

The second flaw is the fact that there is no limit on s 75 liability. The creditor who supplies only a relatively small amount of credit under a regulated agreement can be held liable under s 75 for unlimited damages. Thus, an oven costing £500 might be paid for by use of a regulated credit card and, because it is defective, might burn down the house causing, say, £100,000 worth of damage. The creditor who is not in the business of supplying ovens has nevertheless to pick up the £100,000 bill. It is true that s 75 gives the creditor a right of indemnity against the supplier. However, where the supplier is insolvent, this is of little use. Many creditors have the opinion that if it is right for there to be a s 75 type of liability, it should be confined to the amount of credit advanced in relation to the transaction in question.

A further flaw in s 75 is in relation to sub-s (3). This sub-section was intended to prevent creditors being made liable for relatively trivial claims. As drafted, however, it does not work to rule out claims according to their size, but rather according to the cash price attached to the item in question. Thus, there is in s 75(3) a lower figure of £100, the result of which is that if the cash price of the item in question is £100 or less, no s 75 claim can be made. That is so even if the item in question causes a vast amount of damage.

Thus, the defective toaster which burns down the house will not attract s 75 liability, since its cash price will not have exceeded £100. Section 75(3) seems to be encouraging creditors to give credit for a lot of small items, but not to give a lot of credit for any one item – unless the item costs more than £30,000. The sense of doing this is difficult to see. This is especially so where, in the case of a misrepresentation by the supplier, the debtor may be able to avoid this limitation in s 75 by the simple device of relying upon the deemed agency provision in s 56. Section 56 has no equivalent limitation.

There is a further flaw in the implementation of the policy. It is that, quite apart from the limitation in s 75(3), s 75 does not always work to protect the debtor in circumstances where the supplier is effectively in a joint venture for mutual profit. This is because there are other ways in which the creditor can help to finance the supplier or the supplier's customers without incurring liability under s 75. One of these ways is simply to lend money direct to the supplier. This might, on the one hand, avoid s 75 and, on the other, still leave the creditor reasonably well protected against the risk of the supplier's insolvency by virtue of charges over the supplier's assets granted to the creditor. Another way of arranging the finance is for the finance company to enter into an arrangement with the supplier whereby it is the latter who himself makes the credit agreement with the debtor, but where subsequently the supplier assigns the benefit of the credit agreement to the finance company. Thus, the latter becomes entitled to the receivables (that is, the debtor's repayments) under the credit agreement, but avoids being liable to the debtor. This is because an assignee takes only the benefits of the contract and not the burdens. Of course, where a debtor has a claim under the credit agreement against the supplier, that claim could be used as a set-off against money owed by the debtor (to the assignee, that is, the finance company) and this would then, by a roundabout way, make the finance company 'liable' (that is, by way of set-off) for the supplier's default towards the debtor. That 'liability' would, however, be limited to the amount of credit (and interest) due under the credit agreement.

Thus, there are serious flaws in s 75. It should also be pointed out that there are other 'difficulties' in s 75, which are not least the cross-border implications (for example, those arising out of the use of regulated credit card agreements abroad) and the doubt over the position of the second credit card-holder vis à vis s 75.[1]

Some of the issues discussed here in relation to s 75 are likely, during the course of 2003, to be discussed at a European level as a result of the European Commission's proposal for a revised Directive on Consumer Credit. That proposal was published in 2002. The proposal suggests a type of connected lender liability (such as that which s 75 imposes) which: (a) would not extend to credit cards other than store cards; (b) would, apparently, not include claims for consequential loss; and (c) would require the removal of the lower and upper price limits to the application of s 75 liability. The eventual new Consumer Credit Directive which emerges from this proposal may, however, be very different from that proposed by the Commission.

(b)

It seems reasonably clear that Betty has a good claim in law against Kitch Kitchens for breach of implied (or express) terms of the contract of supply. This appears to have been a contract for the provision of services with some goods being incidentally supplied. Even so, there are still implied terms as to satisfactory quality and fitness for purpose (s 4 of the Supply of Goods and Services Act 1982). In the case of the waste disposal unit, it appears that there is a breach of the term as to satisfactory quality and, in the case of the oven, a breach of the term as to fitness for purpose, since she must have indicated to Kitch Kitchens the particular purpose (installing it in her kitchen) for which she wanted the oven. So far as the cupboards are concerned, it appears that there has been a breach of the condition in s 13 of the same Act, that the work will be carried out with reasonable care and skill. The problem in this case is that it is of no use to Betty that she has a good claim in law against Kitch Kitchens Ltd, because the latter is insolvent.

The issue is what remedies Betty may have against Flash Finance by virtue of the Consumer Credit Act. Section 75 provides that in certain circumstances, the debtor (here, Betty) may bring a claim against the creditor (here, Flash Finance) for breach of contract or misrepresentation by the supplier (here, Kitch Kitchens Ltd). For s 75 to apply, the credit contract must be a regulated debtor-creditor-supplier agreement within s 12(b) or (c). It seems highly likely that the loan agreement satisfies this requirement and falls within s 12(b). It does not fall within s 12(c) since it appears to be an agreement for restricted-use credit, because the loan was to be paid not to Betty, but direct to Kitch Kitchens. The agreement will fall within s 12(b), however, only if it was made under 'arrangements' between Kitch Kitchens and Flash Finance. Since it appears that Kitch Kitchens had a stock of Flash Finance loan proposal forms, it would seem quite likely that there were such arrangements. If there were a commission paid by Flash Finance to Kitch Kitchens (or indeed vice versa), that would be conclusive. Assuming such arrangements exist, Betty has a like claim against Flash Finance as she has against Kitch Kitchens. According to a Scottish case (*United Dominions Trust v Taylor* (1980)), a like claim means that in circumstances where the debtor has a right to rescind the supply contract, the 'like' claim under s 75 is to rescind the loan contract. This case is controversial in the way it reached the result. That, however, is perhaps unimportant in the case of the problem here, since it appears that this being a contract for services (and not a sale of goods contract) the debtor, Betty, will not be seeking to recover all her money paid to Kitch Kitchens, but will wish to make simply a money claim, that is, for damages. That claim being a valid legal claim against Kitch Kitchens, Betty is entitled to succeed with it against Flash Finance.

In this sort of situation, it is quite common for the finance company still to expect the debtor to maintain monthly payments under the loan agreement while the other claim is still being contested and, if the debtor ceases to maintain those payments, the finance company will keep sending reminders and of course there will be default interest which the finance company will show on each successive statement. This operates as a clear pressure upon the debtor who may doubt the likelihood of success with her claim under s 75. Cautious advice to Betty is therefore to maintain her loan repayments whilst also pursuing her claim against Flash Finance.

Note

1   For general criticism of the policy behind s 75, see an article by Dobson at (1978) 128 NLJ 703.

CHAPTER 9

GENERAL PRINCIPLES OF AGENCY

Introduction

The doctrine of privity in contract law normally prevents a person acquiring rights under a contract unless he is a party to it. The long established exception to that rule is the concept of agency. The most important feature of the relationship created by an agency agreement is that where a contract is concluded by an agent on behalf of a principal, the agent's acts are treated as if they were the acts of the principal and the principal becomes a party to the contract through the agreement. Examiners often set questions dealing with the general concept of agency contracts, either in the form of whole essay questions (Questions 27, 28 and 30) or part-essay questions (Question 29).

A contract of agency is governed by the general law of contract and is subject to the same rules as other contracts. However, unlike other types of contract, there are special terms which are implied into agency contracts, such as the fiduciary relationship between the principal and agent as a result of which a number of duties are cast on the agent (Question 27) and, similarly, the agent has rights as against the principal (Question 31). In addition, in relation to one type of agent – the 'commercial agent' – the relationship will be at least partially governed by the Commercial Agents (Council Directive) Regulations 1993. These Regulations, deriving from a European Directive, are particularly important in relation to the rights of the agent on termination of the agreement (Questions 30 and 31). They apply only to self-employed agents engaged to arrange contracts for the sale or purchase of goods.

The questions in this chapter concentrate on the general principles of agency contracts, and those in Chapter 10 deal with the scope of an agent's authority to bind the principal.

Checklist

Students should be familiar with the following areas:

- general concept of agency and its relationship to the doctrine of privity;
- rights and duties of an agent vis à vis the principal;
- ratification – when can it be used and what are its effects?;
- termination of an agency contract;
- the Commercial Agents (Council Directive) Regulations 1993.

Question 27

The duties owed by agents to their principals may or may not be dictated by the express terms of the contracts between them.
Explain the duties of an agent in the context of this statement.

Answer plan

As with any other contract, the express terms of a contract of agency primarily determine the obligations of the parties to it. However, by the very nature of the relationship, the agent stands in a position of trust vis à vis the principal. A fiduciary relationship therefore exists between them and other important duties are implied into the contract, based on the notion of good faith, save insofar as these are not excluded or modified by the express terms of the contract.

In relation to commercial agents falling within the Commercial Agents (Council Directive) Regulations 1993, there is a duty to act 'dutifully and in good faith' which cannot be modified by the contract between principal and agent. Even where an agent acts gratuitously (and therefore there is no question of contractual obligations arising), the agent still owes fiduciary duties and the lack of consideration *per se* is no bar to these arising, and the possibility of a general liability in tort arises.

The following points need to be considered:

- express contractual duties determined by the terms of the contract;
- fiduciary duties which, if not expressly provided for in the contract, are either implied or enforceable *per se*;
- in the case of a gratuitous agent, a general duty of care in tort.

Answer

Any contract between a principal and an agent may expressly impose duties on the agent and, in the absence of any relevant express duties, the obligations of the agent are regulated by a number of duties as a matter of law. Even in the absence of a contract, an agent who acts gratuitously owes fiduciary duties to the principal in the law of tort.

Where there is an agency contract, the terms of that contract will generally dictate the internal obligations between the principal and the agent. In relation to commercial agents falling within the Commercial Agents (Council

Directive) Regulations 1993, however, there is a non-derogable duty on the agent to look after the principal's interests and to act dutifully and in good faith. Subject to this, an agent's duties will include the following.

Obedience

An agent must obey the principal's lawful instructions and must not exceed his authority. This applies to both the paid and gratuitous agent. Where the agent's instructions are ambiguous, however, he will not be liable if he acts on a reasonable interpretation of them (*Weigall & Co v Runciman & Co* (1916); *The Tzelepi* (1991)), although a duty will be imposed on the agent to seek clarification of the instructions.

A paid agent must act according to the terms of the contract and is liable for loss caused either by a failure to act or acts in excess of the authority. In *Turpin v Bilton* (1843), for example, an agent who was instructed to insure his principal's ship but failed to do so was liable in damages to his principal when the ship was lost.

A gratuitous agent is generally under no duty to act so that, whilst liable for exceeding his authority, he cannot be liable for a complete failure to act. There is generally no liability in tort for negligent omissions. However, some academic authorities maintain that liability could arise if the agent does not warn the principal that he has not or does not intend to perform the agency.[1] On this basis, a gratuitous agent acting in *Turpin* above would still have been liable to the principal.

Care and skill

All agents owe a duty of care to their principals to exercise reasonable care and skill in the execution of their authority. A paid agent is expected to exercise care and skill which is usual and proper in the type of business or work for which the agent is employed. An unpaid agent's duty of care arises in tort, and his actions are judged against the skill actually possessed. Whether or not an agent has fulfilled this duty is a question of fact in each case. Any attempt by an agent to exclude or limit liability for failure to exercise care and skill is subject to the Unfair Contract Terms Act 1977.

The standard of care required is whatever is reasonable in the circumstances of each case. Where the agent holds himself out as being a member of a profession, the standard of care and skill expected of him is that of a reasonably competent member of that profession, irrespective of the degree of skill he may personally possess. In deciding what care is reasonable, the court will take into account whether or not the agent is paid.

In *Chaudry v Prabhakar* (1988), P, who had recently passed her driving test, asked a friend, A, to buy a car on her behalf, stipulating that the car must not have been involved in an accident. A, who was not a mechanic and acted gratuitously, bought a one year old car for P. When P discovered that the car had been badly damaged in an accident, P sued A. The Court of Appeal, taking into account that A acted gratuitously, held that on the facts, A had failed to exercise reasonable skill and was liable to P.

Personal performance

As a general rule, an agent must personally perform the task because, in every case, the principal places trust in the agent: 'confidence in the particular person employed is at the root of the contract of agency', *per* Thesiger LJ in *De Bussche v Alt* (1878). This is often expressed in the Latin maxim *delegatus non potest delegare*. There are exceptions to the rule, but if the agent delegates duties without authority to do so, the agent is liable to the principal for breach of duty. The principal is not bound by an unauthorised sub-agent's acts unless the agent had apparent authority to delegate and the principal is thereby estopped from denying the want of authority. Some exceptions to the rule are as follows:

- Where the agent is expressly authorised to delegate. In *De Bussche v Alt*, for example, an agent employed to sell a ship at a specified price at one of a number of specified places was unable to do so and obtained the principal's authority to appoint a sub-agent who subsequently sold the ship according to the principal's instructions. This was held to be a permissible delegation by the agent of his authority.

- Where the agent has implied authority to do so in the circumstances because of a custom in a particular trade or profession. For example, a solicitor practising outside of London generally has authority to appoint a London-based solicitor to conduct litigation on his behalf in London courts (*Solley v Wood* (1852)).

- Where the principal is aware, at the time of making the contract of agency, that the agent intends to delegate part or all of his authority and the principal does not raise objections.

- Where the circumstances necessitate delegation, for example, where a company is appointed as an agent, it must delegate performance to its employees since it must act through human agents.

- Where the task delegated does not require the exercise of discretion, for example, signing documents or sending notices. In *Allam & Co v Europa Poster Services* (1968), for example, it was held that an agent who was instructed to revoke certain licences could delegate to his solicitor the task of actually sending the notices of revocation. Estate agents provide a common example where authority cannot normally be delegated. Selling the principal's property is not a purely ministerial act and, should they delegate their task to sub-agents without authority, they are not entitled to commission on a sale effected by the sub-agents.

No conflict of interest

This fiduciary duty of good faith is paramount and applies whether or not the agent receives payment. The duty is very strict and applies even where it can be proved that there was no actual conflict of interest. It is enough that there is the possibility of conflict. In *Boardman v Phipps* (1966), for example, where the duty was strictly applied, a solicitor, whilst acting as agent, acquired information relating to the value of certain shares. Acting in good faith, he used this information for his own benefit after the principal had declined to use it for his. The House of Lords held that the agent was accountable to his principal for the profit made, because the information that he had acquired and used for his own benefit belonged to his principal.

More generally, this duty is reflected in the principles that an agent should not purchase the principal's property nor act for both parties in a transaction. Where, for instance, an agent is instructed to buy property on behalf of the principal and the agent sells his own property to the principal, the agreement reached will be a breach of the duty owed to his principal. In such a situation, the potential for conflict is clear, since a seller's interest is to get the best price, whilst the buyer's is to pay as little as possible. Even if the agent acts fairly and pays a reasonable price, he will be in breach of duty unless there is full disclosure to the principal and the principal consents to the transaction.[2]

Not to make a secret profit

An agent must not make a secret profit over and above the agreed commission. Again, this rule is strictly applied and it is irrelevant that the agent acted in good faith or that the principal suffered no loss (see *Boardman v Phipps*). If a secret profit is made and discovered, it may be claimed by the principal. The duty applies equally to unpaid agents. In *Turnbull v Garden* (1869), for example, an agent was employed without payment to purchase clothes for his principal's son. He was allowed a trade discount on the transaction by the seller, but sought to charge his principal the full price. The court held that the agent had to account to his principal for the discount that he had received.[3]

Not to take a bribe

A bribe is a particular form of secret profit and arises where a payment between a third party and an agent is kept secret from the principal. If an agent takes a bribe, the principal is entitled to claim the amount of the bribe as money had and received (*Logicrose v Southend United Football Club Ltd* (1988)) or to damages against either the agent or the third party. The principal can also refuse to pay commission to the agent on that transaction (or recover any commission already paid) and summarily dismiss the agent, and can set aside the transaction with the third party. The principal's remedies are cumulative save that, in *Mahesan v Malaysia Government Officers' Co-operative Housing Society Ltd* (1979), the Privy Council held that the principal must choose between recovering the bribe or an action for damages (to prevent the principal receiving a windfall profit). If, however, property constituting or representing the bribe has increased in value, the principal can claim the full value (*Attorney General of Hong Kong v Reid* (1994)).

Futhermore, both parties to the bribe may be liable to prosecution under s 1 of the Prevention of Corruption Act 1916 if proof of corrupt motive can be shown (this is not required for the principal's civil remedies).

To account

An agent must keep his principal's property strictly separate from his own and is treated in equity as though he was a trustee of the property. On the termination of the agency, an agent must account for all such property.[4] For example, in *Lupton v White* (1808), it was held that where an agent fails to keep the principal's property separate, the principal is entitled to a charge on the entire mixed property unless the agent is able to establish who owns what.

An agent is also required to keep proper accounts and present these to his principal.

Notes

1   *Hedley Byrne & Co Ltd v Heller & Partners Ltd* (1964) suggests that liability will be imposed for loss caused by a failure to warn the principal where the agent had voluntarily assumed such a responsibility, although the point remains undecided in English law.

2   Where an agent deals with the principal in breach of his duty, the principal may rescind the contract. His right to rescission subsists until the breach is actually discovered. (In *Oliver v Court* (1820), the principal was able to rescind 13 years after the transaction.)

3   See also *Hippisley v Knee Bros* (1905), where the court found that although the agent, acting in good faith, was in breach of duty, he was allowed to keep his commission on the transaction. Similarly, in *Boardman v Phipps* (1966), the agents were allowed some reimbursement for their expenses.

4   In recent years, sellers of goods have increasingly sought to rely on reservation of title clauses in their contracts of sale by making the buyer the seller's 'agent'. In practice, courts are reluctant to require such buyers to act as true agents in the sense of owing fiduciary duties, preferring that the agent should be a debtor to the principal.

Question 28

When will an agent, who enters into a contract on behalf of a principal, have rights and incur liabilities under the contract concluded with the third party? Is the law on this topic in a satisfactory state?

Answer plan

This question requires you to know and explain the exceptions to the general rule that an agent 'is neither liable under, nor entitled to enforce, a contract he makes on behalf of his principal'. It goes a little further than that, however, in that there are some actions which may be taken by the third party against the agent which are not strictly speaking based on the contract. Examples are liability on a collateral contract, or liability for breach of the implied warranty of authority. The issues to be discussed are:

*   intention to contract personally;
*   custom;
*   undisclosed principal;
*   principal non-existent;
*   collateral contract;
*   implied warranty of authority.

It may also be useful to say a little about the power of the third party to choose whom to sue in a situation where both principal and agent may be potentially liable.

Answer

It is no doubt true to say that in the normal course of events, once the principal and third party have made a binding contract, the agent has no further rights or liabilities against the third party.[1] The agent may, of course, have outstanding claims on or obligations towards the principal, but that is a separate issue, arising from their continuing relationship rather than the specific contract which has resulted from the agent's activities. It is also true, however, that in certain situations, the agent will have rights and liabilities either alongside or in place of the principal, and it is to those exceptions which we now turn. Some of them relate to rights and liabilities on the contract itself; some are independent of the contract.

The first exception which must be considered is where the parties themselves intend that the agent should have personal rights or liabilities. At one time, much stress seemed to be placed on the exact form in which the contract was signed, for example, to sign 'as solicitors' left the agent liable (*Burrell v Jones* (1819)), whereas to sign 'on behalf of' or '*per pro*' was taken to indicate an intention that the agent should not be liable. The more recent approach, set out by Brandon J in *The Swan* (1968), suggests that it is a question of looking carefully at the contract and the surrounding circumstances to try to determine the intention of the parties.[2] *The Swan* involved a one man company, JD Rodger Ltd, which had hired a boat belonging to JD Rodger himself, who was a director of the company. The company gave instructions through JD Rodger for repairs to be carried out. It was held that in all the circumstances, although the order for the work had been signed simply as 'Director' (which carried no implication of personal liability nor, it has to be said, avoidance of liability), JD Rodger, the agent, was personally liable. It was natural for the ship repairers to assume that the shipowner would accept personal liability.

By way of contrast, in *The Santa Caterina* (1977), the defendants requested the plaintiffs to supply bunkers to the ship, *The Santa Caterina*. The plaintiffs forwarded the invoice to the defendants, who denied liability on the basis that they had requested the bunkers as agents of the time charterers of the ship. The Court of Appeal held that, since on the facts the plaintiffs *knew* that the defendants were agents, the onus was on the plaintiffs to introduce evidence to enable an inference to be drawn that the defendants were personally liable. In the absence of such evidence, the court held the agents not personally bound by the contract.

It is also clear that if there is a custom or trade usage (for example, in the tallow trade: *Thornton v Fehr* (1935)) that agents are personally liable or entitled under the contract, the courts will give effect to it, provided that it is consistent with the express terms of the contract and the surrounding circumstances.

The rights and liabilities of the principal and agent against third parties may differ according to whether the agency is disclosed or undisclosed. Agency is disclosed where the agent reveals that he is acting as an agent; it is sufficient that the fact of agency is revealed without the need for the principal to be named. Agency is undisclosed where the agent does not reveal the fact of agency at all and appears to be acting on his own behalf. Where the principal is undisclosed, then it is only fair that the third party who thinks that the agent is the other party should be able to take action against the agent (*Sims v Bond* (1833)). Once this is established, it must also be fair to allow the reciprocal right to the agent.

There may also be rights and liabilities where there is in fact no principal standing behind the agent. This might occur in two ways. It may be that the agent is in fact the principal and is simply pretending to act as an agent. Secondly, the principal may not be in existence at the time the contract is made.

If the agent is simply pretending to be acting for a principal (real or imaginary), while really acting on his own behalf, then there is no doubt that he will be liable on the contract. He will also be able to enforce the contract, provided that he gives due notice of the fact that he was acting on his own behalf, and the contract is not one where the personal characteristics of the other party are important, as they would be, for example, in an employment contract or an underwriting contract (*Collins v Associated Greyhound Racecourses Ltd* (1930)).[3]

More difficulty can arise where the principal was not in existence at the time of the contract. This can happen in relation to contracts made on behalf of a company which has yet to be incorporated. The common law approach was demonstrated by *Kelner v Baxter* (1866), where it was held that the promoters were personally liable for the contract. This has now been given statutory force by s 36 of the Companies Act 1985. The section deals with liability, rather than ability to enforce. At common law, the only authority in this area was *Newborne v Sensolid* (1954), where the decision against allowing the agent to enforce turned on a very pedantic argument about the precise form of the signature on the contract.[4] This kind of technical argument has been disapproved in later cases, and in particular by the Court of Appeal in *Phonogram v Lane* (1982). The balance of opinion seems to be that, following the statutory intervention noted above, the agent should be able to sue as well as being liable where a contract is made on behalf of a company not yet incorporated.

The situations we have looked at so far have involved the agent being liable on the contract itself. There are two situations, however, in which the agent may have a separate type of liability to the third party. The first is where there is a collateral contract between the agent and the third party. The kind of situation where this could arise is exemplified by the case of *Andrews v Hopkinson* (1957). The plaintiff wanted to acquire a car on hire purchase. The dealer said, 'It's a good little bus. I would stake my life on it'. The plaintiff entered into a hire purchase contract with a finance company for the car, arranged through the dealer. When the car turned out to be defective, it was held that the plaintiff, although at first sight having no contractual remedy against the dealer, could in fact sue him on the basis of a collateral contract. At the time, the dealer was in fact held not to be the agent of the finance company, but that has now been changed by statute.[5] The case illustrates how a statement made by an agent which encouraged the third party to enter into the contract could make the agent liable for breach of a collateral contract.

The final way in which the agent may be liable to the third party is for breach of the implied warranty of authority. This will occur where the agent has held himself out as having authority from the principal, when in fact he does not. Of course, in some circumstances, the principal may nevertheless be liable for the contract on the basis of usual or apparent authority.[6] If the principal is not liable, however, the agent will be liable for breach of this implied warranty. The remedies that the third party will be able to recover, however, are limited to what could in practice have been recovered from the principal. Thus, if the principal is insolvent, it may not be worth suing the agent for breach of the implied warranty.

The existence of the warranty does not depend on the agent's awareness of the lack of authority. This was established in *Collen v Wright* (1857) and taken to its logical extreme in *Yonge v Toynbee* (1910). In the latter case, the warranty was held to operate against a solicitor who had continued to act for a client who, unknown to the solicitor, had become mentally incapacitated (which had the automatic effect of terminating the solicitor's authority). The fact that the solicitor had acted in good faith throughout was regarded as irrelevant.

A final issue which may need consideration is the position where the third party has the possibility of suing either the agent or the principal. Judgment cannot, of course, be enforced against both, but suppose judgment has been obtained against the principal, who turns out to be unable to pay. Can the third party then sue the agent in respect of the same loss? Or does he have to make a choice at an earlier stage? The rules are not very clear. It used to be the case that once judgment has been obtained against either principal or agent, that precluded any action against the other. That was changed, however, by the Civil Liability (Contribution) Act 1978, so that there is no longer any automatic effect of this kind. In all situations now, the test is whether the third party has 'elected' to sue one party. If so, this will bar any action against the other. The problem is in deciding what amounts to an 'election'. In *Clarkson Booker Ltd v Andjel* (1964), it was held that what was required was a 'truly unequivocal act'. It might have been thought that the institution of proceedings was such an act, but the Court of Appeal in that case thought that this was only *prima facie* so. The election, to be binding, must be made with knowledge of all relevant facts. In the case before them, the third party had issued a writ against the principal, but had subsequently discovered that the principal was insolvent. It was held that because they were not in possession of the full facts, the issue of the writ against the principal was not a binding election. Proceedings could be started against the agent. The question of the precise requirements for an election remains unclear.

As we have seen, there are various ways in which the agent may have rights against and liabilities towards a third party. Most of the rules seem to operate in a reasonably satisfactory way. Some criticism might be made, however, of the rather strict approach to the implied warranty of authority. Moreover, as has just been pointed out, the rules relating to 'election' are in considerable need of clarification.

Notes

1 'The contract is that of the principal, not that of the agent and, *prima facie* at common law, the only person who can sue is the principal and the only person who can be sued is the principal' (*per* Wright J in *Montgomerie v United Kingdom Mutual Steamship Association* (1891)).

2 The test is, as in most other areas of contract law, objective, that is, the question is not what the two individuals actually intended, but what 'two reasonable businessmen making a contract of that nature, in those terms, and in those surrounding circumstances, must be taken to have intended' (*per* Brandon J in *The Swan* (1968)).

3 In this case, the problem was that an undisclosed principal wanted to take over the contract, but there is no reason why it should not also apply where the agent is looking to step into the shoes of the supposed principal. See also *Schmalz v Avery* (1851).

4 It was taken to have been signed in the name of the company, that is, 'Leopold Newborne (London) Ltd'.

5 That is, s 56 of the Consumer Credit Act 1974.

6 For which see the answer to Question 35.

Question 29

(a) When will an agent, who enters into a contract on behalf of a principal, incur liability to the third party with whom the contract is concluded?

(b) Penelope engages Andrew to sell Penelope's 'Supaklean' industrial carpet cleaning service. The terms of the contract specify that Andrew may only give 30 days' credit to purchasers, and provide for Andrew to be paid 2% commission on all sales arranged by him.

Andrew negotiates contracts with Zubin and Yatin, incurring considerable travelling and subsistence expenses in order to do so. In his negotiations, Andrew discloses his agency to Zubin, but not to Yatin. In addition, Andrew agrees that Yatin can have 40 days' credit.

Andrew communicates his dealings to Penelope and Penelope agrees to allow Yatin 40 days' credit. Contracts are entered into between Penelope and Zubin, and Andrew and Yatin, Penelope subsequently confirming the latter contract directly with Yatin. Subsequently, a dispute arises between Andrew and Penelope, and Penelope refuses to supply the Supaklean service to Zubin and Yatin. She also refuses to have any further dealings with Andrew.

Discuss the legal position of the parties involved.

Answer plan

The first part of this question is similar to that in Question 28, except that there are two parts to this question, so the amount of detail required will be restricted to the time available for answering both parts.

The second part of the question deals with an agent's right to claim remuneration and expenses necessarily incurred in the course of his agency. The question also involves a discussion of an agent's rights and liabilities under a contract which he makes on behalf of an undisclosed principal. Finally, we need to consider whether an undisclosed principal may ratify a contract.

Answer

(a)

An agent will be personally liable on a contract in the following circumstances.

- *Where the agent intends to be a party to the contract*

  This might either be because the contract expressly states that the agent is a party or, on the proper construction of the contract, the agent will be held personally liable on it. In order to escape liability, the contract must make clear that the agent signs only in a representative capacity, for instance, by signing '*per pro*' or 'A as agent for P'. Using descriptive words such as 'director' or 'agent' after a signature may well be insufficient. In *The Swan* (1968), a one man company, JD Rodger Ltd, hired a boat belonging to JD Rodger himself, who was a director of the company. The company gave instructions through JD Rodger for repairs to be carried out. It was held that in all the circumstances, although the order for the work had been signed simply as 'director', JD Rodger, the agent, was personally liable. It was natural for the ship repairers to assume that the shipowner would accept personal liability.

- *Where the agent does not disclose the existence of the principal*

  Here, the agent is both liable on and able to enforce the contract against the third party since the third party, at the time of the contract, believes that the agent is the principal.[1] Merely failing to name the principal does not result in personal liability. An agent's liability ends when the principal fully performs the contract or, having discovered the principal's existence, the third party chooses to enforce the contract against the principal and not the agent.

- *In some circumstances where the agent signs a cheque or other bill of exchange*

  A person who signs a bill of exchange becomes a party to it if his name appears on it, and he therefore incurs liability on it unless the representative nature of the signature is made perfectly clear. Again, merely adding words such as 'agent' or 'director' is insufficient to avoid personal liability. However, in *Bondina Ltd v Rollaway Shower Blinds Ltd* (1986), the Court of Appeal held that, provided a cheque is printed with the company's name and account number, the company and not the person signing is liable on the cheque, even if the representative nature of the signature is not stated.[2]

- *Where an agent executes a contract by deed*

  The agent and not the principal may enforce it. This rule does not, however, apply to a deed executed under a power of attorney, that is, where the agent is appointed by deed (s 7 of the Power of Attorney Act 1971).

- *Where trade usage makes the agent liable*

  It is also clear that if there is a custom or trade usage (for example, in the tallow trade: *Thornton v Fehr* (1935)) that agents are personally liable or entitled under the contract, the courts will give effect to it, provided that it is consistent with the express terms of the contract and the surrounding circumstances.

- *Where the principal does not exist*

  This situation does not usually arise as the result of the literal non-existence of the principal, but as a result of their legal non-existence, almost always involving an agent acting on behalf of a yet-to-be incorporated company. The common law approach was demonstrated by *Kelner v Baxter* (1866), where it was held that the promoters were personally liable on the contract. This has now been given statutory force by s 36 of the Companies Act 1985, where the agent will be personally liable, subject to a term in the contract to the contrary. More generally in these situations, the agent will be liable for breach of warranty of authority under the principle in *Collen v Wright* (1857).

(b)

Andrew's position vis à vis Penelope

Andrew's position here depends on applying the rules relating to an agent's rights against his principal. These are: the right to be remunerated; the right to be indemnified for expenses properly incurred; and the right to a lien over items of the principal's property in his possession.

Because the contracts negotiated by Andrew are for the supply of a service rather than the sale of goods, the Commercial Agents (Council Directive) Regulations 1993 will not apply to this situation. The precise conditions to the right of remuneration will therefore depend on the terms of the agency contract but, in essence, the agent must have acted within the scope of his authority and his acts must have been the effective cause of the event he was employed to bring about. Whether or not the agent's acts were the 'effective cause' will be a question of fact in each case.

In the case of the contract with Zubin, Andrew has fulfilled the criteria for payment and is entitled to his commission.

Unless excluded from doing so by his contract with Penelope (of which there is no evidence), Andrew can also claim his expenses from Penelope in relation to the contract with Zubin, since these have been properly incurred in the performance of the agency. The right to indemnity covers all expenses and liabilities necessarily incurred by the agent whilst acting within his actual authority. Furthermore, should Andrew be in lawful possession of property or documents of title belonging to Penelope, he may protect his rights by exercising a lien[3] over them for unpaid commission and expenses.

The position in relation to the contract with Yatin is more problematic. Andrew exceeded his authority by giving Yatin 40 days' credit. Where an agent acts outside his authority, he is generally not entitled to commission, even though his principal may be bound by the transaction. Although Penelope purported to ratify the contract, at law, an undisclosed principal cannot do so (*Keighley Maxsted & Co v Durant* (1901)). In that case, the agent entered into a contract for the purchase of wheat at a price in excess of the limit on behalf of himself and his principal. The agent did not disclose to the seller of the wheat his intention to contract on the principal's behalf as well as his own. Later, the principal purported to ratify the agent's act. The House of Lords unanimously held that an undisclosed principal cannot ratify. It seems therefore that whatever the position as between Yatin and Penelope or Yatin and Andrew, Andrew is not entitled to commission on the contract made with Yatin.

As for Andrew's expenses, in order to render Penelope liable to indemnify him, he must have acted within the scope of his authority. For the same reasons as above, Andrew will not be entitled to claim for his expenses because he has acted in breach of his instructions.

Andrew's position vis à vis Zubin and Yatin

Where an agent acts with authority and names or sufficiently identifies the principal in such a way that it is clear to the third party that the agent is acting as such, the contract is made between the principal and the third party, and the agent drops out of the transaction entirely. This is Andrew's position with regard to Zubin – he incurs neither rights nor liabilities on the contract made between Zubin and Penelope.

In relation to Yatin, Penelope's purported ratification of Andrew's actions is without legal effect, because a principal can only ratify if he was identified at the time the contract was made (*Keighley Maxsted & Co v Durant* (1901)). Thus, the position is exactly the same as it was when the contract was made – Yatin thought the contract was made with Andrew and, therefore, Andrew is contractually liable to Yatin. No question of breach of warranty of authority arises here, because Andrew was, at law, the principal when the contract was entered into. It is clear that an agent is personally liable on a contract where it has been negotiated on behalf of an undisclosed principal. If the agent is unable to supply the Supaklean service under the contract made personally with Yatin, Andrew will be liable to pay damages for breach of that contract.

Penelope's position vis à vis Zubin and Yatin

Once again, the position in relation to Zubin is straightforward. Andrew acted within his authority and identified Penelope as his principal; the contract was therefore solely between Penelope and Zubin. Thus, if Penelope refuses to supply the Supaklean service to Zubin, she is in breach of this contract and Zubin has a right of action against Penelope alone.

In relation to Yatin, Penelope is able to rely on the rule in *Keighley Maxsted & Co v Durant* (1901) that an undisclosed principal cannot ratify.

Notes

1   Where the agent acts on behalf of a foreign principal, it used to be the rule that only the agent was liable on and able to enforce the contract but, since *Teheran Europe Co Ltd v ST Belton* (1968), it has been recognised that the court will now consider all the facts to decide if the contract has created privity between the principal and the third party, and the foreign nationality of the principal will be only one factor to be taken into account.

2   It should be noted, however, that in modern practice, cheques are rarely negotiated (being used largely as an alternative to cash) and usually include details of the company's name and account number on the face of the document. Thus, the party seeking to enforce it is usually the party to whom the cheque is given and that party will have sufficient notice that the intention is that it is the company, and not the person signing, who should be liable on the cheque. Since bills other than cheques are more likely to be negotiated and therefore less likely to include printed details of account numbers, etc, a person signing it will incur liability unless some other intention is clearly expressed.

3   Agents normally exercise a particular lien, that is, the agent is entitled to retain the principal's property until debts relating to that property are discharged (cf a general lien exercised by certain types of agents, for example, bankers and solicitors).

Question 30

'Agents are in a vulnerable position in relation to their principals and, accordingly, stand in need of protection. The Commercial Agents (Council Directive) Regulations 1993 have gone some way towards providing agents with an appropriate level of protection, but much more remains to be done.'

Critically evaluate this statement and, in particular, consider the contribution made by the Commercial Agents (Council Directive) Regulations to the protection of the agent.

Answer plan

This is a straightforward question which simply requires you to demonstrate a good understanding of the 1993 Regulations. Topics which will need to be covered are:

- definition of a 'commercial agent';
- duties of a commercial agent as regards the principal;
- duties of the principal as regards the agent, including the payment of commission;
- rights of termination, including the agent's right to compensation or indemnity.

There is some case law on the Regulations, most of which deals with the issue of compensation. The cases of *Page v Combined Shipping and Trading Co Ltd* (1997), *Moore v Piretta* (1999), *Ingmar GB Ltd v Eaton Leonard Technologies Inc* (2000) and *Hackett v Advanced Medical Computer Systems Ltd* (1999) will need to be mentioned.

Answer

The Commercial Agents (Council Directive) Regulations 1993 were introduced to give effect to a European Directive intended to provide protection for a particular type of agent, and to ensure equivalent treatment across the European Union. In England, the Regulations sit alongside the common law, supplementing it in some areas and replacing it in others. In general, an agent covered by the Regulations is better protected as regards relations with the principal than under the common law. The Regulations do not affect the relationships between principal or agent and third parties with whom the agent negotiates.

The Regulations only apply to a particular type of agent, described in reg 2 as a 'self-employed intermediary who has continuing authority to negotiate the sale or purchase of goods' for a principal. The Regulations do not, therefore, apply to agents who are employed by the principal, or who act for a single transaction, or who do not act in relation to sale of goods contracts. In addition, the Regulations specifically exclude company officers, partners and insolvency practitioners from their scope. Their extent is therefore limited, and there are many agents who in the broadest sense might be regarded as 'commercial' but who will fall outside the Regulations. Their relationships with their principals continue to be governed solely by the common law.

The duties of the commercial agent as regards the principal are set out in reg 3. Overall, the duty is to 'look after the interests of his principal and to act dutifully and in good faith'. This seems to add little to the common law duties to follow instructions and to comply with an agent's fiduciary obligations (for example, to avoid conflicts of interest not to make a secret profit). There are two specific duties mentioned in reg 2, however, which seem to go a little further. The first is to 'make proper efforts' to negotiate and conclude transactions. This seems to amount to a duty of 'due diligence', expecting the agent to be rather more pro-active than the common law would require. The second obligation is to communicate 'all necessary information' to the principal. This has no equivalent under the common law. Again, it is requiring the agent to be pro-active in providing information, rather than the common law approach of prohibiting the concealment of relevant information (for example, as regards secret profits).

Turning to the duties of the principal in relation to the agent, reg 4 sets out some general duties which mirror those imposed on the agent under reg 3. Thus, the principal is also required to act 'dutifully and in good faith' in his dealings with the agent. There is no parallel to this under the common law, where the principal's main general obligation is simply to act in accordance with the contract. More specific duties relating to information and documentation are, however, set out in the rest of reg 4. These require, first, that the principal should obtain for (and presumably communicate to) the agent, the information 'necessary for the performance of the agency contract'. This is very general, and the precise limits of the information are not clear, though it will obviously cover practical information such as the details of prospective buyers or sellers. There is also a specific obligation to notify the agent if the volume of transactions is likely to be significantly lower than the agent could have expected. Finally, the principal must inform the agent of any action taken in relation to a transaction arranged by the agent. Thus, the agent must be told whether the principal has accepted or refused the transaction, or not executed it. These actions have potential consequences for the agent's remuneration and as regards the agent's relationship with the third party with whom the transaction has been negotiated, and therefore it is desirable that the agent should have this information. The common law does not impose any such obligations on a principal.

Similarly, the final obligation contained in reg 4 has no equivalent under the common law. This is that the principal must provide the agent with the relevant documentation relating to the goods concerned. This is an unexceptional and uncontroversial duty (which might indeed be implied by the common law on the basis of 'business efficacy'). If the agent is to deal with goods on behalf of the principal, relevant documentation necessary to the transaction (for example, documents of title or customs clearance) must be made available. Breach of any of these obligations (which cannot be changed by the contract between principal and agent) will amount to a breach of contract by the principal – but the Regulations do not provide for any specific remedies.

The most important obligation is for the principal to remunerate the agent. The obligation to do so is at common law regulated by the contract between the principal and agent, and that largely remains the case in relation to commercial agents, except that where the contract is silent as to payment, the Regulations provide that the agent is to be paid 'reasonable remuneration', which is not necessarily the common law position (*Kofi Sunkersette Obu v Strauss & Co* (1951)). Where the agent is paid wholly or partly on the basis of commission, however, the Regulations contain some provisions (in regs 7–12) as to how this is to be calculated and paid (though the rate of commission is left to the parties).

The entitlement to commission will arise when a transaction has been concluded 'as a result of [the agent's] action'. Presumably, this will be approached in the same way as the question of whether the agent's actions were the 'effective cause' of the transaction under the common law. The Regulations also give the agent the right to commission, however, in two situations where there has not been any direct involvement in negotiating a transaction (reg 7). Both apply for as long as the agency contract between agent and principal subsists. The first is where the principal concludes a transaction with a third party previously 'acquired' by the agent as a customer for transactions of the same kind. So, once a customer has been found by the agent, all subsequent transactions with the principal raise the possibility of commission. Secondly, where the agent has exclusive rights in a particular geographical area, or with a specific group of customers, the agent will be entitled to commission on all transactions of the relevant type entered into by the principal with customers from that area or group. Neither of these rights would apply under the common law unless specifically provided for in the agency contract.

The Regulations also contain provisions relating to transactions completed after the termination of the agency (reg 8). For example, where an order is received prior to termination, though the transaction is not concluded until after termination, the agent may be entitled to commission. In addition, commission may also be recovered where a transaction is mainly attributable to the agent's efforts, and is entered into within a 'reasonable period' of the termination of the agency. The language here is rather vague and, as yet, there has been no case law on it. It clearly goes further than the common law, but the precise scope of the agent's rights is difficult to determine without some clarification of the terms used in the Regulations.

Regulation 10 contains detailed provisions as to when commission becomes due, and by when it should be paid. These override any common law rules or anything in the agency contract which is less favourable to the agent. They mean that there should not be undue delay in paying an agent his commission.

The right to commission on a concluded transaction is lost in only one circumstance – when the transaction is not executed for a reason for which the principal is not to blame (for example, frustration or withdrawal by the third party) (reg 11). The Regulations make no provision for the right to commission to be lost as a result of the agent acting contrary to instructions, even where this is in bad faith. The agent will, of course, be in breach of the duty of good faith and if this has resulted in loss to the principal, compensation could be sought, but commission cannot be withheld on this basis.

Finally, in relation to commission, there are obligations imposed by reg 12, going beyond anything that would be implied under common law, for the principal to supply information to the agent in order to allow him to check what commission is due.

As has been seen, the provisions so far discussed supplement the common law in various ways and to some extent supersede it. The most significant difference, however, is in relation to the payment of compensation on termination of the agency agreement. Under the common law, this is governed by general contractual principles, so that what the agent will recover, even if the agency has been terminated in breach of contract, will normally be based simply on the rules governing the assessment of contractual damages. The Regulations take a very different approach, however.

First, as regards termination by notice, the Regulations specify minimum periods for such notice, which will override anything less favourable contained in the agency contract (reg 15). The most important provisions, however, are contained in reg 17, which deals with the rights to compensation or indemnity where the contract is terminated (other than as a result of the fault of the agent (reg 18)). An agent wishing to make a claim under these provisions must give notice within one year of the termination of the agency. It was held in *Hackett v Advanced Medical Computer Systems Ltd* (1999) that no particular formality is required. A letter which gave a clear indication of an intention to seek compensation was sufficient, even if it did not specify the Regulations which would be relied on.

Regulation 17 provides for the agent to seek recompense on an 'indemnity' basis or 'compensation'. Unless the agency contract specifies otherwise, however, the compensation rather than the indemnity approach will be taken. The European origins of these remedies are shown in the fact that the indemnity approach is derived from the German system, whereas the compensation approach follows the French system.

The operation of the indemnity provisions was considered in *Moore v Piretta* (1999). The judge had no doubt that they should effectively be dealt with as a self-contained system, without reference to common law principles. It would, however, be appropriate to look at the way in which German law dealt with indemnities for commercial agents, since the Regulations were clearly based on the German system. The basis of the indemnity provisions is to provide compensation calculated by reference to the amount of increased business which the agent has brought to the principal, by introducing customers. There is a cap on what can be awarded, however, based on what the average of what the agent has received over previous years, up to a maximum of five. This cap was applied to limit the payment to the agent in *Moore v Piretta*.

The terminology of the compensation provisions makes them appear superficially closer to the common law contractual approach. Indeed, in *Page v Combined Shipping and Trading* (1997), the Court of Appeal appeared, *obiter*, to endorse the application of common law principles to the operation of the Regulations. Commentators have, however, doubted that this is the right approach. Recent cases in Scotland have adopted an approach based on French law. Rather than taking the English approach of putting the parties in the position that they would have been in had the contract been performed, this involves assessing the value of what the agent has lost by the termination, by considering what commission would have been earned in future years.

In *Ingmar GB Ltd v Eaton Leonard Technologies Inc* (2000), after the termination of a commercial agency contract between the claimant (a UK company) and the defendant (a Californian company), the claimant sought compensation under the 1993 Regulations for damage suffered as a result of the termination of its relations. The defendant maintained that the Regulations did not apply, since a clause in the contract stated that Californian law governed the contract. The question referred to the European Court of Justice (ECJ) was whether Directive 86/653, as implemented in the laws of the Member States, was applicable in the circumstances. The ECJ said that the regime set up by the Directive was mandatory in nature. Furthermore, the purpose of that regime, apart from protecting commercial agents, was to ensure their freedom of establishment and undistorted competition in the internal market. Accordingly, the ECJ held that commercial agents are entitled to an indemnity or compensation in the event of breach of their relations with the undertaking which they represent in the Community, irrespective of the law by which the two parties intended the contract to be governed.

In conclusion, it is the case that the common law is still important in relation to many aspects of commercial agency agreements. In certain areas, however, particularly in relation to the information to be provided to agents, the payment of commission and the consequences of termination, the European approach set out in the 1993 Regulations operates to provide rather more protection for the agent than would otherwise be the case.

Question 31

(a) When is an agent entitled to claim commission?

(b) Pavaro Ltd engages Addam to act for it in the sale of machinery manufactured by Pavaro Ltd. The contract provides that Pavaro Ltd shall pay Addam '... 3% commission on the value of all sales of machinery pursuant to this agreement ...' and that '... no sales shall be made through the intermediation of any other agent so long as this present agreement shall last'.

Addam negotiates a sale to Kentucky Ltd and has delivered to Pavaro Ltd a letter from Miniac Ltd expressing its intention to place an order with Pavaro Ltd (through Addam) in the near future. In addition, Laventi Ltd places an order directly with Pavaro Ltd, having entered into preliminary negotiations with Addam some six months ago, negotiations which ended because, at the time, the specifications of the machinery available from Pavaro Ltd did not meet Laventi Ltd's requirements. Subsequently, Miniac Ltd makes a formal offer to purchase machinery, which Pavaro Ltd rejects because it fears that the machinery may be used to manufacture armaments.

After this sequence of events, Pavaro Ltd cancels the contract with Addam by giving notice in accordance with the terms of the contract, and refuses to pay commission which Addam claims is owed to him. Addam claims commission on the sales to Kentucky Ltd and Laventi Ltd, and damages in respect of Pavaro Ltd's refusal to sell to Miniac Ltd.

Discuss the legal position.

Answer plan

Both parts of the question concern the right of an agent to claim commission. The conditions for such payment at common law are as follows:

- the agent is acting with the principal's authority;
- the contract expressly or impliedly provides for commission to be paid;
- the event has happened on which payment was made conditional;
- the acts of the agent were the effective cause of that event happening.

The provisions of the Commercial Agents (Council Directive) Regulations 1993 in relation to the payment of commission to commercial agents will also need to be noted.

Answer

(a)

The general rule is that an agent is only entitled to commission if that has been agreed with the principal. There are, however, instances where the court will imply a term giving the agent a right to be paid for his services even if there is no express agreement.

If the contract is silent as to *when* commission is payable, the normal intention of the parties is that the agent can claim commission when the contract of sale is concluded, particularly where the agent is acting in the course of a profession or business. As regards commercial agents falling within the Commercial Agents (Council Directive) Regulations 1993, the time for payment of commission is dealt with by reg 10. In the absence of any more favourable agreement, commission will be payable when either the principal or the third party has 'executed the transaction', and at the latest when the third party has executed his part of the transaction (or should have done if the principal had executed his part as he should have). At common law, it is only rarely, however, that a court will interfere where to do so varies or is contrary to the express terms of the agency contract. For example, in *Kofi Sunkersete Obu v Strauss & Co Ltd* (1951), the contract provided for the agent to receive £50 per month as expenses but that the scale of commission was solely at the company's discretion. The Privy Council in that case was not prepared to intervene to determine the rate and basis of the commission that the agent claimed he had earned.

The principal's duty to pay commission only arises where the agent has earned it. If the agent acts contrary to his instructions, therefore, under common law, no right to commission will arise. For example, in *Marsh v Jelf* (1862), an auctioneer was employed to sell property by auction and was held not to be entitled to commission when he sold the property by private contract. If the agent himself is in breach of his instructions under the contract of agency, but a contract of sale has been concluded between the principal and a third party, the agent may still be entitled to his commission if his breach was done honestly and in good faith (but he does forfeit his commission if he acted in bad faith).[1] As regards a commercial agent payable by commission, the right will only be lost if a contract concluded between the principal and a third party is not executed for a reason for which the principal is not to blame (for example, frustration or where the third party withdraws) (reg 11 of the Commercial Agents (Council Directive) Regulations 1993). The Regulations make no provision for the right to commission to be lost as a result of the agent acting contrary to instructions, even where this is in bad faith. The agent will of course be in breach of the duty of good faith and if this has resulted in loss to the principal, compensation could be sought, but commission cannot be withheld on this basis.

An agent will only earn his commission when he has been the direct or effective cause of the event upon which the principal has agreed to pay commission. The relevant phrase in the Commercial Agents (Council Directive) Regulations is where a contract 'has been concluded as a result of [the agent's] action' (reg 7). It is to be assumed that this will be interpreted in the same way as 'effective cause'. The question of causation is ultimately a question of fact in the absence of judicial definition of 'effective cause'. If some event breaks the chain of causation between the agent and the event on which payment of commission depends, then the agent will not be entitled to commission. Thus, in *Coles v Enoch* (1939), A was employed to find a tenant for P's property. T overheard a conversation between A and an interested party and, although A only gave T a general description of the location, T found the property himself and made an offer directly to P which was accepted. The court held that A was not entitled to commission since his actions had not been the direct cause of T's agreement with P.

A commercial agent may also be able to claim commission in relation to contracts between the principal and a customer previously introduced by the agent, even though the agent has not taken any action in relation to the later contracts (reg 7(1)(b) of the Commercial Agents (Council Directive) Regulations 1993).

In some cases, an agent will be entitled to commission where the principal willfully breaks his contract with a third party whom the agent has introduced and whom the principal has accepted. In *Alpha Trading Ltd v Dunnshaw-Patten* (1981), a principal was introduced to a buyer for a quantity of cement. The principal accepted the introduction and contracted with the buyer accordingly. In order to take advantage of a rising market, the principal decided not to perform the contract of sale (preferring instead to pay damages for breach of contract). The agent claimed damages for lost commission. The Court of Appeal held that the agent was entitled to commission because it was an implied term of the agency contract that the principal would not deprive the agent of his commission by breaking the contract with the third party. As noted above, this common law principle also operates under reg 11 of the Commercial Agents (Council Directive) Regulations 1993. If a contract is not performed for a reason for which the principal is to blame, the commercial agent is still entitled to commission.

Where a person is appointed 'sole agent', he is entitled to be paid even if the sale is not effected by him but by some other agent.[2]

(b)

On the assumption that Pavaro Ltd's termination of Addam's contract is justified, this question involves an agent's right to receive commission (more generally discussed in part (a)). Since Addam is a self-employed agent engaged under a continuing authority to sell goods for Penelope, he is a 'commercial agent' within the Commercial Agents (Council Directive) Regulations 1993. The common law position will therefore be modified by the provisions of these Regulations.

Kentucky Ltd

In relation to the contract placed by Kentucky Ltd, it is clear that (as required by the Regulations) the transaction was concluded as a result of Addam's action or, in common law terms, his actions were the effective cause of the sale and therefore Addam is entitled to 3% of the sale price as commission. The contract is quite specific as to the commission payable, and Addam's role in effecting the sale is unequivocal.

Miniac Ltd

Here, the issue is not one of commission, since no contract was concluded on which commission would be payable, but one of whether the principal has the right to take actions which prevent the agent from earning his commission. In the absence of an express term in the agency contract, might the courts be prepared to imply such a term in the circumstances of this question? Decided cases show that they are reluctant to do so. This situation is not one which is dealt with by the Regulations.

In the leading case of *Luxor (Eastbourne) Ltd v Cooper* (1941), agents were instructed to sell two cinemas and commission of £10,000 was payable on completion of a sale. The agents introduced a prospective purchaser who was willing and able to proceed with the purchase, but the owners of the cinemas refused to sell to him. The agents alleged the existence of an implied term preventing the owners interfering with an agent's ability to earn his commission. The House of Lords held that no such term could be implied. It was not necessary to achieve business efficacy in the contract and, given the size of the commission in relation to the work involved,[3] the agents were held to have taken the risk that the owners might not proceed with any sale arranged by the agents. However, a contrary view was taken by the court in *Alpha Trading Ltd v Dunnshaw-Patten Ltd* (see above).

The commission claimed by Addam is probably of a different order to that claimed by the agent in *Luxor*. Nor was there a deliberate breach of an existing contract or, on the facts, any evidence of a pecuniary motive behind Pavaro Ltd's refusal to proceed as there was in *Alpha Trading*. Thus, both cases can be distinguished on the facts. It would appear to be a situation in which general principles are most likely to apply – unless there is an express term stopping Pavaro Ltd from doing anything which prevents Addam earning his commission, Pavaro Ltd is able to do so. An action by Addam for damages is thus likely to fail.

Laventi Ltd

The issue involved in this third situation is whether the sale of machinery to Laventi Ltd has been concluded as a result of Addam's actions (as required by the Regulations). If it has, then Addam is entitled to receive commission.

It is assumed that English courts, in tackling this issue, will adopt the common law approach of asking whether the agent's actions were the 'effective cause' of the contract. 'Effective cause' has not been judicially defined. It concerns the question of causation which depends on the facts of each case. Although Addam was responsible for the initial contact and negotiations with Laventi Ltd, there is arguably no direct connection between these and the subsequent sale because, at the time of the initial negotiations,

Pavaro Ltd did not have machinery which matched Laventi Ltd's requirements. On this basis, Addam cannot be said to be the effective cause of the sale and he would therefore not be entitled to commission.

The term of the contract '... no sales shall be made through the intermediation of any other agent so long as this present agreement shall last' appears to amount to a 'sole agency'. A sole agency agreement is a variant of a standard agency agreement because it prevents the principal selling goods through other agents. However, a 'sole agency' agreement does not prevent the principal himself from selling goods. If, therefore, after the termination of the agency contract, Pavaro Ltd and Laventi Ltd enter into new negotiations, whereby Pavaro Ltd concludes the contract with Laventi Ltd for goods now matching Laventi Ltd's requirements, the effective cause of the sale is not the introduction by Addam (although to some degree it remains), but Pavaro Ltd itself. Thus, Addam is not entitled to commission on this transaction. This is not affected by anything in the Regulations.

Notes

1 See also *Hippisley v Knee Bros* (1905), where the court found that although the agent, acting in good faith, was in breach of duty, he was allowed to keep his commission on the transaction. Similarly, in *Boardman v Phipps* (1966), the agents were allowed some reimbursement for their expenses.

2 This takes the form of damages for breach of the term that he should be the 'sole' agent.

3 £10,000 was, in 1941, the equivalent of the remuneration for a year's work by the Lord Chancellor.

CHAPTER 10

RELATIONSHIP WITH THIRD PARTIES

Introduction

This chapter is concerned with the scope of an agent's authority and when a principal will be liable, or be able to sue, on a contract made by the agent without authority. The different types of authority must be understood, in particular, apparent authority (sometimes known as 'ostensible' authority) and usual authority.

Checklist

The following issues are important:

- the concepts of implied authority (in particular, apparent and usual);
- the concept of the undisclosed principal;
- duties of an agent;
- rights and obligations between principal and agent vis à vis third parties;
- implied warranty of authority.

Question 32

On 1 October, Tristan, an art dealer in London, appoints Sonia as his agent in Sheffield and that same day, he sends a letter to Artrus Ltd, a company dealing in paintings in Sheffield, confirming Sonia's appointment and her authority to buy and sell pictures on his behalf. In fact, Sonia is under an express instruction not to deal with any pictures alleged to have been painted by Warholle, because of the risk of forgery. On 10 November, Sonia, purporting to act on behalf of Tristan, contracts with Artrus to buy from it 'The Pink Coyote', a genuine Warholle painting, for £17,000. On 12 November, Sonia visits the office of Belgravia Galleries and, without mentioning Tristan, contracts to sell it 'The Pink Coyote' for £23,000. Sonia intends to keep the profit from this transaction for herself. On 16

November, Artrus discovers what Sonia is trying to do, and tells Tristan that it intends to withdraw from the contract and keep 'The Pink Coyote'. On 17 November, Tristan purports to ratify Sonia's actions of 10 and 12 November.

Consider the rights and liabilities of all parties.

Answer plan

Part of this problem is concerned with authority and, in particular, apparent authority. This relates to the effect of Sonia's actions on 10 and 12 November, and whether they can be regarded as falling within the scope of her authority so as to bind Tristan. The approach to the issue of apparent authority should be the same as is outlined in the answer plan for Question 35.

The second issue that should be looked at is Sonia's attempt to make a secret profit out of her position as Tristan's agent. The duty of the agent to act in good faith and account for any secret profit (for example, *De Bussche v Alt* (1878)) needs to be noted here. Sonia may also be said to have broken another duty of an agent in her failure to follow instructions.

Finally, there is Tristan's attempt to ratify what Sonia has done. The general requirements of ratification should be stated, that is:

- the agent must purport to act for the principal (*Keighley Maxsted & Co v Durant* (1901));
- the principal must be in existence at the time of the contract (*Kelner v Baxter* (1866)); and
- the principal must have capacity at the time of contract and at the time of ratification (*Grover and Grover v Matthews* (1910)).

These should be applied to the problem, and you should also note the effects of ratification, in particular, its retrospective nature (*Bolton Partners v Lambert* (1889)).

The answer could well conclude with a summary of the position of each of the parties.

Answer

This question raises issues relating to the extent of an agent's authority, the duties of an agent and the power of a principal to ratify an agent's unauthorised acts. These will be looked at in turn in discussing the rights and liabilities of all the parties.

In making the contracts of 10 and 12 November, Sonia is acting outside the actual authority given to her by Tristan, in that she has been forbidden to deal in pictures by Warholle. This does not necessarily mean, however, that her actions cannot bind Tristan. This is because she may have 'apparent' authority (also known as 'ostensible' authority or 'agency by estoppel'). The requirements for this, as set out by Slade J in *Rama Corp Ltd v Proved Tin and General Investment* (1952), are: (a) that there is a representation of authority by the principal to the third party;[1] (b) that the third party relies on that representation; and (c) that the third party alters his position in reliance on the representation. This approach was followed by the Court of Appeal in *Freeman and Lockyer v Buckhurst Park Properties (Mangal) Ltd* (1964), which made it clear that the representation could be by conduct, rather than by a statement. Here, however, as far as Artrus is concerned, there was a clear and apparently unequivocal representation as to Sonia's authority in Tristan's letter of 1 October. Provided that Artrus could show that it was important to it that Sonia was Tristan's agent – in other words, that it was relying on Tristan's representation – then the apparent authority would seem to operate. This would mean that if, on 10 November, Artrus had sought the £17,000 from Tristan, it would have had every chance of success. This does not mean, however, that Tristan can necessarily enforce the contract against Artrus. The doctrine of apparent authority has developed to protect third parties. It is unlikely that the courts would allow it to be used against a third party in a situation such as this. That is why it will become important to look later at Tristan's power to ratify Sonia's actions.

In relation to the contract with Belgravia Galleries, the position is different. We are not told of any letter being sent to it about Sonia's authority. Moreover, Sonia apparently purports to contract on her own behalf. Even if she had been acting for Tristan, so that Tristan was an undisclosed principal, this would not affect the position. There can be no apparent authority without a representation from the principal to the third party, and it is difficult to see how this could occur if the third party is unaware of the existence of the principal. The possibility of Tristan's ratifying what Sonia has done will be considered later.

Turning to Sonia, what is her position? Her actions have involved breaches of two of the duties which an agent owes to a principal. First, she has disobeyed an instruction not to deal with Warholle pictures.[2] She will be liable for any loss flowing from this. This rule has been applied strictly, even in cases where there was some doubt as to whether, even if the agent had carried out his instructions, the principal would have avoided the loss. An example of this is *Fraser v Furman* (1967), where the agent failed to take out an insurance policy on the principal's behalf, but argued that even if he had taken it out, the insurer would have been able to avoid paying out because of a minor omission on the part of the principal. The Court of Appeal refused to get involved in that argument, and held the agent liable.

Secondly, Sonia is in the process of breaching one of her fiduciary duties, that is, the duty not to make a secret profit out of her position as agent. If she does, she will be liable to account to the principal for the profit. This is what happened in *De Bussche v Alt* (1878), where an agent, engaged to sell a ship, bought it himself at the minimum price specified by the principal and shortly afterwards sold it at a substantial profit. This profit had to be handed over to the principal. Here, if Sonia completed her transactions as she planned, the £6,000 profit on the resale of the picture would have to be handed over to Tristan. There is no suggestion in the facts that Sonia has taken any bribe. This type of secret profit is dealt with even more severely, with the principal being entitled to dismiss the agent, and sue both the agent and the third party for any losses resulting (*Logicrose v Southend United Football Club* (1988)), but it does not appear to be relevant on these facts.

Although Sonia has been acting beyond her instructions, and has been trying to make a profit for herself, Tristan has now apparently recognised that the contracts which Sonia has negotiated in relation to 'The Pink Coyote' amount to a good bargain. He is therefore trying to take the benefit of them himself by ratifying Sonia's actions of 10 and 12 November. Can he do this?

The power of a principal to ratify the unauthorised acts of an agent is well established. There are, however, certain limitations. First, the agent must have purported to act for a principal. This was established in *Keighley Maxsted & Co v Durant* (1901). The agent was authorised by the principal to buy wheat for their joint account at a certain price. He made a contract with the third party (Durant) at a higher price. He intended this to be for the joint account, but did not tell Durant this. The next day, the principal ratified what the agent had done, but subsequently refused to take delivery. An action by Durant against the principal failed because the agent had not purported to act for the principal, and ratification was therefore impossible.[3] Provided that the agent says that the contract is on behalf of a principal, however, it does not matter that in fact the agent is acting on his own account. In *Re Tiedemann and Ledermann Freres* (1899), it was held that in these circumstances, the principal could still ratify.

The second limitation on the power to ratify is that the principal must have been in existence at the time of the contract between the agent and the third party. This problem arises where contracts are made on behalf of companies which have not yet been incorporated. In *Kelner v Baxter* (1866), the promoters of a company which had not yet been incorporated made a contract to buy stock for it. When the company was incorporated, there was an attempt to ratify this contract. It was held that this was ineffective, and the promoters remained personally liable.

The third requirement is that the principal must have been able to make the contract at the time of the contract and at the time of ratification. The first part of this will be a problem where, for example, a minor attempts to ratify a contract which the minor would not have had capacity to make. The second part will also apply where at the time of ratification the contract would simply not have been possible. In *Grover and Grover v Matthews* (1910), for example, there was an attempt to ratify a contract of fire insurance after a fire had destroyed the property which was the subject of the insurance. It was held that ratification was impossible, because at that stage, the principal would not have been able to make the insurance contract.

How does all this apply to the facts of the problem and to Tristan's attempts to ratify Sonia's actions? The second two requirements appear not to create a problem, so we must concentrate on the first – that is, that the agent must purport to act for a principal. In relation to the contract made on 10 November, this is no problem. Sonia clearly says that she is acting for Tristan, and we have seen that the fact that she is in reality acting for her own benefit is irrelevant (*Re Tiedemann and Ledermann Freres*). When Sonia makes the contract with Belgravia Galleries on 12 November, however, she makes no mention of Tristan or any other principal. This contract cannot therefore be ratified by Tristan. So, it seems that Tristan can take over the contract to buy 'The Pink Coyote', but not the contract to sell. What about Artrus' attempt to withdraw, which comes before the ratification? This does not matter, because ratification is retrospective; it was so held in *Bolton Partners v Lambert* (1889), where it was said that the contract, once ratified, had to be treated as if it had been made with proper authority from the start. Similarly, in *Re Tiedemann and Ledermann Freres*, the third party had tried to withdraw on the basis of the false pretence about whom he was contracting with (which is similar to the situation here), but was prevented from doing so by the subsequent ratification of the contract.

Where does all this leave the various parties?

Tristan has a contract to buy 'The Pink Coyote' at £17,000, but no contract for resale. He may also be able to take action against Sonia for her various breaches of duty.

Sonia has a contract with Belgravia Galleries to sell it 'The Pink Coyote'. She will have difficulties fulfilling this contract, since 'The Pink Coyote' now belongs to Tristan. She is also likely to face action by Tristan, as noted above.

Artrus is obliged to sell 'The Pink Coyote' at £17,000 to Tristan, and seems to have no possibility of any action against anyone else. Tristan's ratification of Sonia's actions prevents it from pursuing her.

Belgravia Galleries has a contract to purchase 'The Pink Coyote' from Sonia which, as we have noted, Sonia will have difficulty fulfilling. It will be able to sue her for breach of contract.

Finally, the best outcome for all concerned, apart from Artrus, might be for Tristan to get together with Belgravia Galleries, and see if they can come to a similar arrangement to that negotiated by Sonia.

Notes

1   In *Armagas v Mundogas* (1986), the House of Lords emphasised that for apparent authority to exist, the representation must come from the principal, not from the agent. In this case, the vice president of a company had indicated that he had authority to agree a deal for the sale and charter-back of a ship. His plan was to make a secret profit out of the transactions. When his deceit came to light, the third party argued that the shipowners were bound by the agent's apparent authority. The House of Lords disagreed, holding that there was no representation of authority from the principal as opposed to the agent, and that therefore apparent authority could not arise.

2   This assumes that Sonia has a contractual relationship with Tristan.

3   The lower courts disagreed on the result, but this was the unanimous decision of an eight person House of Lords.

Question 33

Sebastian, the owner of a shop selling antique British goods, has several red telephone boxes for sale. Sebastian is an eccentric and is well known for his dislike of Americans. Rocky, an American, knows that Sebastian is unlikely to sell a telephone box to him and therefore asks his friend, Alison, to visit Sebastian's shop and to purchase one of the telephone boxes on his behalf, promising to buy it from Alison for 10% more than she paid for it. Alison takes Sebastian out for lunch (the bill for which came to £25) and buys from him a telephone box for £300. She also agrees to buy an old chimney pot for £100. Rocky is delighted with the telephone box and also wants to take up Alison's offer to sell the chimney pot for £120. Sebastian learns of Alison's association with Rocky and purports to cancel both agreements.

Consider the rights and liabilities of all parties.

Answer plan

Part of this question is concerned with the problem of 'who is an agent?'. It is not always easy to recognise an agent. It is the effect in *law* of the conduct of the parties that must be considered in order to determine whether the agency relationship has come into existence. This question requires you to analyse the nature of the relationship between Rocky and Alison, and to consider whether Alison is acting as an agent or buying in her own name and reselling to Rocky. If it is the latter, then the agreement is not one of agency (*Lamb v Goring Brick Co* (1932); *AMB Imballaggi Plastici SRL v Pacflex Ltd* (1999)).

If Alison is an agent, she has acted on behalf of Rocky in such a way that the agency is wholly undisclosed. Many of the cases dealing with the effects of undisclosed agency are old, but will need to be discussed. There is a general right for the undisclosed principal to intervene on and enforce the contract made on his behalf, but there are restrictions on that right, as in *Said v Butt* (1920).

Answer

This question raises issues relating to the nature of the relationship between a principal and his agent, the concept of the undisclosed principal and the right of an agent to be remunerated and indemnified for expenses in the performance of an agency agreement. These will be looked at in turn in discussing the rights and liabilities of Rocky, Alison and Sebastian.

Rocky asks Alison to buy a telephone box which Alison does not own or possess at the time of the contract. It is a difficult question of fact whether this agreement between them involves Alison as the 'seller' of goods acting for Rocky as the 'buyer', or as an agent acting for Rocky as the 'principal'.

If Alison is held to be buying and reselling on her own account, then she is not a true agent in law (*Lamb v Goring Brick Company* (1932); *AMB Imballaggi Plastici SRL v Pacflex Ltd* (1999)). Accordingly, Sebastian would be in breach of his agreement if he refuses subsequently to sell the telephone box to her. If the opposite is true, that is, Alison is procuring the telephone box for Rocky as Rocky's true agent and Alison is authorised to create privity between Rocky as principal and Sebastian as the third party, Rocky may intervene and enforce the contract made on his behalf, subject to certain restrictions which will be discussed.

On the facts, it is likely that Alison is acting as an agent. A particularly important factor in favour of this is the fact that Alison's remuneration in carrying out Rocky's instructions has been fixed at 10% of the purchase price.

Further, Alison's duty to buy a telephone box on Rocky's behalf is not absolute, in the sense that she will not be liable to Rocky if she does not obtain the telephone box; her duty is to use her care and skill as an agent to endeavour to obtain what Rocky wants (*Anglo-African Shipping Co of New York Inc v J Mortner Ltd* (1962)).

The essence of an agency agreement is the agent's power to affect the principal's legal position vis à vis third parties. Alison has been authorised by Rocky to buy a telephone box, but does not reveal the fact of agency to Sebastian at all and purports to be acting on her own behalf. The general rule is that there is no need for an agent to identify his principal. Provided that an agent has his principal's actual authority for his actions, the undisclosed principal may enforce a contract made by his agent with a third party.[1] This rule may appear harsh, since its effect on this question is that Sebastian deals with Alison in ignorance of the presence of an American being interested in the contract. The doctrine does, however, carry certain restrictions to protect the position of the third party and, in some cases, the undisclosed principal is entirely prohibited from intervening on the contract.

In *Said v Butt* (1920), the principal was a theatre critic who had been banned from a particular theatre after a bad review. He wanted to obtain a ticket for the opening night of a new play and, knowing that the theatre manager would not let him have one, employed an agent to obtain one for him. When he arrived at the theatre, he was refused entry. He then sued for breach of contract. The court held that he was not entitled to enforce the contract, on the basis that if the identity of the person with whom the third party is contracting is material to the making of the contract, the failure to disclose the fact that the agent is acting on behalf of a principal will deprive the principal of the right to sue on the contract. Applying this case to the question here, it would appear that Rocky will not be able to sue Sebastian on the contract if Sebastian refuses to sell the telephone box. Certainly, courts are likely to favour the interpretation of the situation which best protects the third party where third party rights in goods are in issue.

However, there have been criticisms of the decision in *Said v Butt* on the basis that personal dislike of the undisclosed principal should not normally prevent him intervening on a contract. In *Dyster v Randall & Sons* (1926), the agent, without revealing the fact that he was acting on behalf of a principal, entered into a contract for the sale of land. The court held that the identity of the person contracting with the third party was not material and, therefore, a valid contract was made with the principal who could sue for specific performance. Again, in *Nash v Dix* (1898), although the third party would not have sold the property concerned to the undisclosed principal, the court held that the identity of the contracting party was immaterial. Since Sebastian's objection to the contract for the sale of the telephone box is not based on a particular dislike of Rocky, but on his dislike of Americans generally, this would not amount to personal reasons. Rocky will be entitled to intervene on the contract and sue Sebastian for specific performance.

As far as the chimney pot is concerned, Rocky will be able to enforce the contract on the basis that Alison was not acting as his agent at the time of her agreement to purchase it from Sebastian (and is thus free to resell to whoever she wishes).[2]

We are also told that Alison takes Sebastian out for lunch, presumably to conduct her negotiations for the purchase of the goods. The general rule is that all agents are entitled to be reimbursed expenses necessarily incurred in the course of performing their duties. This is so whether or not the agent is acting under a contract of agency. Alison thus has the right to be indemnified for the expenses of lunch, such expenses having been incurred whilst acting within her actual authority to persuade Sebastian to sell goods to her on Rocky's behalf.

If Alison has taken possession of the goods, she is entitled to protect her rights to remuneration and indemnity by retaining the telephone box and the chimney pot until the amounts outstanding relating to the goods are discharged.[3]

To summarise the positions of the parties: Sebastian has a contract with Rocky to sell him the telephone box and a contract with Alison to sell her the chimney pot. If Sebastian cancels either contract, he will be liable to damages to Rocky and Alison respectively. Alison is entitled to her 10% commission vis à vis the telephone box, has agreed to resell the chimney pot to Rocky for a profit of £20 and has a lien over the goods in her possession until she is paid. Alison is further entitled to be indemnified for the cost of lunch.

Notes

1 Similarly, the third party may enforce the contract made by an agent against his principal.

2 Ratification does not apply here, since one of the requirements is that an agent must purport to act for the principal at the time the contract was made (*Keighley Maxsted & Co v Durant* (1901)). Clearly, Alison did not disclose the agency at the time she agreed to buy the goods from Sebastian. (See Questions 32 and 36 on the restrictions on the right of a principal to ratify.)

3 Alison is entitled to a particular lien, that is, she may retain Rocky's property until debts relating to that property are discharged (cf a general lien exercised by certain types of agents, for example, bankers and solicitors).

Question 34

Annabel, who owned a shop named 'Annabel Fruits and Flowers', sold the business earlier this year to Pansiflora, which appointed Annabel as manager and renames the business 'Annabel Flower Specialists'. A sign was put up stating 'Under new management, part of the Pansiflora group'. Annabel knows that Pansiflora does not sell fruit at any of its business outlets.

Annabel, however, continues to sell at the shop fruit grown in her own garden. Marcus, who bought some apples from her, is claiming that the fruit was infected, causing him severe stomach pains which prevented him from working for two weeks. Marcus is an architect and lost the opportunity to bid for a lucrative contract during that period. He is threatening to sue Pansiflora.

Nesbitt, Annabel's former landlord, accepts five bouquets of flowers in part-settlement of Annabel's unpaid rent.

Annabel is persuaded by Gisele on one occasion to sell some doughnuts which she had baked. Gisele gives Annabel £10 for doing this.

Advise Pansiflora.

Answer plan

Part of this question is concerned with the types of authority, in particular, usual or apparent authority, and the extent to which a principal can be bound by contracts which the agent has made without authority. This relates to Annabel selling fruit and the fact that it is unclear whether Pansiflora had given her any instructions in this respect. If Marcus does not have a claim against Pansiflora, Annabel may be personally liable (*The Swan* (1968)). The amount of damages Marcus may recover will also need to be discussed.

As for Nesbitt, Annabel has used her position as manager to satisfy a personal debt. If Pansiflora sues Nesbitt for the value of the five bouquets of flowers, set-off may offer a partial defence to such a claim. This will depend on whether Pansiflora is held to be a disclosed or undisclosed principal.

In accepting £10 from Gisele, Annabel is in breach of one of her fiduciary duties, that is, the duty not to make a secret profit out of her position as agent. The consequences of such a breach need to be discussed.

Answer

This question concerns the issue of an agent's authority and, in particular, the extent to which a principal can be bound by contracts which the agent has made without authority.

As far as selling fruit is concerned, Pansiflora did not give any express instructions to Annabel. The general rule is that where an agent is expressly appointed, the scope of his authority depends on the construction of the agreement. If the terms of the agreement are ambiguous, the court will generally construe them in a way which is most favourable to the agent as long as the agent construes his instructions reasonably (*Weigall v Runciman* (1916)). Therefore, it could be argued that Annabel was entitled to continue to sell fruit. The more likely view, however, is that Annabel should have known that Pansiflora would not permit the selling of fruit, partly because of the renaming of the business to 'Annabel Flower Specialists' with no mention of 'fruit', and partly because Annabel knew that Pansiflora did not sell fruit at any of its outlets. Furthermore, it would be reasonable to expect Annabel, faced with an ambiguity in her agency agreement, to seek clarification from Pansiflora (*European Asian Bank v Punjab & Sind Bank (No 2)* (1983)). Therefore, not only did Annabel have no actual express authority to sell fruit, but it could be said that Annabel should have known of the restriction not to sell fruit.

However, if it is usual for a flower shop manager such as Annabel to have certain authority, then Pansiflora will be liable to a third party even if Annabel knows that she is prohibited or restricted from acting in the way she did unless the third party had notice of the limitation (see *Watteau v Fenwick* (1893)). This doctrine of usual authority, however, may only be relied on by a third party where the agent makes a contract within the scope of the usual authority of an agent in that position. Pansiflora may rely on the fact that a business named 'Annabel Flower Specialists' does not imply that anything other than flowers would be sold in that shop, and a manager of such a shop would not have the authority to sell fruit. Pansiflora may thus escape liability on this basis.

The other possibility is that Marcus could argue for the existence of apparent authority (also known as 'ostensible' authority or 'agency by estoppel'). From the decisions in *Rama Corp v Proved Tin and General Investment Ltd* (1952) and *Freeman and Lockyer v Buckhurst Park Properties (Mangal) Ltd* (1964), the factors which must be present to create apparent authority include a representation that the agent has authority, which must be made by the principal. Such a representation must have been relied on by the third party claiming apparent authority.

The essence of a principal's representation is that the agent is authorised to act on his behalf. It is an authority which 'apparently' exists, having regard to the conduct of the parties. The principal's representation need not depend on previous course of dealings, as in *Summers v Solomon* (1857), but could it be argued that simply by employing Annabel as the manager, Pansiflora is representing that Annabel has authority to do all the things that a flower shop manager would normally do, including selling fruit? The answer on the facts is likely to be in the negative, on the ground that a third party such as Marcus would not expect the manager of a well known flower shop chain to have the authority to sell anything but flowers. Since the sign which was put up clearly states that 'Annabel Flower Specialists' is part of the Pansiflora group, it is unreasonable for Marcus to believe that he is dealing with a manager who possesses the necessary authority to sell fruit.

Marcus does not seem to be on strong ground against Pansiflora. This does not mean, however, that Marcus has no claim at all. Annabel may be personally liable to Marcus if the intention was that Annabel should be personally liable. The intention is to be gathered from the nature and terms of the contract and the surrounding circumstances. An objective test is applied so that if Annabel sells apples to Marcus in circumstances that make it reasonable to assume that Annabel was contracting personally, Marcus will have an action against Annabel.

In *The Swan* (1968), the defendant owned a boat called *The Swan* which was hired to a company of which he was a director. The company instructed the plaintiff to repair the ship on company notepaper which was signed by the defendant as director of the company. The company could not pay, and the question was whether the defendant was personally liable on the contract to repair the ship. The court held that the defendant contracted as agent for the company, but since it was reasonable for the repairer, who knew that the defendant owned the boat, to assume that the owner would accept personal liability for such repair, the defendant was personally liable on the contract. Applying this case to the question, if Annabel sold the apples in such a way that Marcus reasonably assumed that Annabel was selling in her personal capacity, then Annabel will be personally liable to Marcus in damages.

If, as is more likely, Annabel is held not to have contracted personally but to have contracted as an agent, Annabel cannot be made personally liable on the contract. However, since Annabel had no authority to sell fruit, Annabel will be liable to Marcus who has contracted with her on the faith of her representation of authority. The nature of her liability depends on whether Annabel had knowledge that she had no authority to sell fruit[1], or whether she merely acted negligently or in good faith and under the honest but mistaken belief that she was contracting with Pansiflora's authority. The latter is the more likely, rendering Annabel liable to Marcus for breach of the implied warranty of authority.

The amount of damages recoverable depends on the nature of the wrong committed. Essentially, the measure of damages will be either the loss which flowed directly as a natural or probable consequence or the loss which was foreseeable by the parties as a probable consequence, of the breach of warranty. It seems, therefore, that Marcus will be able to sue Annabel for damages. Whether or not Marcus can recover for the lost opportunity to bid for the 'lucrative' contract will depend on whether this opportunity was made known to Annabel at the time the contract was made. This seems unlikely, in which event, Marcus will not be able to recover damages on the basis that the damage was too remote (*Victoria Laundry (Windsor) Ltd v Newman Industries Ltd* (1949)).

As far as Nesbitt is concerned, can Pansiflora recover from Nesbitt the price for the bouquets of flowers? The right of a third party to set-off a liability against a principal will only apply where the principal has induced the third party to believe that the agent is acting as a principal and not as an agent, that is, where the principal is undisclosed. Did Nesbitt know of the existence of Pansiflora? Clearly, Nesbitt knew that Annabel had owned the business, but the question is really whether Nesbitt had *actual* notice[2] of the existence of Pansiflora. This will depend on whether Nesbitt noticed the sign which had been put up – that the business was now part of the Pansiflora group. If Nesbitt had actual notice, then Nesbitt has no right of set-off and Pansiflora is entitled to recover the price of the bouquets of flowers from Nesbitt.

As far as accepting £10 for selling Gisele's doughnuts is concerned, Annabel is in breach of one of her fiduciary duties, that is, the duty not to make a secret profit out of her position as agent.[3] Unless Annabel has revealed all the circumstances to Pansiflora and Pansiflora consented to her retaining the profit, she will be liable to account to Pansiflora for the profit. If an agent takes a bribe, the principal is entitled to claim the amount of the bribe as money had and received (*Regier v Campbell-Stuart* (1939)).[4]

Notes

1   In which event, Annabel acted fraudulently and will be liable in the tort of deceit (*Polhill v Walter* (1832)). This will be the case if Annabel *knew* Pansiflora's policy of restricting the types of goods sold at its outlets.

2   It is clear from *Greer v Downs Supply Co* (1927) that in respect of the existence of an undisclosed principal, the kind of notice that is required in order to be effective is actual notice, and constructive notice will be insufficient to affect the position of the third party.

3   The facts do not suggest that the £10 was a bribe. This type of secret profit is dealt with more severely, with the principal being entitled to summarily dismiss the agent and sue both the agent and the third party for any losses resulting. If an agent takes a bribe, the principal is entitled to claim the amount of the bribe as money had and received (*Logicrose v Southend United Football Club* (1988)).

4   Annabel holds the £10 on constructive trust (*Boardman v Phipps* (1966)). See also Question 27 on the duties owed by an agent.

Question 35

In April, Prashant appoints Alison as the manager of his restaurant. He tells her not to buy dairy products from a new company, Offwhite & Co, because he has heard that its products are of poor quality. In May, Slick, a representative of Offwhite & Co, visits the restaurant and as a result, Alison orders £100 worth of dairy products. Slick is unaware of Prashant's instruction to Alison. When, later in the day, Prashant discovers what Alison has done, they have an argument and Alison resigns. The following day, Alison goes to Thinbit Ltd, Prashant's regular supplier of wines and spirits, and purchases three cases of vodka on credit in Prashant's name. She then absconds with the vodka.

Advise Prashant as to his liability to Offwhite & Co and Thinbit Ltd.

Answer plan

This question is concerned with the issue of an agent's authority, and in particular the extent to which a principal can be bound by contracts which the agent has made without authority.

The two contracts concerned here raise different points, though there is some possibility of overlap. In relation to the contract with Offwhite & Co, there is the possibility of Prashant being liable on the basis of 'usual' authority, as in *Watteau v Fenwick* (1893). This will involve looking at what is the usual authority of a restaurant manager.

The contract with Thinbit Ltd, on the other hand, will only be binding on Prashant if Alison can be said to have 'apparent' authority. This is sometimes referred to as 'ostensible' authority or 'agency by estoppel'. It involves the principal having made a representation of the agent's authority which is then acted on by the third party. *Freeman and Lockyer v Buckhurst Park Properties*

(Mangal) Ltd (1964), which is one of the leading authorities on this area, will need discussion, though the case of *Summers v Solomon* (1857) is closer to the facts in the problem.

The overlap arises from the fact that it might also be possible to treat the contract with Offwhite as being binding on the basis of apparent authority, if it can be established that there was some representation of authority by Prashant on which Offwhite & Co could rely.

Answer

An agent frequently has the power to make contracts which are binding on his principal. Problems arise, however, where the agent exceeds the authority given. In what circumstances can the principal still be liable? There are two main ways. First, if it is customary for an agent of a particular type to have certain authority, then restrictions on that authority will be ineffective unless the third party knows about them. This is also referred to as 'usual' authority, or sometimes 'implied' authority.[1] An example of this type of authority which will be discussed below is the case of *Watteau v Fenwick* (1893). The second type of extended authority which we will need to consider is 'apparent' authority, which arises where the principal has made some representation of the agent's authority on which the third party has relied. An example of this is the case of *Freeman and Lockyer v Buckhurst Park Properties (Mangal) Ltd* (1964). We will need to examine whether either type of authority will lead to Prashant being bound to either of the two contracts made by Alison.

In relation to the contract with Offwhite & Co, the most obvious type of authority to consider is usual authority. In *Watteau v Fenwick* (1893), the defendants owned a beerhouse which was managed by a man named Humble.[2] Humble was under instructions not to buy cigars for the business from anyone other than the defendants. In breach of this instruction, Humble bought cigars on credit from the plaintiff. At the time of the contract, the plaintiff thought that Humble was the owner of the beerhouse. When he discovered the truth, however, he sought payment from the defendants. The defendants resisted on the basis that Humble had no authority to bind them to this contract. On the contrary, he was acting in breach of express instructions not to act in this way. The court nevertheless found the defendants liable. They said that it was within the usual authority of the manager of a beerhouse to be able to buy cigars from any source. The fact that Humble had been instructed not to do so was irrelevant, since the plaintiff was unaware of this restriction. He was entitled to rely on Humble's usual authority, and thus the defendants were obliged to pay for the cigars.

The issue of what constitutes usual authority is a question of fact, which will have to be decided in each case. The decision in *Watteau v Fenwick* can, for example, be contrasted with the earlier case of *Daun v Simmins* (1879), where it was held that where a public house was 'tied' to a particular brewer, the third party should have realised that the freedom of the manager to purchase would be restricted.

Watteau v Fenwick has been the subject of considerable criticism, in that it applied this approach to a situation where the third party was unaware that he was dealing with an agent. This, however, does not detract from the general principle. Even if it only applies where the principal is disclosed, it is still a type of authority which can bind the principal even where the agent has exceeded his actual authority.

Applying this to the problem, we find that Alison, the manager of a restaurant, has, like Humble in *Watteau v Fenwick*, failed to follow an express limitation on the contracts she is entitled to make. It is not clear whether Slick knew that he was dealing with an agent. If he did not, it is possible that the court would refuse to apply *Watteau v Fenwick* on the basis that, despite what happened in the case itself, the concept of usual authority should not be applied to situations involving an undisclosed principal. It seems more likely, however, that Slick would have realised that he was dealing with a manager rather than the owner of the restaurant. In that case, the next issue to decide concerns the limits of the usual authority of the manager of a restaurant.

As indicated above, this is a question of fact, not of law. In other words, it would be necessary to look at evidence as to what was normally accepted as being within the scope of the authority of someone like Alison. If it was found that such managers usually had authority to purchase goods from suppliers chosen at their own discretion, then Prashant will be likely to be found liable for this contract. If the opposite is found, or if it is not possible to determine any particular usual authority for such managers, then Offwhite will probably have to pursue Alison rather than Prashant. The only other possibility is if Offwhite could argue for the existence of apparent authority. Consideration of this point, however, will be left until after the discussion of the position as regards Thinbit Ltd.

In respect of the contract for the vodka, there is no possibility of using usual authority, because Alison is no longer an agent when she makes the contract. The only possibility here will be for Thinbit to argue that Alison had apparent authority to make this contract (the phrases 'ostensible authority' and 'agency by estoppel' are also used to describe this concept). As defined by Diplock LJ in *Freeman and Lockyer v Buckhurst Park Properties (Mangal) Ltd* (1964), this requires a representation by the principal,[3] intended to be acted on by the third party, and in fact acted on, that the agent does have authority to make the contract.[4] The representation need not be in the form of words;

conduct will be sufficient. In *Freeman and Lockyer v Buckhurst*, a person had been allowed to act as managing director of a company by the other directors, although he had never been appointed as such in the manner required by the company's Articles of Association. It was held that the directors' actions in allowing him to act in this way amounted to a representation to the outside world that he had authority to do so. The company was therefore bound by his actions. The case which is closest to the facts of the problem, however, is *Summers v Solomon* (1857). Solomon owned a jewellers shop and employed a manager to run it. Solomon regularly paid for jewellery that had been ordered by the manager from Summers. After the manager had left Solomon's employment, he ordered jewellery in Solomon's name from Summers and then absconded with it. It was held that Solomon was bound to pay for the jewellery. His previous conduct in paying for the jewellery had amounted to a representation of the manager's authority. That representation had not been contradicted or withdrawn, and so Summers was still entitled to rely on it.

At first sight, this decision would seem clearly to mean that Prashant will have to pay Thinbit for the vodka. There are, however, two questions that need to be asked. We are told that Thinbit is Prashant's regular supplier. What we do not know, however, is what the usual ordering procedures were. In particular, was it usual for goods to be ordered on credit? If so, did Alison follow the usual procedures in placing this order and immediately taking the goods away? If the answer to either of these questions is no, Prashant may escape liability. If it was not usual for goods to be ordered on credit, then there is less in the way of a representation of authority for what Alison has done in this case. Secondly, if Alison has not followed the normal procedures, should Thinbit not have been put on notice that something unusual was happening, and therefore made some attempt to confirm that Alison was acting with authority? If, however, these issues are not resolved in Prashant's favour, then it seems certain that he will be bound by Alison's apparent authority and will have to pay for the vodka.

The final point to consider is whether the contract with Offwhite could fall under the heading of apparent authority as well. The problem here is that of finding a representation. We are told that Offwhite is a new company, and therefore there will have been no previous dealings. It might be argued, however, that simply by employing Alison as a manager, Prashant is representing that she has authority to do all the things that a restaurant manager would normally do, including, perhaps, making contracts to buy dairy products. This was the kind of approach adopted in *United Bank of Kuwait v Hamoud; City Trust v Levy* (1988), where it was held that a firm that employed X as a solicitor was representing to the world that X had authority to engage in all transactions on the firm's behalf which came within the normal scope of a solicitor's responsibilities.[5] If this was followed here, it would be another argument for making Prashant responsible for Alison's contract with Offwhite.

The advice to Prashant in relation to these two contracts must be that he is on fairly weak ground. The doctrines of usual and apparent authority taken together mean that it is very likely that he will have to meet the obligations under the contracts with both Offwhite & Co and Thinbit Ltd. His only remedy then will be to try to trace Alison, and attempt to recover his losses from her.

Notes

1   Though it is probably preferable to restrict 'implied' authority to filling out the relationship between principal and agent, as in *Waugh v Clifford* (1982), rather than as indicating the extent to which the agent may bind the principal to a third party despite a clear breach of the authority given by the principal.

2   Humble had in fact previously been the owner of the beerhouse.

3   It was confirmed in *Armagas v Mundogas* (1986) that the representation must be by the principal. A representation by the agent will not be sufficient. But cf *First Energy (UK) Ltd v Hungarian International Bank* (1993) (discussed in Question 36).

4   Note also *Rama Corp Ltd v Proved Tin and General Investment* (1952), where Slade J identified the need for: (i) a representation; (ii) reliance on the representation by the third party; (iii) an alteration of position resulting from such reliance.

5   Cf also *Gurtner v Beaton* (1993). This approach if used widely would, of course, render the concept of usual authority virtually redundant.

Question 36

In June 2002, Nicholas approached Charmaine, 'New Business Manager' of Duncoutts Bank plc, seeking a loan of £100,000 to start up a business making garden furniture. Charmaine told Nicholas that approval was needed from Head Office for loans over £50,000. She sought approval for him, but Nicholas' application was rejected.

In February 2003, Nicholas, together with his wife, Chloe, again approach Charmaine, this time seeking a loan of £75,000 to set up an internet business selling garden furniture. On 5 March 2003, Nicholas and Chloe receive a letter from Charmaine, addressed to them both, stating 'I am pleased to inform you that your loan can proceed' and asking them to call in to deal with the paperwork. In fact, the papers are made out in Nicholas' name alone, since the loan is secured on property which is in his sole ownership. Chloe resigns from her well paid job as an engineer so that she can devote her time to the new business.

Before the money is paid, however, Duncoutts Bank informs Nicholas that Charmaine has agreed the loan without authorisation. Although they have in the recent past ratified some loans of more than £50,000 arranged by Charmaine without authorisation, in this case they are not prepared to do so because of the risks involved in internet businesses.

Advise Nicholas and Chloe.

Answer plan

There are two main issues to discuss in this question:

- did Charmaine have apparent authority to make the loan to Nicholas?;
- if she did not, what remedies might Nicholas and Chloe have against Charmaine?

The first issue requires consideration of whether any representation has been made by Duncoutts Bank plc to Nicholas as to Charmaine's authority, as required by *Freeman and Lockyer v Buckhurst Park Properties (Mangal) Ltd* (1964) and *Armagas v Mundogas* (1986). The case of *First Energy (UK) Ltd v Hungarian International Bank Ltd* (1993) on the extent to which an agent can represent his own authority will also need to be considered.

As regards the second issue, since there is no basis for making Charmaine liable on the loan contract, this will involve consideration of the remedies available against her in tort, or for breach of the implied warranty of authority. As far as Chloe's reliance on the implied warranty is concerned, the effect of the decision in *Penn v Bristol and West Building Society* (1997) will need to be considered.

Answer

This question concerns the extent to which agents may bind their principals even when acting outside their actual authority. It also raises the question of what remedies a third party will have if the agent has acted without authority, and this has led to loss.

The best outcome for Nicholas and Chloe in this situation would be for it to be found that Duncoutts Bank plc was obliged to make Nicholas the loan for the business, despite the fact that Charmaine had not sought approval for it. If that is not possible, however, they may well wish to seek a remedy against Charmaine personally.

There is no doubt that Charmaine has acted beyond her actual authority in arranging the loan to Nicholas. She did not have authority to approve loans of over £50,000, and Nicholas was aware of this as a result of their previous dealings. Although Duncoutts Bank has ratified some loans of over £50,000 made recently by Charmaine, there is no suggestion that her actual authority has changed. Duncoutts Bank is not obliged to ratify any contract, and is quite entitled to 'pick and choose' which ones it is prepared to accept. The fact that it does not wish to become involved in Nicholas' internet business is therefore a decision which it is free to take.

Nicholas may argue, however, that Charmaine has bound Duncoutts Bank to the loan agreement on the basis of apparent authority. The requirements for apparent authority were established by *Freeman and Lockyer v Buckhurst Park Properties (Mangal) Ltd* (1964). There must be a representation (by words or conduct) from the principal to the third party, which is relied on by the third party and which leads to an alteration of position by the third party. There is no doubt here that Nicholas has relied on an assumption that Charmaine had authority, and changed his position by entering into the loan contract. The more difficult question is whether the assumption has been created by any representation from Duncoutts Bank to him. In some situations, it can be argued that by placing a person in a particular position (for example, New Business Manager) this in itself amounts to a representation of authority or, alternatively, that agents in such a position might be argued to have the 'usual' authority attaching to that position. That cannot apply here, however, since Nicholas is aware of the limitation on Charmaine's authority as a result of their dealings in June 2002. Nor can it be said that the ratification by Duncoutts Bank of other loans of over £50,000 amounts to a representation, since there is no evidence that Nicholas is aware of these.

Could it be argued that the letter which Charmaine wrote to Nicholas is a representation that she has authority to agree the loan? It may well have this implication, but the problem is that it emanates from Charmaine, rather than from Duncoutts Bank. In *Armagas v Mundogas* (1986), the House of Lords emphasised that, for apparent authority to exist, the representation must come from the principal, not from the agent. In this case, the vice president of a company had indicated that he had authority to agree a deal for the sale and charter-back of a ship. His plan was to make a secret profit out of the transactions. When his deceit came to light, the third party argued that the shipowners were bound by the agent's apparent authority. The House of Lords disagreed, holding that there was no representation of authority from the principal as opposed to the agent, and that therefore apparent authority could not arise.

This case would suggest that Nicholas will not be able to rely on apparent authority, since he has only had dealings with Charmaine, and there has been no direct representation from Duncoutts Bank. The subsequent decision of the Court of Appeal in *First Energy (UK) Ltd v Hungarian International Bank Ltd* (1993) must, however, also be considered. The facts of this case bear some similarity to those of the problem. A branch manager of a bank had, in contravention of limitations on his actual authority, agreed arrangements with a third party for the provision of credit facilities to customers of the third party's business. The third party knew that the manager had no personal authority to enter into such arrangements on behalf of his principal, but assumed from a letter written by the manager that the appropriate approvals had been obtained. Although this appeared to amount to a representation by the agent, and therefore to fall foul of the decision in *Armagas v Mundogas*, the Court of Appeal felt able to distinguish the earlier case. It held that an agent who does not have apparent authority to enter into a particular transaction may nevertheless have apparent authority to communicate to a third party that such a transaction has been approved. Part of the reason for this was a feeling that it would be unreasonable to expect a third party to have to check in such situations whether the Board, or whatever other body within the principal company was appropriate, had in fact given approval to the transaction. It may well be, therefore, that it would be held here that Charmaine did have apparent authority to communicate to Nicholas that the necessary approval for his loan had been obtained. If that is the case, then Nicholas will be able to insist that the loan goes ahead, or claim compensation if it does not.

What is the position, on the other hand, if the strict requirements as laid down in *Armagas v Mundogas* are held to apply in this situation, so that Charmaine did not have apparent authority, even to the limited extent found to exist in *First Energy (UK) Ltd v Hungarian International Bank Ltd* (1993)? Nicholas will then have to seek a remedy from Charmaine herself. This is not a situation where Charmaine would be liable for the loan contract itself. Nicholas will rather be looking for compensation for any losses which he may have suffered. There are two ways in which this might be possible. First, there is the possibility of an action in tort for deceit or negligent misstatement under the *Hedley Byrne v Heller* (1964) principle, as modified in *Caparo v Dickman* (1990). If Charmaine is found to have made a statement as to the fact that the transaction had been authorised which she knew was false, or which she made without proper care, this could give an action for damages.

Alternatively, and this is particularly applicable if Charmaine's misrepresentation was innocent (that is, neither deliberately deceitful nor negligent), Nicholas may be able to sue for breach of the implied warranty of authority which is held to be given by agents (see, for example, *Collen v Wright* (1857)). This may enable him to recover all losses which have resulted from the fact that Charmaine was in fact acting without authority.[1] It is possible to obtain either expectation or reliance damages under this action.

Finally, what is Chloe's position? She was not a party to the purported contract with Duncoutts Bank, but this does not necessarily mean that she would have no action against Charmaine. In reliance on Charmaine's letter, she has given up her job, and can therefore claim to have suffered loss. It is clear that she could bring an action in deceit, if it is clear that Charmaine's misrepresentation was made to her and she acted on it. Similarly, an action for negligent misstatement would also be possible, provided that Chloe could be said to be owed a duty of care by Charmaine under the principles of *Caparo v Dickman* (1990). This would not seem to be too difficult on the facts. Charmaine's letter was addressed to both Nicholas and Chloe; Chloe was therefore within the group whom Charmaine could have expected to rely on the statements in the letter. The type of action she took (giving up her job) was reasonably foreseeable, and she could therefore claim for damages consequent upon this.

What about a claim under the breach of the implied warranty of authority? It might be thought that this would not be applicable, since Charmaine was not in the end someone whom Chloe was purporting to bring into a contractual relationship with her principal. The decision in *Penn v Bristol and West Building Society* (1997), however, suggests that this may not be an obstacle. In this case, a solicitor agent's innocent misrepresentation of authority to a building society was held to give rise to liability for breach of the implied warranty, even though the building society's loss resulted not from attempting to contract with the solicitor's principal, but from lending money to someone who was entering into such a contract. It was held to be sufficient that the representation of authority had been made to the building society and that it had acted on it to its detriment. Applying that to the situation in the problem, the representation of authority was clearly made to Chloe, and she has acted on it to her detriment by giving up her job. On this basis, Chloe, like Nicholas, could also seek damages for breach of the implied warranty from Charmaine.

In conclusion, therefore, it seems that either Charmaine will be found to have apparent authority, so that the loan agreement with Duncoutts Bank will be enforceable or, if she did not have such authority, both Nicholas and Chloe will be able to recover compensation from her on the basis of an action in tort or for breach of the implied warranty of authority.

Note

1   The existence of the warranty does not depend on the agent's awareness of the lack of authority. This was established in *Collen v Wright* (1857) and taken to its logical extreme in *Yonge v Toynbee* (1910). In the latter case, the warranty was held to operate against a solicitor who had continued to act for a client who, unknown to the solicitor, had become mentally incapacitated (which had the automatic effect of terminating the solicitor's authority). The fact that the solicitor had acted in good faith throughout was regarded as irrelevant.

Question 37

On 4 January 2002, Purplewell Ltd employed Anthony as the manager of its new bookshop in Manchester. The contract was for a fixed term of three years and stated that Anthony was to receive £15,000 per year and a 5% bonus if sales exceeded £50,000 in any one year. The contract forbade Anthony from selling books not supplied or ordered by Purplewell's head office.

Advise Purplewell in the following circumstances:

(a) Anthony sells a copy of *How to Pass Exams* by Hitchcock to Stephanie, a student, who only agrees to buy it on Anthony's personal guarantee that Stephanie will pass her exams if she follows the instructions in the book. She fails her exams.

(b) Anthony is out of stock of *Uncommon Law* by Cartwright and is told by Purplewell's head office that it would take four weeks before Anthony can expect fresh supplies of the book. Anthony approaches Tim, who owns a bookshop, and obtains from Tim 10 copies of *Uncommon Law* on credit.

(c) On 1 March 2003, Purplewell informs Anthony that the bookshop in Manchester is to be closed down due to a restructure of the company. The sales for the Manchester bookshop for 2002 were £55,000.

Answer plan

This question concerns the issue of an agent's authority and, in particular, the extent to which a principal can be bound by contracts which the agent has made without authority. We have been asked to look at the agency contract from the principal's point of view.

We are concerned here with the two contracts which Anthony made with third parties. Although the contracts raise different points, there is some possibility of overlap. In relation to the contract with Stephanie, Purplewell will only be bound if Anthony can be said to have had 'express' or 'usual' authority. This will involve looking at Anthony's express contractual obligations as well as his implied duties owed to his principal. As far as the contract with Tim is concerned, Purplewell may be liable on the basis of 'usual' authority, as in *Watteau v Fenwick* (1893). We will need to look at what is the usual authority of a bookshop manager. The concept of 'apparent' authority will need to be discussed, as in *Summers v Solomon* (1857).

The final part of the question concerns Anthony's entitlement to claim remuneration where his employment contract is brought to an end earlier than the fixed term. Note that Anthony is not a 'commercial agent' because he is not self-employed.

Answer

The relationship between an agent and his principal is a contractual one and as such, it imposes upon both parties rights, duties and obligations. An agent frequently has the power to make contracts which are binding on his principal. Problems arise, however, where the agent exceeds the authority given when contracting with a third party. This question concerns two types of authority. First, if it can be said that the nature and extent of Anthony's express contract with Purplewell Ltd includes the giving of a personal guarantee to customers, then Purplewell will be bound by the contract made with Stephanie ('express' authority). Secondly, if it is customary for a bookshop manager such as Anthony to have certain authority, then restrictions on that authority will be ineffective unless the third party knows about them ('usual' authority). This is sometimes referred to as 'implied' authority.[1] We will need to examine whether either type of authority will lead to Purplewell being bound to either of the two contracts made by Anthony.

(a) Stephanie

In relation to the contract with Stephanie, it does not appear that Purplewell had in any way incorporated into the employment contract with Anthony a term that Anthony should have the right to give personal guarantees to customers. Certainly, Anthony is contractually bound to sell books and Purplewell has invested Anthony with actual express authority to act on Purplewell's behalf. Although Anthony may have express authority to promote Purplewell's books to customers, the giving of a personal guarantee that, by using *How to Pass Exams*, a customer *will* pass exams seems likely to fall outside his express contract of agency.

It seems that Anthony's guarantee to Stephanie is a personal one and will not bind Purplewell.

Furthermore, an agent has an implied duty, which is over and above his express contractual duties, to act in good faith in pursuance of the principal's interest. Anthony does not appear to be acting in the best interests of Purplewell. Even if Anthony expressly named Purplewell at the time of the contract with Stephanie, Purplewell has the option of whether or not to ratify the guarantee.[2]

It seems unlikely that Purplewell will wish to ratify Anthony's guarantee even if Purplewell was named at the time of the contract, since this would clearly be to Purplewell's detriment. Accordingly, if Stephanie decides to sue on the personal guarantee, Purplewell is entitled to hold Anthony personally liable. The guarantee which Anthony gave Stephanie is a personal one and will not bind Purplewell.

(b) Tim

In respect of the contract for the purchase of 10 copies of *Uncommon Law* from Tim, the most obvious type of authority to consider here is usual authority. In *Watteau v Fenwick* (1893), the defendants owned a public house and had appointed a man named Humble as its manager. The defendants forbade Humble from buying cigars for the business from anyone other than the defendants. In breach of this, Humble bought cigars on credit from the plaintiff. The plaintiff sought payment from the defendants, who resisted on the basis that Humble had no authority to bind them to this contract because Humble had acted in breach of express instructions not to buy cigars from anyone other than the defendants. The court nevertheless found the defendants liable to pay for the cigars. The court considered that it was within the usual authority of the manager of a public house to be able to buy cigars from any source. Since the plaintiff was unaware of Humble's restriction to do so, the plaintiff was entitled to rely on Humble's usual authority.[3]

Watteau v Fenwick has been the subject of considerable criticism on the basis that the approach was applied to a situation where the third party was unaware that he was dealing with an agent.[4] It has been argued that the principle should only apply where the principal is disclosed. Even so, the general principle is clear. 'Usual' authority can bind the principal even where the agent has exceeded his actual authority.

How does all this apply to the facts of the problem? Anthony has, like Humble in *Watteau v Fenwick*, failed to follow an express restriction on the contracts he is entitled to make. It is not known whether Tim knew that he was dealing with an agent. If he did not, it is possible that the court would refuse to apply *Watteau v Fenwick* on the basis that the concept of usual authority should not be applied to a situation involving an undisclosed principal, despite the facts of that case itself. It seems more likely, however, that Tim would have realised that Anthony was dealing as a manager rather than as the owner of the bookshop. In that case, the issue that needs to be discussed is what constitutes the usual authority of a bookshop manager. This is a question of fact which will have to be decided in each case. If it is normally accepted that bookshop managers have the authority to purchase books from suppliers chosen at their own discretion, then Purplewell will be likely to be found liable for this contract. If it is not possible to determine that bookshop managers have this usual authority, then Tim will probably have to pursue Anthony for payment rather than Purplewell.

The only other possibility is if Tim could argue for the existence of apparent authority (also known as 'ostensible' authority or 'agency by estoppel'). This requires a representation by the principal which is intended to be acted on by the third party, and is in fact acted on, that the agent does have authority to make the contract (*per* Diplock LJ in *Freeman and Lockyer v Buckhurst Park Properties (Mangal) Ltd* (1964)). In *Summers v Solomon* (1857), Solomon owned a jewellery shop and employed a manager to run it. Solomon regularly paid for jewellery ordered by the manager from Summers. After the manager left Solomon's employment, he ordered jewellery from Summers and then absconded with it. The court held that Solomon was bound to pay for the jewellery on the basis that his previous conduct in paying for the jewellery had amounted to a representation of the manager's authority. Summers was entitled to rely on that representation since he was unaware that the manager's authority had been withdrawn.

Applying this to the contract with Tim, the problem here is that of finding a representation. We are told that the Manchester bookshop is a new business and, therefore, there will have been no previous course of dealings. Could it be argued that simply by employing Anthony as the manager, Purplewell is representing that Anthony has authority to do all the things that a bookshop manager would normally do, including buying books from suppliers chosen at their own discretion? This approach was favoured by the court in *United Bank of Kuwait v Hamoud* (1988) and *Gurtner v Beaton* (1993). If followed here, it would make Purplewell liable for Anthony's contract with Tim, and Purplewell will have to pay for the books.

(c) Anthony

The contract here is that Anthony is to receive £15,000 per year for three years and a 5% bonus payment if sales exceeded £50,000 in any one year. It would seem that Purplewell's decision to close down the Manchester bookshop amounts to a breach of the agency contract by Purplewell. It is unlikely that either of the contracts made with Stephanie or Tim will render Anthony guilty of misconduct entitling Purplewell to dismiss him. In the circumstances, Anthony will be entitled to claim remuneration from Purplewell for the full period of three years, since it has been expressed in the contract that Anthony was to be employed for that period.

The sales for 2002 exceeded £50,000 and it seems that Anthony will be entitled to his 5% bonus. Is Purplewell liable to pay compensation to Anthony for his removal of the opportunity to earn bonuses for 2003 and 2004? One test is whether or not the agency contract is one of service. Phillimore J in *Northey v Trevillion* (1902) indicated that if the contract is one of service, then the agency contract cannot be terminated without compensation to the agent. In *Turner v Goldsmith* (1891), the agent was employed for a period of five years on a commission basis by the principal to sell shirts. The principal's factory which manufactured the shirts accidentally burnt down. The court held that the principal was still liable to pay the agent a reasonable sum representing what the agent would have been likely to earn by way of commission. Since Anthony's contract contains an express term about the length of service and duration of the liability to pay bonuses, it seems that Anthony will also be entitled to recover a reasonable sum for loss of bonus which Purplewell's decision to close down the Manchester bookshop will prevent him from earning.[5]

Notes

1　It is preferable to restrict the use of the type of authority here to 'usual' authority rather than using the phrase 'implied authority', since the latter should be regarded as merely filling out the relationship between principal and agent (see *Waugh v Clifford* (1982)).

2　If Purplewell decides to ratify Anthony's guarantee, Purplewell will have to adopt unequivocally all of Anthony's actions after his full disclosure (*Keighley Maxsted & Co v Durant* (1901)).

3　If a third party knew or should have known of the restriction on the freedom of the manager to purchase from any source, it is unlikely that the third party may rely on the manager's 'usual' authority (*Daun v Simmins* (1879)).

4   At the time of the contract, the plaintiff thought that Humble was the owner of the public house.

5   See also Question 31.

Question 38

Frank approaches his bank for advice on how best his affairs could be managed while he goes abroad for six months. The bank suggests that he give his brother Denzil, also a customer at the same branch, power of attorney for this period. Frank, however, has never trusted his brother in business affairs and tells the bank this. He appoints his sister Margaret as his attorney, using the correct procedure, and instructs her in the strongest possible terms not to give any money to Denzil in his absence. During Frank's absence, however, Denzil puts pressure on Margaret to lend him some money and she eventually draws two cheques on Frank's account in favour of Denzil, which the bank pays.

On his return, Frank discovers the payments and wishes to recover the money from either Margaret or the bank. Advise him.

Answer plan

The legal position in this situation involves the duties of Margaret as an agent and her failure to follow Frank's instructions; the extent of her authority in relation to the drawing of the cheques and their payment by the bank; and the effect of the bank's knowledge of Frank's distrust of his brother.

The bank will only be entitled to debit Frank's account with the cheques if Margaret can be said to have 'apparent' authority. This is sometimes referred to as 'ostensible' authority or 'agency by estoppel'. It involves the principal having made a representation of the agent's authority which is then acted on by the third party. *Freeman and Lockyer v Buckhurst Park Properties (Mangal) Ltd* (1964), which is one of the leading authorities on this area, will need to be discussed.

Answer

The most basic duties of an agent owed to his principal include the duty to obey the principal's lawful instructions and the duty not to exceed his authority. Allied to this is the agent's duty to act with care and skill in following the principal's instructions. Even if Margaret is acting gratuitously, she owes a fiduciary duty to her principal in the law of tort in the absence of a contract (*Chaudry v Prabhakar* (1988)). Failure to follow instructions or failure to exercise care and skill renders the agent liable to the principal for any loss thereby caused. On the facts, it is clear that Margaret has not obeyed Frank's instructions.

There is no question of Margaret having express authority to draw the cheques, because Frank specifically told her not to give Denzil any money. Apparent authority might exist, however, because Margaret has Frank's power of attorney and it is probable that it expressly allows, or necessarily implies, a power to draw cheques. Apparent (or 'ostensible') authority does not depend on the agreement between the principal and agent, but on the facts as they appear to third parties which operate to prevent the principal denying that the agent had authority to act. As Lord Denning said in *Hely-Hutchinson v Brayhead* (1968), apparent authority is the authority as it 'appears to others'. Specifically, it requires: (a) there to be a representation by the principal to the third party that the agent has his authority; (b) a reliance by the third party on that representation; and (c) an alteration of the third party's position as a result of the reliance (*Freeman and Lockyer v Buckhurst Park Properties (Mangal) Ltd* (1964)). The authorities are divided as to whether this last requirement also requires the third party to have acted to their detriment.

Should Frank proceed against his bank rather than Margaret, the issue is whether Margaret had Frank's authority to draw the two cheques. As an agent, Margaret's authority may be actual or apparent. Actual authority arises by virtue of the agreement between the principal and agent, and requires either express authorisation (verbally or in writing) or implied authority (inferred from the circumstances).

As a power of attorney must be given in a deed, Margaret's authority is subject to the usual strict rules of construction which apply to deeds. Her authority will be limited to the purpose for which it was given. Even if the power of attorney is expressed in general terms, it will be limited to what is absolutely necessary to perform the authorised acts. In *Jacobs v Morris* (1902), for example, an agent was authorised to purchase goods for his principal and to draw and sign bills of exchange. The agent borrowed money on the security of some bills of exchange and appropriated the money. The agent was held to have exceeded his authority and his principal was not liable on the bills. Again, in *Midland Bank Ltd v Reckitt* (1933), a solicitor was given power of attorney to draw cheques on his principal's account and to apply the money for his principal's purposes. The power also contained a ratification clause by which the principal purported to ratify in advance anything the solicitor might do acting under the power of attorney. The solicitor drew some cheques on his principal's account and paid them into his own badly overdrawn account at the same bank. The House of Lords held that the deed must be construed strictly and the power could not be extended to cover the acts of the agent which were beyond the purposes set out in the deed.

The power of attorney is a clear representation by Frank that Margaret had his authority and the bank has relied on it. The bank has also altered its position to its detriment by paying the cheques. Thus, it would appear that the bank was entitled to debit Frank's account with the cheques unless the bank had knowledge that Margaret is acting in breach of her instructions.

Any limitation of an agent's apparent authority only affects a third party if that third party has actual notice of it. If a third party has actual notice, it must take the consequences of its actions and, if it is deemed to have constructive notice, it is not then inequitable for the principal to deny the agent's authority. In *Midland Bank Ltd v Reckitt*, for example, the bank was also held to have acted negligently. Applying this to the question, the bank is in breach of its duty of care in that, knowing of Frank's distrust of Denzil, the bank did not query the cheques before paying the monies. In *Barclays Bank v Quincecare Ltd* (1988), it was suggested that a bank would be negligent if it obeyed the mandate where the circumstances are such as to put on inquiry and provide reasonable grounds for suspecting that an attempt was being made to defraud the customer. The bank is certainly aware of Frank's distrust of Denzil and knows that Frank was intending to be abroad for six months. Under these circumstances, the bank should have known of, or had a reckless disregard to, Margaret's lack of authority.

However, recent cases seem to suggest that where a principal, having placed his trust in the agent, puts him in a position to commit the fraud, the principal must bear the loss unless the circumstances are exceptional. The circumstances here *do* appear exceptional, because the degree of knowledge the bank possessed about Margaret's lack of authority should have required them to enquire about the two cheques drawn on the account. It seems, therefore, that Frank will have a good claim against the bank in the tort of negligence, since the bank has ignored facts which would make a reasonable banker suspicious.[1]

Note

1   If the bank is not able to rely on Margaret's apparent authority and the bank is held liable to repay Frank, it may be able to bring an action against Margaret for breach of warranty of authority (*Collen v Wright* (1857)) or in the tort of deceit. Under the principle in *Collen v Wright*, the agent's liability does not arise under the agency contract, but under a separate contract between the agent and the third party, the essence of which is the agent's assertion of authority that he does not have.

CHAPTER 11

FOB CONTRACTS

Introduction

The central feature of an fob (free on board) contract is that the seller fulfils his obligations when he delivers goods conforming to the contract over the ship's rails. He must bear all the costs up to that point. Although he is not under a duty to insure the goods once he has delivered them, the seller is under a statutory duty to give notice to the buyer so that the buyer has an opportunity to insure. Examiners often set questions dealing with this duty under s 32(3) of the Sale of Goods Act 1979.

The primary duty of the fob buyer is to nominate an effective ship to carry the goods. Unless and until he does so, the seller is not obliged to deliver the goods. Examination questions often involve the buyer's inability to nominate an effective ship and the related problem of where there is a delay in the arrival of a ship which the buyer has nominated to carry the goods.

Questions on international sale of goods contracts invariably involve the financing arrangements between the parties, and the rules in relation to documentary credits are important. It should be remembered that the buyer in such transactions has two distinct rights of rejection: first, the right to reject documents arises when the documents are tendered; and, secondly, the right to reject the goods arises when they are landed and when, after examination, they are not found to be in conformity with the contract.

This chapter deals mainly with fob contracts, although it is usual to have parts of questions involving other types of international sale contracts (Question 40, for instance, deals with both an fob as well as a cif contract) or, indeed, with other topics on the commercial law syllabus, such as the principles of agency (see Question 39).

The UN Convention on Contracts for the International Sale of Goods (the Vienna Convention 1980) now plays, and will play, a very important role in regulating contracts for the international sale of goods (see Question 43).

Chapter 12 deals mainly with cif contracts.

Checklist

The following topics should be prepared in advance of tackling the questions:

- the duties of the parties to an fob contract (both under common law and INCOTERMS 2000);
- the requirements of proper shipping documents;
- the strict rules in relation to documentary finance.

Question 39

Salton Associated Ltd entered into an fob contract to purchase 8,000 tennis balls from Jays plc, payment to be made by a letter of credit. Salton Associated's bank, Rednex Bank, opened a letter of credit in favour of Jays plc which provided for payment at the counter of Rednex Bank in Manchester on presentation of the shipping documents. Jays plc presented documents at Rednex for payment. It was an extremely busy time of the year for Rednex and the documents lay unchecked for six days. When an employee of Rednex found the time to check the documents, he discovered that the commercial invoice described the purchaser of the goods as Salton Associates. Whilst he was of the view that it was probably a typographical error which he could dismiss as irrelevant, he decided that he ought to check the matter with Salton Associated. He telephoned Andrew, the managing director of Salton Associated, in order to obtain his instructions. The call was answered by Esta, Andrew's secretary. Esta stated that Andrew was in a meeting but that she would pass on the information to Andrew and call back with his response. Esta decided that Andrew was too busy to be bothered with such a minor issue and so she called Rednex an hour later and said that Andrew had decided that Rednex should pay, notwithstanding the discrepancy. Rednex honoured the credit and then debited Salton Associated's account. When the goods are delivered to Salton Associated, it is discovered that the consignment is of rubbish and not tennis balls.

Salton Associated now claims that Rednex should not have honoured the letter of credit on the ground of the discrepancy in the commercial invoice, and on the separate ground that Jays had defrauded Salton Associated by shipping rubbish and not tennis balls.

Advise Rednex Bank.

Answer plan

This question concerns banker's documentary credits and the principles of agency.

Whether Rednex is entitled to be reimbursed by Salton Associated will depend on the contractual nature of the bank's undertaking to Salton Associated and its position in relation to the strict rules of documentary finance. It will therefore be important to discuss the two general principles of the doctrine of strict compliance (*Equitable Trust Co of New York v Dawson Partners* (1927)) and autonomy of credit (*Power Curber International v National Bank of Kuwait* (1981)).

We will need to consider the issue of an agent's authority and, in particular, the extent to which a principal can be bound by statements which the agent has made without authority. This will involve looking at Andrew's and Esta's express contractual obligations owed to their principal, Salton Associated. Regarding Andrew, the concept of 'apparent' authority will need to be discussed, as in *Summers v Solomon* (1857). As far as Esta is concerned, Salton Associated may be liable on the basis of 'usual' authority, as in *Watteau v Fenwick* (1893). We will need to look at what is the usual authority of a managing director's secretary.

Answer

When Jays tendered the shipping documents to Rednex Bank, the commercial invoice showed Salton Associates as the purchaser of the goods. As far as the bank is concerned, it is not obliged to pay the seller if the documents do not comply with the terms of credit (*Equitable Trust Company of New York v Dawson Partners Ltd* (1927)). As Lord Sumner said in that case: 'There is no room for documents which are almost the same, or which will do just as well.' This follows the doctrine of strict compliance. Rednex has no discretion, in that it must comply strictly with the buyer's instructions as to payment. The bank's right to reimbursement from Salton Associated depends on it taking up a faultless set of documents and, since the invoice indicates another name as the buyer, Rednex was entitled to refuse to pay Jays, no matter how minor the discrepancy.

Although we are told that English law applies, we do not know whether the Uniform Customs and Practice for Documentary Credits (1993, ICC Brochure 500) (UCP) has been expressly incorporated into the contract. If it has, although Art 37 of the UCP permits the description of the goods in the bill of lading to be described in general terms to be sufficient compliance as long as the goods are correctly described in the commercial invoice (*Soproma v Marine and Animal By-Products* (1966); *Midland Bank v Seymour* (1955)), it is most unlikely that a variation, no matter how slight, would be permitted where the name of the purchaser was stated incorrectly (*JH Rayner v Hambro's Bank* (1943)).

The courts have, however, recently allowed some flexibility as regards the doctrine of strict compliance. In *Karaganda Ltd v Midland Bank plc* (1999), the bank rejected the documents presented by the seller for two reasons. First, the invoice policy tendered was to be marked 'original' and it was not, nor was it 'negotiable or blank endorsed' as was required. Secondly, a certificate of quality was required from 'Griffith Inspectorate' and that tendered by the sellers indicated that the documents were issued by 'Daniel Griffith'. In relation to the insurance policy, the court held that the bank had wrongly rejected the documents since, although Art 20(b) of the UCP required certain documents to be marked as original, it did not apply to documents which were clearly original and the failure to name an assured did not mean that the policy was unenforceable – it was sufficient that it was valid against the insurer. As far as the certificate of quality was concerned, the court interpreted 'Griffith Inspectorate' to mean documents by a member of the Inspectorate Group and documents issued by Daniel Griffith satisfied the condition. Thus, the bank was not entitled to refuse payment to the seller.

Even with the new approach that the courts appear to be taking, it is unlikely that an incorrectly named purchaser on the invoice is sufficient compliance. Therefore, Rednex could have rejected the shipping documents.

However, instead of rejecting them, Rednex sought clarification from Salton Associated. Certainly, if a bank is faced with discrepancies, it may consult with its customer as to whether its customer is prepared to waive them (*Bankers Trust v State Bank of India* (1991)). However, it remains the bank's decision to accept or reject the documents. Under Art 13(b) of the UCP, a bank has seven banking days following the receipt of the documents in which to examine them in order to decide whether to accept or reject. If a bank refuses to accept the documents, it must give notice of refusal, specifying the reason for rejection (which could have enabled Jays to amend the name of the buyer and re-tender the commercial invoice in accordance with the letter of credit).

If the UCP was not incorporated into the contract, the common law rule is that a bank is allowed a reasonable time to examine the documents to ensure compliance. What amounts to a reasonable time depends on the facts of each case. The court in *Bankers Trust v State Bank of India*, however, indicated that a reasonable time to examine the documents would not be extended to include the time taken by the bank's customer to decide whether it was prepared to waive the discrepancies found by the bank. Rednex sought instructions to clarify the issue six days following the receipt of the shipping documents.[1]

This is likely to fall within a reasonable time allowed for examination of the documents (certainly, it falls within the seven day rule under Art 13(b) of the UCP).

The bank's employee tried to contact the managing director of Salton Associated. We are not told whether Andrew had express authority to bind Salton Associated in such matters, but it is very likely that a managing director would have apparent authority to do so (*Summers v Solomon* (1857)).[2] 'Apparent authority' is authority as it 'appears to others' (*per* Lord Denning in *Hely-Hutchinson v Brayhead* (1968)). As defined by Diplock LJ in *Freeman and Lockyer v Buckhurst Park Properties (Mangal) Ltd* (1964), this requires a representation by the principal, intended to be acted on by the third party, and in fact acted on, that the agent does have authority to make the contract. The representation need not be in the form of words; conduct will be sufficient. In *Freeman and Lockyer v Buckhurst*, a person had been allowed to act as managing director of a company by the other directors, although he had never appointed as such in the manner required by the company's Articles of Association. It was held that the directors' actions in allowing him to act in this way amounted to a representation to the outside world that he had authority to do so. The company was therefore bound by his actions. Applying this case to the question, it seems reasonable for Rednex to rely on Salton Associated's representation that Andrew was entitled to make these decisions.

However, we are told that the managing director, Andrew, was not contactable at that time but his secretary, Esta, promised to obtain Andrew's response. Without informing Andrew of the bank's query, Esta took it upon herself to communicate a response saying that Andrew authorised payment to Jays. Clearly, Esta was not expressly authorised to do so, but is Rednex entitled nevertheless to rely on Esta's statement to estop Salton Associated from arguing that Rednex had not acted in accordance with its credit instructions? It could be argued that the usual authority of a managing director's secretary includes communicating the usual business decisions of his/her boss, so that in appointing Esta as Andrew's secretary, she would have the usual authority to communicate Andrew's decisions. As Wills J said in *Watteau v Fenwick* (1893): 'The principal is liable for all the acts of the agent which are within the authority usually confided to an agent of that character, notwithstanding limitations, as between the principal and agent, put upon that authority.' It appears therefore that Salton Associated will be bound by Esta's statement (*Kinahan v Parry* (1911)) and Salton Associated, having waived the discrepancy in the commercial invoice, cannot now resile from the acceptance of the documents by its bank.

Assuming that the other shipping documents were in order, Rednex was correct in making the payment to Jays. Rednex is thus entitled to be reimbursed by Salton Associated.

When Salton Associated took delivery of the goods, however, it was discovered that the goods were not as contracted for – the consignment was for tennis balls, not rubbish.

We are not told whether any of the shipping documents indicated that the shipped goods were anything other than tennis balls. An fob buyer to whom documents have been tendered is not entitled to refuse to pay until he has examined the goods for the purpose of determining whether the goods are of the contract quality. In any event, banks are not concerned with the underlying sales transaction even if reference is made to it in the letter of credit. The bank is concerned only that the documents tendered by the seller correspond to those specified in the instructions (*Power Curber International v National Bank of Kuwait* (1981); Arts 3 and 4 of the UCP).

Under the principle of autonomy of credit, a bank must examine all documents with reasonable care to ascertain that they appear on their face to be in accordance with the terms of credit. A bank is not responsible for the genuineness or accuracy of the documents, merely whether they comply. In *Gian Singh v Banque de L'Indochine* (1974), the signature on the certificate was forged (as was the passport used to verify the signature). The court held that the bank was right to pay. It had carried out its duty reasonably. There is no requirement that a bank checks the authenticity of documents.

The only exception to this rule is where, although the documents are apparently in order on their face, it is proved to the bank that they are fraudulent and that the beneficiary (that is, the seller) was involved with fraud. In this case, the bank may refuse to pay under the terms of the credit (*Tukan Timber v Barclays Bank* (1987)). *Sztejn v Henry Schroder Banking Corp* (1941) involved an irrevocable credit for the shipment of bristles. The seller shipped crates of rubbish. The documents presented to the bank, however, described the goods as bristles. The buyer discovered the fraud and applied for an injunction to restrain its issuing bankers from accepting the documents. The court held that the bank was entitled not to pay, because the fraud had been brought to its attention.

So, a bank need not pay under the terms of the credit if it knows the documents are forged. Even so, the defence of fraud can be raised only against a party who committed it and, if it is not the seller's fraud, the bank cannot reject the documents (*United City Merchants (Investments) v Royal Bank of Canada* (1982)).

Salton Associated could have obtained an injunction to restrain Rednex from paying Jays plc under the letter of credit because of fraud. Courts, however, are reluctant to grant injunctions in such cases, preferring the buyer to pursue his claim against the seller under the sales contract (*Discount Records v Barclays Bank* (1975)).

Thus, if there was nothing in the shipping documents to indicate that anything other than tennis balls were shipped and the fraud exception does not apply, and the discrepancy in the invoice was waived by an authorised agent of Salton Associated, Rednex is entitled to be reimbursed by Salton Associated. This does not, of course, preclude Salton Associated from rejecting the goods against Jays plc since, on arrival, the goods are found not to conform to the contract (*Kwei Tek Chao v British Traders and Shippers* (1954)).

Notes

1   In *Bankers Trust v State Bank of India,* expert evidence was adduced that major UK clearing banks aim to accept or reject documents within three working days of their receipt.

2   The phrases 'ostensible' authority and 'agency by estoppel' are also used to describe this concept. See Chapter 9.

Question 40

Crusty plc, a wholesalers based in London, enters into two separate contracts for the purchase of 5,000 (3,000 deluxe models and 2,000 super models) video recorders cif London from Sonita (Japan) Ltd, and the purchase of 1,000 dolls houses fob Rotterdam from Marten. Both contracts called for September/October shipment and payment by irrevocable letter of credit at Ambrose Bank on presentation of the shipping documents. The contract with Marten contained a clause requiring the dolls houses to be delivered in time to catch the Christmas trade.

An irrevocable letter of credit in favour of Sonita (Japan) Ltd was opened on 5 September and the bank paid on presentation of a received for shipment bill of lading, an insurance policy and an invoice. When the video recorders arrived in London, 2,000 super models were immediately delivered to Carmen Ltd, which had agreed to buy them from Crusty plc, and the deluxe models were transferred to Crusty's warehouse. Three weeks later, Carmen returned all 2,000 video recorders on discovering that the electrical wiring was faulty.

A revocable letter of credit in favour of Marten was opened on 27 August and the bank paid on presentation of the shipping documents, which included a bill of lading dated 31 October and a certificate of quality dated 1 November. The dolls houses arrived in London on 28 November but, due to a shortage of staff at the docks, Crusty plc was not notified of this until 26 December.

Both contracts are governed by English law.

Advise Crusty plc as to its remedies.

Answer plan

Both parts of the question require you to discuss the opening of the documentary credit. Although the cases do not lay down a conclusive rule either in the cases of fob or of cif contracts, you will need to discuss the time at which documentary credit must be available to the seller.

The bank's position needs to be dealt with. Both Sonita and Marten have presented the shipping documents to Ambrose Bank, but neither set of shipping documents is in accordance with Crusty's instructions to the bank. The contractual nature of the bank's undertaking to Crusty and the bank's entitlement to reimbursement will need to be discussed.

It is not uncommon to find international sale questions involving certain provisions of the Sale of Goods Act 1979. In this question, you will need to discuss the buyer's remedy where there has been a breach of s 14(2) and (3) but where he may have accepted the goods under s 35.

The final part of the question involves stipulations as to time of delivery in fob contracts.

Answer

The general rule is that documentary credit must be opened in accordance with the contract of sale. The contracts with Sonita and Marten do not provide a date for the opening of the credit. They do, however, stipulate a period for the shipment of the goods. It is clear from *Pavia & Co SpA v Thurmann-Nielsen* (1952) that in these circumstances, the documentary credit must be opened at the very latest on the first day on which shipment may take place. The reason for this is that the seller is not bound to tell the buyer the precise date when is he going to ship, but whenever he does ship the goods, the seller must be able to draw on the credit.[1]

As far as Sonita is concerned, the documentary credit was not opened until 5 September. Following the *Pavia* case, Sonita is not obliged to ship the goods and may terminate the contract and claim damages.[2] However, we are told that Sonita presents the shipping documents to the bank for payment.

Thus, Sonita must have shipped the goods, although the credit was not opened until 5 September, and may be taken to have waived the breach or at least agreed to a variation of the contract.[3]

The credit in favour of Marten was opened on 27 August, and this appears to have allowed a reasonable time before the shipment date (*Sinason-Teicher Inter-American Grain Corp v Oilcakes and Oilseeds Trading Co Ltd* (1954)).

However, the contract stipulated that the credit to be opened is to be irrevocable credit, whereas the credit which was actually made available is a revocable one, that is, one where the bank is free to revoke its undertaking to pay the beneficiary at any time before payment is due. In these circumstances, Marten is entitled to claim damages for a breach of the terms of the contract, such a breach qualifying as a condition.[4] As with Sonita, Marten appears to have either waived the breach or has agreed to a variation to the contract, because he does ship the goods and presents the documents to the bank for payment.

We are told that the contracts are governed by English law. It is also assumed that, as is usual, the documentary credits expressly incorporated the 1993 Uniform Customs and Practice for Documentary Credits (UCP) published by the International Chamber of Commerce. It appears from the question that Sonita has already been paid on presentation of the shipping documents and nothing turns on the fact that some of the goods are faulty.[5] However, it seems that the bank has paid against a received for shipment bill of lading. Such a bill of lading is not good tender under a cif contract because the buyer cannot confirm that the goods have been loaded within the shipment period. The bank's duty is to examine all documents with reasonable care to ascertain that they appear on their face to be in accordance with the terms of the credit. Ambrose Bank does not seem to have scrutinised the documents carefully. Therefore, Crusty is not bound to take the shipping documents from the bank.[6] However, we are told that Crusty has taken physical delivery of the goods. This in turn means that Crusty must have ratified the bank's actions (otherwise the bank would not release the shipping documents to Crusty), and such ratification prevents Crusty from treating the shipping documents as anything but regular as against the bank.

Carmen returns the 2,000 super model video recorders. Faulty electrical wiring renders the goods unsatisfactory and will give Crusty a remedy for breach of s 14(2) of the Sale of Goods Act 1979 against Sonita. Furthermore, the use of video recorders is well known, so that faulty electrical wiring would render Sonita in breach of the implied term under s 14(3) whereby goods should be reasonably fit for that use. The often sought remedy for breach of s 14(2) and (3) is rejection of the goods and damages. However, this is subject, of course, to s 15A, which provides that where the buyer is not a consumer and the breach is so slight that it would be unreasonable for him to reject the goods, the breach may be treated as a breach of warranty. Faulty electrical wiring, even if easily put right, would hardly appear to be a slight breach. However, rejection will not be available for those goods which have been accepted. Section 35 of the Sale of Goods Act 1979 provides that the buyer may be deemed to have accepted the goods, thus losing the right to reject, where *inter alia* he does some act 'inconsistent with the seller's ownership' or where after a reasonable period he retains the goods without indicating that he rejects them. It is unclear whether before the delivery to Carmen, Crusty had an opportunity to examine the super model video recorders for the purpose of seeing whether they conformed to the contract. If Crusty resells the goods, having inspected them, and Carmen then rejects them, it might be argued that Crusty has lost the right to reject the goods, it being argued that it had retained them for more than a reasonable length of time (three weeks) before rejecting them (*Bernstein v Pamson Motors* (1987)). On the other hand, it has been held (*Truk (UK) Ltd v Tokmakidis* (2000)) that where goods are bought for resale, the reasonable period of time before the right to reject the goods is lost will normally last for the time it takes to resell the goods, plus a further period of time for the ultimate purchaser to test the goods.

Thus, in determining whether Crusty has accepted the goods, the important factor becomes one of whether Carmen has accepted the goods vis à vis Crusty. This in turn depends upon whether the three weeks which it took Carmen to reject the goods amounts to more than a reasonable period of time and, since s 35 was amended by the Sale and Supply of Goods Act 1994, one of the relevant factors is whether that period allowed Carmen a reasonable opportunity to examine the goods for the purpose of ascertaining whether they complied with the contract. Whereas, prior to the 1994 amendment, a three week period was held to amount to more than a reasonable period of time (*Bernstein v Pamson Motors*, above), it seems likely that the court would now find that it does not. Thus, Carmen, it is submitted, is not restricted to a claim for damages but was entitled to reject the goods, and Crusty was similarly entitled. If, as soon as Carmen intimated to Crusty its rejection of the goods, Crusty immediately informed Sonita that it was rejecting the goods, then Crusty will not have lost its right to reject the goods. If, on the other hand, Crusty failed for some time to inform Sonita that it was rejecting the goods, that delay will have increased the chances of Crusty being held to have accepted the goods.

Assuming that Carmen validly rejected the goods, Carmen will also have a claim for damages against Crusty. The *prima facie* measure of those damages will be the difference between the contract price of the goods and (if it is higher) the market price (of goods which comply with the contract) on the day of delivery. If Crusty has also validly rejected the goods, that will also be the *prima facie* measure of damages that Crusty can claim against Sonita. If Crusty has not validly rejected the goods, then it is entitled only to damages. Those damages will, however, include any consequent losses which Crusty has incurred in relation to the sub-sale to Carmen. In the case of a breach of term as to quality in a contract where goods are bought for resale, the courts are prepared to take into account the effect of a sub-sale upon the losses incurred by the buyer (*Bence Graphics v Fasson UK* (1997)).

As discussed above, the opening of the credit on 27 August was not too late. However, Crusty is in breach of the contract in that the credit was not an irrevocable one, but Marten ships the goods and is paid by the bank on presentation of the shipping documents.

Ambrose Bank is only entitled to be reimbursed sums it pays out if it pays on receipt of documents which strictly comply with Crusty's instructions. Ambrose Bank has paid against the bill of lading which is dated 31 October (and thus appears to fall within the shipment period) but also a certificate of quality dated 1 November. On the face of the documents, read together, the goods could not have been shipped on 31 October. The bank is thus liable to Crusty, since the documents do not comply with the terms of the credit which stipulate for a September/October shipment (*Soproma v Marine & Animal By-Products* (1966)). Because Crusty appears to have ratified the bank's wrongful act, does Crusty have a second right to reject, that is, to reject the goods themselves on the ground that they are not of contract description? The general rule is that where a buyer who accepts documents in ignorance of a defect in them and later discovers the defect and takes delivery of the goods, he will be taken to have waived his right to reject not only the documents, but also the goods on account of that defect (see *Kwei Tek Chao v British Traders and Shippers* (1954), where the facts were almost identical). Thus, since the certificate of quality is dated 1 November, even though the bank and Crusty do not read the documents carefully, Crusty may not now reject the dolls houses on the ground that they are not of contract description.

May Crusty nevertheless reject the goods since they did not arrive in time to catch the Christmas trade? In *Frebold and Sturznickel (Trading as Panda OGH) v Circle Products Ltd* (1970), German sellers sold toys to English buyers under an fob contract on terms that the goods were to be delivered in time for the Christmas trade. The goods arrived at the destination on 13 November. Due to an oversight (for which the sellers were not responsible), the buyers were not notified of the arrival of the goods until 17 January. The court held that the sellers were not in breach, since they had delivered the goods in such a way that would normally have resulted in the goods arriving in time for the Christmas trade. Applying this case to the question, the dolls houses did in fact arrive in London on 28 November and therefore in time for the

Christmas trade but, because of a shortage of staff at the docks, which could not have been the fault of Marten, Crusty did not know of the arrival until some time after. It seems, therefore, that Crusty will have no remedy against Marten, since Marten had delivered the goods in accordance with the requirements of the contract. Crusty's remedies may be in suing the port authorities, the carriers or their agents or other parties responsible.

Notes

1   This principle applies to both cif and fob contracts. It has been argued that, since an fob buyer had the option as to the time of shipment, the documentary credit need only be opened at a reasonable time before the date nominated by the buyer in the shipping instructions. Lord Diplock in *Ian Stach Ltd v Baker Bosley Ltd* (1958) thought that such a rule would lead to uncertainties and concluded that the *prima facie* rule is that the credit must be opened, at the latest, on the first day of the shipping period.

2   The measure of damages, it seems, is not limited by the market price rule in s 50(3) of the Sale of Goods Act 1979, but may extend to the seller's lost profits, provided that they are not too remote under the rule in *Hadley v Baxendale* (1854); *Trans Trust SPRL v Danubian Trading Co Ltd* (1952).

3   The difference between a waiver and an agreement to a variation is that the former entitles the seller to reinstate the requirement on giving the buyer reasonable notice, and the latter will prevent the seller unilaterally to restore the original position. The significance of the distinction does not arise in this question.

4   See note 2, above.

5   Even if the bank knew that the goods were faulty at the time Sonita presented the shipping documents, it is well established that the courts will not allow revocation at all where the credit is irrevocable.

6   The bank is also prevented from returning the documents to the seller.

Question 41

Samantha enters into three separate contracts for the sale of 4,000 tons of cranberries to Cyrus, 5,000 tons of potatoes to Damion and 1,500 tons of olive oil to Michael. Each contract calls for shipment in May, fob Manchester and contains a clause permitting the buyer, on giving reasonable notice, to call for delivery at any time within the shipment period.

On 5 May, Cyrus informs Samantha that he has nominated *The Winser* to take delivery of the consignment, ready to load on 11 May. Samantha protests at the length of notice and since she is not able to have the consignment packed in time, she purchases 4,000 tons of already packed cranberries from a third party at 5% above the normal market price. Samantha is able to send the cranberries to the docks at Manchester on 11 May. *The Winser* is not ready to load and Cyrus nominates *The Winslet* to take the consignment on 28 May. By this time, the cranberries have deteriorated due to rain seeping through the packaging. Cyrus refuses to load the consignment.

On 8 May, Damion nominates *The Dilly* and asks Samantha to have the consignment ready to load on 20 May. The general market price of potatoes has unexpectedly dropped by half since the contract was made. Due to a strike at the farm, Samantha is not able to send the potatoes to the docks at Manchester until 23 May, and Damion uses this as a reason for refusing to load the consignment.

On 25 May, Michael informs Samantha that *The Forseasons* will be ready to load on 30 May. When Samantha tries to load the goods, she is informed that recent regulations require an export licence for the supply of olive oil in excess of 1,000 tons. Michael refuses to accept a smaller quantity when asked by Samantha.

The contracts are governed by English law.

Advise Samantha.

Would it have made any difference if Samantha had contracted to sell the olive oil fob INCOTERMS Manchester?

Answer plan

This question requires a review of the duties of both parties to an fob contract. In particular, the part of the question regarding the cranberries involves the buyer's duty to nominate an effective ship and the seller's duty to ensure compliance with the implied terms as to quality under the Sale of Goods Act 1979. The situation with the potatoes concerns a seller's failure to load within time.

The part of the question dealing with the olive oil is a little unusual, since it involves a partial prohibition on the export of goods imposed *after* the contract of sale was concluded. The issue is whether the contract is brought to an end because of frustration or whether the contract subsists for that part of the contract where performance was possible. Please note that frustration and prohibition of export have separate origins and consequences.

Since there are three parts to the question, the amount of detail required will be restricted to the time available for answering all the parts.

Answer

In the absence of further information regarding express terms in the contract, the basic duties of the parties depend on commercial practice as recognised by English law. Under a 'classic' fob contract, the primary duties of the buyer are to nominate an effective ship to carry the goods, to notify the seller of such nomination in time for him to load the goods and to pay the agreed price (*Pyrene & Co v Scindia Navigation Co Ltd* (1954); *The El Amria and El Minia* (1982)). Once the buyer has nominated a ship, the buyer is required to deliver goods which comply with the terms of the contract to the port in time for loading to take place during the contract period.

Cranberries

Cyrus informs Samantha on 5 May that *The Winser* has been nominated to take delivery of the consignment on 11 May. Although Samantha protests at the short notice, this is normally irrelevant since the buyer in an fob contract has the option of when to ship during the contract period. More particularly, there is an express term in the contract allowing the buyer to call for delivery at any time. It is clear, however, that if the buyer nominates a ship in such a way that the seller is not given reasonable time to have the goods ready for loading, the seller is entitled to claim damages[1] for the failure of the buyer to nominate a suitable ship. The question of whether Cyrus has given Samantha adequate notice is one of fact.

In an fob contract, the timing of the nomination of an effective ship is normally of the essence, that is, it is a condition of the contract. If Cyrus's notice of nomination is unreasonable, Samantha is entitled to treat the contract as repudiated and will be entitled to damages (*Bunge & Co Ltd v Tradax England Ltd* (1975)).[2] However, by delivering to the docks on 11 May, Samantha has probably waived her right to treat the contract as repudiated.

Samantha has had to purchase the cranberries at 5% above the normal market price. This additional cost cannot be recovered from Cyrus since, under a 'classic' fob contract, the seller is responsible for all the expenses of getting the goods over the ship's rail (*AG v Leopold Walford (London) Ltd* (1923)).

Cyrus subsequently nominates *The Winslet*. A buyer is entitled to substitute a fresh nomination provided there is time to do so in accordance with the contract. Cyrus's first nomination is not irrevocable (*Agricultores Federados Argentinos v Ampro SA* (1965)). Thus, Cyrus is entitled to nominate a second ship.

The cranberries deteriorate before loading and Cyrus refuses to load the consignment on this basis. The implied terms as to satisfactory quality and as to fitness for a particular purpose under s 14(2) and (3) of the Sale of Goods Act 1979 apply to an fob contract, and breach of either term may entitle the buyer to reject the goods and claim damages, provided the buyer is not a consumer and the breach is not so slight that it would be unreasonable for him to reject the goods (s 15A of the Sale of Goods Act 1979).[3] Since the seller is responsible for the goods prior to loading, it appears that Cyrus is *prima facie* entitled to refuse to accept delivery of the defective cranberries on 28 May.

If the cranberries deteriorate due to unsuitable packaging, this would amount to a breach of s 14(3). Where the seller knows that goods are to be shipped, he is under an obligation to ensure that the goods are packaged in such a way that they can endure the sea transit (*Wills v Brown* (1922)). It seems, therefore, that Cyrus may be able to reject the cranberries and will be entitled to recover damages for non-delivery from Samantha.[4]

Potatoes

Samantha is not able to send the consignment of potatoes to the docks until three days after *The Dilly* is ready to load. In a 'classic' fob contract, it is the buyer who has the option of when to ship within the contract period (*Bowes v Shand* (1877)) and, once shipping instructions have been received, the seller must load within a reasonable time. It seems that 12 days' notice is reasonable in this question, since we are told that the delay in sending the potatoes to the docks was due to a strike at the farm. A failure to load on 20 May is a breach of a condition of the contract and is a ground for rejection (*The Mihalis Angelos* (1971)), because time is of the essence in commercial contracts.

Damion could have chosen to affirm the contract and claim damages for the loss occasioned by the delay but, due to the drop in the market price of potatoes, it seems more likely that Damion will wish to reject the goods. He will also have a claim against Samantha in damages for non-delivery.

Olive oil

As for the consignment of olive oil, we are told that Samantha is only aware of the recent prohibition on the export of such goods without a licence when she tries to load the goods on 30 May. It appears that the prohibition was imposed after the conclusion of the contract. Such a prohibition does not make the contract illegal *ab initio*, but may discharge it under the doctrine of frustration. Since the contract specifically provides that the olive oil is to be exported from Manchester (and within the country which is imposing the prohibition), the contract between Samantha and Michael may be frustrated (*Tsakiroglou v Noblee Thorl* (1962)). However, where the prohibition is qualified, as in this question (making a previously unrestricted export of goods subject to a licensing requirement), the contract is not automatically discharged. The court may decide to impose a duty on one of the parties to make reasonable efforts to obtain the licence. In the absence of an express provision as to licence, there is no general rule putting the burden of obtaining a licence on one party or another, and each case would depend on the facts.[5] *Pagnan SpA v Tradax Ocean Transportation* (1986) provided that in such cases, the court will ask itself whether the duty imposed on the seller to obtain a licence is absolute or is only to use due diligence. If the duty is to be imposed on Samantha, then Samantha will only be able to rely on the prohibition as a ground of discharge if she can show that reasonable efforts to procure the licence would have failed. Certainly, Samantha only knew of the prohibition on 30 May, giving her only 24 hours to obtain the licence before the end of the shipment period.

The prohibition, however, is only partial, in that the regulations merely restrict the amount which a seller is allowed to export to 1,000 tons of olive oil without a licence. In the circumstances, although in the normal course of events, a seller is not obliged to accept a smaller quantity of goods than that contracted for, the contract is not discharged but the prohibition may excuse partial performance. Samantha must supply 1,000 tons of olive oil but is excused from supplying the remaining 500 tons.[6] If Michael refuses to accept delivery of 1,000 tons of olive oil, Samantha will be entitled to recover damages under s 50(3) of the Sale of Goods Act 1979.

Had the INCOTERMS 2000 applied, the seller is placed under an obligation to obtain the export licence at his own risk and expense (A2). In the present case, while INCOTERMS would have cleared the uncertainty in respect of the party responsible for obtaining an export licence, Samantha will still have to show that reasonable efforts to procure the licence would have failed in order to rely on the prohibition as a ground of discharge.

Notes

1   The seller cannot claim the purchase price if the goods have not been shipped, even if non-shipment is the result of the buyer's failure to give effective shipment instruction: *Colley v Overseas Exporters* (1921).

2   The measure of damages will be that set out under s 50(3) of the Sale of Goods Act 1979 for non-acceptance.

3   Damages will be for non-delivery of goods under s 51(3) of the Sale of Goods Act 1979.

4   If the question had not included a reason for the goods deteriorating, the issue would be whether a seller can recover damages for losses incurred because the buyer substitutes another ship.

5   See *Brandt & Co v Morris & Co* (1917) (where the court held that the buyers were obliged to obtain the export licence on the basis that a ship which could not legally carry goods was not an effective ship) and *Pound & Co Ltd v Hardy & Co Inc* (1956) (where the court found that the sellers were obliged to obtain the export licence since the licence could only be obtained by persons registered in the exporting country and as between the parties it was the sellers who were registered).

6   The effect of the partial prohibition is the same as that of physical impossibility caused by the failure of a specified crop.

Question 42

Dafyd in Cardiff sells 3,000 metric tons of salt to Heinz in Hamburg, fob Liverpool calling for February shipment. Payment is to be made by irrevocable letter of credit confirmed by Dafyd's bank, Snowball Bank, in Cardiff. On 17 February, Heinz notifies Dafyd that shipping space is available on *Island Princess*, expected ready to load on 24 February and on the same day, Heinz arranges an irrevocable confirmed credit with Snowball Bank and Snowball informs Dafyd of this on 19 February.

Dafyd had been relying on the credit to enable him to raise the finance to purchase the salt and, now having to buy it at short notice, pays a higher price than he would otherwise have done. Dafyd arranges for the consignment of salt to arrive at the dock on 23 February, but then receives a fax message from Heinz cancelling the nomination of *Island Princess* and informing Dafyd that another ship will be nominated in a few days to take the goods. Heinz faxes Snowball Bank with instructions not to pay if the goods are shipped on *Island Princess*.

Island Princess is, however, ready to take the goods on 24 February and the owners of the vessel, who also received a fax message from Heinz purporting to cancel the nomination, refuse to accept the cancellation. Dafyd has incurred expensive overnight storage and, being reluctant to incur more, also refuses to accept the change in nomination. Dafyd and the owners of *Island Princess* notify Heinz by fax. The salt is shipped on *Island Princess*.

Dafyd tenders the bill of lading to Snowball Bank, which refuses to pay because of Heinz's subsequent fax message.

Dafyd decides to send the bill of lading to Heinz, but Heinz (having heard that some of the cargo on board *Island Princess* has been damaged by heavy storms) rejects the bill and notifies Dafyd by fax.

Advise Dafyd.

Answer plan

The first part of the question is straightforward enough. It requires a discussion of whether the opening of the credit was in accordance with the terms of the contract. As is usual in exam questions, we are not given sufficient information about the terms of the contract so that we should discuss the general rule in *Pavia & Co SpA v Thurmann-Nielsen* (1952).

The more difficult part of the question concerns Heinz's cancellation of *Island Princess*. In normal circumstances, an fob buyer is entitled to substitute the nomination of a ship and there is nothing to suggest otherwise here. What is unusual is that both the seller and the carrier here have refused to accept the cancellation and the goods are in fact shipped on *Island Princess*. The question is whether Heinz must accept the goods on board *Island Princess* as in accordance with the contract or whether he may he wash his hands clean of this shipment. It should be noted, however, that there is no clear authority on what happens when both the carrier and the consigner disagree with the consignee regarding nomination, substitution and cancellation.

Answer

The primary duty of an fob buyer is to nominate an effective ship to carry the goods. The buyer must do so in time for the seller to load the goods within the contractual shipment period. Once the buyer has nominated an effective ship, that is, one that is capable of taking the cargo, the seller is under a duty to deliver goods which comply with the terms of the contract.

Payment under the contract of sale of salt is to be made by irrevocable credit and confirmed by Snowball Bank in London. The contract between Dafyd and Heinz does not, however, provide a date for the opening of the credit. Heinz made these arrangements, it seems, on the same day as notifying Dafyd of the shipping details, that is, 17 February, but Snowball Bank only informed Dafyd that the letter of credit was opened on 19 February. Following *Pavia & Co SpA v Thurmann-Nielsen* (1952), if this does not allow Dafyd sufficient time to make the necessary arrangements and load the goods, Dafyd is not obliged to ship the goods and is entitled to treat the contract as repudiated by Heinz and claim damages. However, Dafyd has chosen not to accept Heinz's breach as discharging the contract because he ships the goods. The contract therefore remains open to the benefit of both parties.

However, Lord Diplock in *Ian Stach Ltd v Baker Bosley Ltd* (1958) thought that such a situation would lead to uncertainties and concluded that the *prima facie* rule is that the documentary credit must be opened at the latest on the first day of the shipping period. It seems, therefore, that Dafyd could have taken issue on this point against Heinz so that Dafyd could have terminated the contract and claim damages. It is clear from the facts, however, that Dafyd has waived the breach or at least agreed to a variation of the contract,[1] because he buys the salt and arranges for it to be delivered to the port of shipment.

As discussed, Dafyd may no longer take issue with Heinz because the documentary credit was opened late. It also seems that Heinz had arranged for an irrevocable confirmed credit with Snowball Bank as he was obliged to do so. Once an irrevocable credit has been confirmed, the confirmation will constitute a definite undertaking of the confirming bank in addition to the undertaking of the issuing bank. The rule is that once an irrevocable confirmed credit has been opened, no party (certainly not the buyer alone) may vary or cancel such credit.

Heinz cancels his nomination of *Island Princess*. It is clear from the decision of *Agricultores Federados Argentinos v Ampro SA* (1965) that an fob buyer who has the option as to the time of shipment is entitled to withdraw the nomination of a ship and to substitute it with another ship, as long as he does so within such time as to make it possible for the seller to load the goods within the shipment period. *Prima facie*, therefore, Heinz was entitled to cancel the nomination. It has been suggested, however, that where a seller acts in reliance on the nomination of a vessel in such a way that he would be gravely prejudiced by its cancellation, the seller may recover damages for such loss, though the precise legal basis for such a claim is by no means clear.[2] Certainly, Dafyd may claim damages from Heinz for the expensive storage charges incurred as from 24 February, since this was the date that

Island Princess was expected ready to load. Dafyd may not, however, claim for the storage charges incurred before 24 February because the fob seller is responsible for all charges up to the point of delivery which, in the absence of contrary provision, is the point of shipment.

It is unclear, however, whether Heinz does in fact nominate a substitute ship, because unless he does so in such a way as would allow Dafyd sufficient time to load the goods in February, Dafyd will be entitled to treat the contract as repudiated and claim damages against Heinz.

Dafyd does load the goods onto *Island Princess*. It seems that Dafyd has acted on his own behalf, albeit in good faith.

In any event, the owners of *Island Princess* are refusing to accept the cancellation of shipping space. In the absence of express terms allowing Heinz to do so, the owners are entitled to treat the contract as a subsisting one and claim against Heinz the agreed contract price.[3]

It appears that since Heinz still had time within the shipment period to nominate a substitute ship, he was within his rights not to accept the goods shipped on *Island Princess*. He may, as discussed above, be liable to Dafyd for any losses incurred between the time of the first nomination and the substitute nomination. The letter of instruction to Snowball Bank would have stipulated *inter alia* for goods of the contract description to be shipped on a vessel nominated by Heinz, and Snowball Bank's refusal to pay against the documents which do not indicate a vessel nominated by the buyer is therefore justified. The discussion is not that the credit was revoked, merely that Dafyd's documents do not strictly comply with the instructions to the bank to pay.

Since Heinz is entitled to refuse to accept the shipment, the question of Dafyd's duty to give sufficient shipping particulars in order to allow Heinz the opportunity to insure the goods during its sea transit under s 32(3) of the Sale of Goods Act 1979 does not arise. Only if he accepts the documents (and thus has property in the goods) would the question of risk be relevant. If he refuses to accept the documents, property does not pass to Heinz and, even if he had risk in goods as from shipment, all rights and liabilities re-vest in Dafyd. Thus, any damage to the goods before and during the sea transit will be at Dafyd's risk.

Furthermore, Dafyd is not entitled to send the documents directly to Heinz for payment because the contract has provided for payment by letter of credit and that is the only acceptable method of tender: *Soproma v Marine & Animal By-Products* (1966).

We are not told whether Heinz does in fact nominate a substitute ship in February. If he does not, Dafyd will be entitled to treat the contract as repudiated by reason of Heinz's fundamental breach of his duty to give effective shipping instructions. Dafyd will also be entitled to claim damages for non-acceptance under s 50 of the Sale of Goods Act 1979. Heinz will not be able to argue in his defence that even if he had nominated a substitute ship Dafyd would not have been able to deliver the goods (which were already on board *Island Princess*). This is because Dafyd appears to have agreed to sell generic goods and thus he is at liberty to appropriate 3,000 tons of salt from another source in order to fulfil his obligations under the contract with Heinz.

Notes

1   The difference between a waiver and an agreement to a variation is beyond the scope of commercial law syllabuses and, in any event, the significance of the distinction does not matter in this question.

2   Lord Heward CJ in *Cunningham v Monroe* (1922) said that it was 'not exactly estoppel' and based the reasoning on a principle analogous to that in *Hughes v Metropolitan Railway* (1877).

3   On the other hand, the owners of *Island Princess* could have accepted Heinz's repudiation of the contract and claim for damages instead. If they had done so, they would have been under a duty to mitigate their loss, for instance, by trying to sell the shipping space to someone else.

Question 43

'The Vienna Convention on Contracts for the International Sale of Goods should be adopted by the United Kingdom. The advantages of taking this step will considerably outweigh the disadvantages.'
    Critically evaluate this statement.

Answer plan

This question gives you an opportunity to consider the arguments for and against adoption of the CISG. The amount of detail required will be restricted to the time available. So, do not get carried away!

Adoption of the CISG would provide important benefits to UK exporters and importers of manufactured goods and raw materials. Parties negotiating international sales contracts often find the 'choice of law' issue to be among the most contentious. Each party is familiar with its own domestic sales law, and prefers that its local rules apply to the transaction. A widely acceptable and accepted uniform and generally understood set of rules avoids all of those problems. The CISG attempts to eliminate obstacles to cross-border contracts by putting into place internationally accepted substantive rules on which contracting parties, courts and arbitrators may rely.

Answer

The Vienna Convention on Contracts for the International Sale of Goods (CISG) now accounts for two-thirds of all world trade international sales law[1] and, in practice, supersedes the sales law of many of the countries with which the UK trades. Adopting the CISG gives parties the advantage of a widely accepted and increasingly understood text. The CISG does not seek to deprive parties of the freedom of contract; its provisions merely act as a gap filler governing the parties' rights and obligations where their contract is silent on these issues. There are considerable differences between the contract laws of individual countries, and a common core has to be found. An attempt is made by CISG to eliminate obstacles to cross-border contracts.

The CISG recognises the basic principle of contractual freedom in the international sale of goods. Article 6 enables parties to exclude the application of the CISG and parties have the right to pick and choose those parts of the CISG by which they agree to be bound. The CISG depends in important ways on standards such as reasonableness and good faith, which are familiar ideas and concepts to English lawyers. Another important feature of the CISG is its very limited use of technical legal terms and concepts. It has the characteristics of simplicity, practicality and clarity. It is free of legal shorthand, free of complicated legal theory and easy for business people to understand.

Application

The CISG only applies to international commercial sale of goods. Each of the following elements constitutes an important limitation on the scope of the CISG's applicability. First, the sale must be international in character, that is, it involves parties whose places of business are in different States. Secondly, the CISG covers the sale of goods and does not automatically apply to service contracts. Finally, the CISG only applies to commercial transactions, that is, sales between merchants of goods. Amongst other limitations, it does not cover consumer sales, auction sales, sales of negotiable instruments or securities, nor does it cover sales of ships or aircraft.

Formation of contracts

The CISG does not subject the contract of sale to any requirement as to form. There are, however, aspects of the CISG relating to irrevocable offers and counter-offers which are novel – novel, that is, to English lawyers.

Under English law, the offeror's right to withdraw an offer is not restricted where the offeree has not given consideration, even if the offer is expressed to be irrevocable (*Payne v Cave* (1789)). Under Art 16 of the CISG, an offer can be made expressly irrevocable because a time for acceptance is fixed; this is contrary to *Routledge v Grant* (1828). An offer is also irrevocable if it was reasonable for the offeree to rely on the offer as irrevocable and the offeree has acted in reliance on it.

The rationale behind Art 16 is that commercial interests are enhanced by the greater certainty of dealing that arises from irrevocability. It is interesting to note that the law of major trading countries, including the United States and much of Europe, is consistent in this respect with the CISG.

Under English law, an acceptance which is not the mirror image of an offer does not give rise to a contract – it is regarded as a counter-offer, not an acceptance (*Hyde v Wrench* (1840)). Under Art 19 of the CISG, a reply to an offer which purports to be an acceptance but contains additional or different terms which do not materially alter the terms of the offer constitutes an acceptance rather than a counter-offer. This is subject to the absence of a timely objection by the offeror. Article 19 is designed to maintain the contract if the differences between the offer and 'acceptance' are immaterial. Such a provision would do away with the problem in English law of 'battle of the forms'.

Furthermore, under the CISG, an acceptance of an offer becomes effective at the moment the indication of assent reaches the offeror; to that extent, the postal acceptance rule would be abolished.

The CISG thus facilitates serious dealing, removes the differences arising from different forms of communication and takes account of new technology. Whilst none of the changes should present any difficulty, care should be taken in respect of irrevocable offers.

The CISG is neither concerned with the validity of the contract nor the rights of third parties. Possible issues left to be determined by national legal systems are thus many: contractual capacity, mistake, penalty and liquidated damages clauses, illegal and unconscionable contracts, for instance, which may make a contract or a contract term void or voidable.

Concept of fundamental breach

The CISG imposes a much stricter standard for rejection and cancellation (referred to as 'avoidance'). Under the CISG, a buyer cannot reject defective goods unless there has been a fundamental breach. 'Fundamental breach' under the CISG[2] is quite distinct from the concept under English law. English law permits a buyer to reject the goods or the tender of documents if they fail to comply with conditions of the contract (subject to qualifications, such as s 15A of the Sale of Goods Act 1979). By contrast, the CISG restricts a buyer's right to avoid the contract in circumstances where the buyer would be substantially deprived of what he is entitled to expect under the contract.

(a) *Partial/excessive delivery*

Articles 51–52 of the CISG regulate partial and excessive performance and these differ in detail from existing English law. For example, under the CISG, a shortfall in the quantity delivered justifies the buyer's avoidance of the contract only if the failure amounts to a fundamental breach and, in the case of excess performance, only the excess can be rejected. By contrast, s 30 of the Sale of Goods Act 1979 allows the buyer to reject the whole delivery, unless the shortfall (or excess) in the quantity of goods delivered to the non-consumer buyer is so slight that it would be unreasonable for him to do so.

(b) *Anticipatory breach*

Under the English doctrine of anticipatory breach, the innocent party is entitled to avoid the contract by reason of the other party's repudiatory breach. Under Art 72 of the CISG, the right to avoid for anticipatory breach arises only if 'it is clear that one of the parties will commit a fundamental breach' (Art 72).

Delivery of conforming goods

Under the CISG, the seller must deliver the goods, hand over any documents relating to them and transfer the property in the goods as required by the contract. These duties are unlikely to cause difficulty for English lawyers.

The basic obligation of conformity of the goods is that the seller must deliver goods which are of the quantity, quality and description required by the contract (including packaging). Conformity is spelled out in terms of fitness for ordinary purpose and for any particular purpose known to the seller, unless the buyer did not reasonably rely on the seller's skill and judgment. Again, these duties are unlikely to cause difficulty for English lawyers, but the wording of the obligations differs from the Sale of Goods Act

1979 – for instance, there is no reference to conditions and warranties – but the substance appears not to differ in any significant way.

The rules relating to the consequence of non-conformity are, however, new. The CISG buyer loses the right to rely on a lack of conformity of the goods unless notice is given within a reasonable time after discovery of the defect or within two years of the actual delivery of the goods (whichever is the earlier).

Remedies

Remedies are critical in the effective operation of law in an area such as this. It is not surprising that the CISG gives them a great deal of emphasis, introducing a range of remedies not to be found in English law.

(a) *Seller's right to cure*

The CISG emphasises saving the contract by enabling the seller to cure the breach. The CISG permits a seller to remedy a tender of defective documents (Art 34) and non-conforming goods (Art 37) up to the time fixed for delivery, as long as the exercise of these rights does not cause the buyer unreasonable inconvenience or unreasonable expense.

Article 48 gives a seller the right to remedy 'any failure to perform' if he can do so without unreasonable delay and without causing the buyer unreasonable inconvenience. This right to remedy applies to a breach by failure to deliver on time. The procedure to be followed is that the seller must give notice to the buyer suggesting a new deadline for delivery. If the buyer does not answer within a reasonable time, the seller has the right to perform and the buyer has the obligation to accept performance within the new deadline. Since the seller's notice to the buyer is assumed under the CISG to include a request that the buyer consent or refuse his consent, this means that a buyer who does not respond to a notice that the seller will deliver late will be in breach if the buyer refuses to accept delivery.

(b) *Price reduction*

Under Art 50, if the seller delivers goods which do not conform to the contract, whether or not the price has already been paid, in addition to recovering damages, the buyer may unilaterally reduce the price in the same proportion as the value that the goods actually delivered bears to the value that conforming goods would have had at that time. If the goods are delivered late, but they did conform to the contract, Art 50 does not apply.

The right to reduce the price is a substantial right and there are situations in which Art 50 can provide better relief than a damages claim (for example, in the case of a falling market). This is good news for the buyer but bad for the seller (the seller may, of course, revise the limitation of liability clause in the contract to reduce the effect of Art 50).

(c) *Damages*

The basic right to damages under Art 74 of the CISG[3] is stated in terms of foreseeability and appears to conform with the basic rule of damages in *Hadley v Baxendale* (1854). There is under the CISG an obligation on a party relying on breach to mitigate the loss.

(d) *Specific performance*

Articles 46 and 62 of the CISG permit both the buyer and seller to require performance of the other party's obligations under the contract. However, this is subject to the qualification that a court need not grant an order for specific performance unless it would do so under its own law in non-CISG cases involving similar contracts of sale. English courts have invariably been reluctant to grant specific performance where damages are an adequate remedy (*Harnett v Yielding* (1805)).

Passing of risk

While the CISG deals with passage of risk of loss or damage, it does not contain provisions governing what we call transfer of 'title' or 'property'. Of course, the Sale of Goods Act 1979 contains detailed provisions specifying when title passes. Although the CISG does not regulate the transfer of property, it does provide a clear basis on which relevant arrangements, including insurance, can be made. Under the CISG, risk in general passes on the handing over of the goods to the carrier (Art 67) or to the buyer if he is taking direct delivery (Art 69).

Frustration

The CISG[4] deals with the issue of the excusing of a non-performing party because of impossibility in a similar way to the doctrine of frustration in English law. However, Art 79 operates only to prevent an action in damages. It does not bring the contract to an end, which is unlike the English law position (*Hirji Mulji v Cheong Yue Steamship Co* (1926)). However, if a failure to perform is a fundamental breach, the other party may declare the contract avoided.

Conclusion

Because the CISG is still so new, the ramifications of its provisions are uncertain. However, with so many nations having become parties to it, and with so many alternative sources and markets available to purchasers of manufactured goods or producers of raw materials, British exporters and importers are no longer in a position to have their way with respect to choice of law and forum selection. The attitudes and lack of a widely accepted alternative that made the 'laws of England' the common contractual choice of law in international commercial transactions are gone, or are changing. A seller or buyer who refuses to deal on the CISG terms may find himself losing business opportunities to competitors who will.

Notes

1   As at 3 December 2002, the following 64 countries subscribe to the CISG:

Argentina, Australia, Austria, Belarus, Belgium, Bosnia and Herzegovina, Bulgaria, Burundi, Canada, Chile, China, Colombia, Croatia, Cuba, the Czech Republic, Denmark, Ecuador, Egypt, Estonia, Finland, France, Georgia, Germany, Ghana, Greece, Guinea, Honduras, Hungary, Iceland, Iraq, Israel, Italy, Kyrgyzstan, Latvia, Lesotho, Lithuania, Luxembourg, Mauritania, Mexico, Moldova, Mongolia, the Netherlands, New Zealand, Norway, Peru, Poland, Romania, Russian Federation, Saint Vincent and Grenadines, Singapore, Slovakia, Slovenia, Spain, Sweden, Switzerland, Syrian Arab Republic, Uganda, Ukraine, United States of America, Uruguay, Uzbekistan, Venezuela, Yugoslavia and Zambia.

2   A breach is fundamental, according to Art 25 of the CISG:

'... if it results in such detriment to the other party as substantially to deprive him of what he is entitled to under the contract, unless the party in breach did not foresee and a reasonable person of the same kind in the same circumstances would not have foreseen such a result.'

3   Article 74:

'Damages for breach of contract by one party consist of a sum equal to the loss, including the loss of profit, suffered by the other party as a consequence of the breach. Such damages may not exceed the loss which the party in breach foresaw or ought to have foreseen at the time of the conclusion of the contract, in the light of the facts and matters which he then knew or ought to have known, as a possible consequence of the breach of contract.'

4   Article 79 states the basic rule:

'A party is not liable for a failure to perform any of his obligations if he proves that the failure was due to an impediment beyond his control and that he could not reasonably be expected to have taken the impediment into account at the time of the conclusion of the contract or to have avoided or overcome it or its consequences.'

Question 44

Nina agrees to sell to Bertha in Bristol 1,000 kilograms of anchovies packed in boxes, 25 kilograms in each box, fob Antwerp, payment by letter of credit on tender of documents to Safestreet Bank. The contract called for October shipment. On 3 October, Bertha nominates *The Witness* to take the goods and Nina arranges for the consignment to arrive at the docks shortly afterwards. Bertha had not booked shipping space on *The Witness* but Nina finally manages to persuade the master to take the goods on 31 October. The following day, a fire breaks out on *The Witness* and the boxes containing the anchovies are wetted whilst the fire is being extinguished. The boxes are unloaded and repacked in boxes of 50 kilograms. They are reloaded on 2 November. The master of the ship issues a bill of lading for '20 x 50 kilograms anchovies shipped on 31 October'.

When Nina presents the documents to Safestreet Bank, she is refused payment on the ground that the bill of lading shows incorrect packaging. Nina takes the bill of lading back to the master of *The Witness*, who agrees to have the anchovies repacked on the voyage and issues a fresh bill of 40 boxes of 25 kilograms of anchovies.

When the boxes arrive in London, Bertha discovers that the anchovies had been infected with fungus, causing the anchovies to deteriorate.

Advise the parties.

Answer plan

Although Bertha nominates a ship, she has not booked shipping space. This is not a fundamental breach of the contract, since Nina does manage to load the goods on the ship nominated by Bertha. The problem is that the goods are damaged and then unloaded and the question of risk will need to be addressed.

Shipping documents have always played a key role in international sale contracts and the second part of this question requires you to discuss whether the bank may refuse to pay against documents which indicate incorrect packaging. The issue of packaging falls squarely within the implied term as to description under s 13 of the Sale of Goods Act 1979. Because the anchovies deteriorate, s 14 of that Act will also need to be discussed.

Answer

In the absence of further information about the express terms, the contract between Nina and Bertha is a 'classic' fob contract. The primary duties of the buyer are to nominate an effective ship to carry the goods, to notify the seller of such nomination in time for the seller to load goods and to pay the agreed price. The seller's primary duty is to deliver goods which comply with the terms of the contract once the seller has given his shipping instructions.

Where documentary credit is involved, the rule is that the letter of credit must be opened at the very latest before the first day of the shipment period. This is clear from *Pavia & Co SpA v Thurmann-Nielsen* (1952). In this question, we are not told when Safestreet Bank advised Nina of the opening of the credit and, if this was on or after 1 October, Nina is entitled to refuse to ship the goods and may treat the contract as discharged and claim damages against Bertha. We are told that Nina does in fact ship the goods, thus choosing not to treat the late opening of credit (if indeed it was opened on or after 1 October) as discharging the contract.

Although Bertha nominates *The Witness*, she has not in fact booked shipping space for the goods. It is the prime duty of an fob buyer to give 'effective' shipping instructions, that is, it must be possible and lawful for the seller to comply with them (*Agricultores Federados Argentinos v Ampro SA* (1965)). The essential point is that the seller must be instructed as to the way in which he can perform his duty to put the goods on board. Nina, nevertheless, manages to persuade the master of *The Witness* to take the goods. Bertha's nomination of *The Witness* is therefore adequate since the named ship can in fact take the goods, irrespective of her failure to make advance arrangements with the master. Nothing turns on this point, since if Bertha had not reserved shipping space in advance, she runs the risk that her shipping instructions may be ineffective, but she does not commit any breach of contract as long as Nina is in fact able to ship the goods in accordance with the shipping instructions. Despite the fact that Nina only managed to persuade the master of *The Witness* to take the goods on the last day stipulated within the contract shipment period, all the boxes were in fact loaded by the end of that day.

A fire breaks out on *The Witness* the next day, 1 November, and the boxes are unloaded. Once goods have been loaded, risk normally passes to the buyer because the seller has fulfilled his obligation to deliver the goods and nothing remains to be done by him under the contract except to tender the shipping documents for payment. Thus, Nina need not have involved herself with the events that occurred after 31 October, and it would have been Bertha's decision whether or not to claim for any damage against the underwriters if she had taken out an insurance policy.[1] Because the goods are unloaded, a problem has arisen. For whatever reason, the anchovies have now been packed in boxes of 50 kilograms per box whereas the contract had stipulated for 25 kilograms per box. The bill of lading issued by the master states '20 x 50 kilograms anchovies shipped on 31 October'.

The requirement that goods must correspond to their description used to be a strict one, entitling the buyer to reject for quite trivial discrepancies, and to do so even though the failure of the seller to deliver goods of the contract description does not in the least prejudice the buyer (*Arcos Ltd v Ronaasen & Son* (1933)).[2] This is no longer the case due to s 15A of the Sale of Goods Act 1979. The buyer who is a non-consumer can no longer reject where the breach is so slight that it would be unreasonable for him to do so.

Safestreet Bank was entitled to refuse to pay against the documents which Nina presents, since the bill of lading does not comply with the terms of the credit because it indicates incorrect packaging. This stems from the principle of strict compliance in documentary financing. As Lord Sumner said in *Equitable Trust Co of New York v Dawson Partners Ltd* (1927): 'There is no room for documents which are almost the same, or which will do just as well.' Safestreet Bank has no discretion, in that it must comply strictly with the buyer's instructions as to payment.[3] The bank's right to reimbursement from Bertha depends on it taking up a faultless set of documents and, since the bill of lading indicates incorrect packaging, Safestreet Bank was entitled to refuse to pay Nina, no matter how minor the discrepancy may appear.

Safestreet Bank's duty is to examine all the documents with reasonable care to ascertain whether they appear on their face to be in accordance with the terms of credit. It not responsible for the genuineness or accuracy of the documents, merely whether they comply and Safestreet Bank has rightly refused to pay Nina.

It appears that Safestreet Bank has notified Nina of the reason for rejection and Nina does have an opportunity to put right any defect and represent the document again, provided that there is time to do so in accordance with the contract of sale and the credit. Nina thus takes the bill of lading back to the master of *The Witness* who issues a fresh bill now stipulating that the cargo is of 40 boxes each containing 25 kilograms of anchovies as was required under the contract.

We are not then told what the parties' actions were, but it is reasonable to assume that Nina then re-tenders the documents to Safestreet Bank which then pays against them, since the bill of lading now indicates the correct packaging. As far as the date of shipment is concerned, the bill of lading shows 31 October and thus the documents appear on their face in apparent good order and comply with the terms of the credit. In order for Bertha to have taken possession of the goods on arrival, Bertha will have reimbursed Safestreet Bank because a bank will not release the documents until payment by its principal. Once Safestreet Bank has taken reasonable care in scrutinising the documents, it will not be liable to Bertha if the documents later turn out to be forged.

Bertha discovers that the anchovies have deteriorated due to fungus infection. Although she has previously accepted documents, Bertha may be entitled to reject the goods. An fob buyer has two distinct rights of rejection. As Devlin J made clear in *Kwei Tek Chao v British Traders and Shippers* (1954), the right to reject documents arises when the documents are tendered, and the right to reject goods arises when they are landed and when, after examination, they are not found to be in conformity with the contract.

This would be the case if the goods suffered from some qualitative defect not apparent on the face of the documents. In *Mash & Murrell v Joseph Emanuel* (1961), Cyprus potatoes were sold cif Liverpool. The potatoes were sound when shipped but were found to be rotten on arrival. On the facts of the case, it was found that the deterioration was a result of fungus infection before or at the time of shipment. The court held that the seller was liable for the deterioration. As Diplock J said in that case: '... when goods are sold under a contract such as a cif contract or fob contract which involves transit before use, there is an implied warranty not merely that they shall be [satisfactory] at the time they are put on the vessel, but that they shall be in such a state that they can endure the normal journey and be in a [satisfactory] condition on arrival ...'

It therefore seems that because anchovies are normally capable of enduring a sea transit, Nina will be liable for any deterioration apparent on arrival. This implied warranty is distinct from the implied term under s 14 of the Sale of Goods Act 1979, the former relating to an undertaking that the goods can endure sea transit as opposed to s 14(2) and (3), which are implied terms relating to satisfactory quality and fitness for purpose.

Bertha may thus be entitled to reject the goods for breach of the implied terms as to satisfactory quality and fitness for purpose under s 14 of the Sale of Goods Act 1979, provided that the breach is not so slight so as to treat it as a breach of warranty (s 15A of the Sale of Goods Act 1979). If the anchovies no longer have commercial value, as it appears in this case, Bertha is likely to be entitled to reject the goods despite the fact that Nina has already been paid against documents.

Furthermore, according to the House of Lords in *Bowes v Shand* (1877), stipulations as to the time of shipment form part of the description of the goods and that breach of such stipulations entitles the buyer to reject. Although *Bowes v Shand* was decided before the Sale of Goods Act 1893, subsequent cases have acknowledged that the time of shipment is part of the description of the goods and is within s 13 of the Sale of Goods Act (*Avon & Co v Comptoir Weigmont* (1920)). Since the goods were not in fact shipped within the contract period, Bertha may be able to reject the goods on the ground that they did not constitute an October shipment. However, it is arguable whether Bertha can reject the goods, since s 15A of the Sale of Goods Act 1979 provides that where the breach is so slight that it would be unreasonable for the buyer to reject the goods and the buyer does not deal as a consumer, the breach is to be treated as a breach of warranty and not as a breach of condition. Since time is of the essence in commercial contracts, it is submitted that the breach will not be perceived as so slight for it to be treated as a breach of warranty.

Notes

1   An fob seller is not obliged to take out insurance cover for the goods, but s 32(3) of the Sale of Goods Act 1979 imposes on him an obligation to 'give such notice to the buyer as may enable him to insure [the goods] during their sea transit'. If the seller does not do so, the goods are deemed to be at the seller's risk. However, *Wimble Sons & Co v Rosenberg* (1913) established that in a classic fob contract, that is, where the buyer nominates the vessel and gives the shipping instructions, the buyer will normally have sufficient information to enable him to insure so that the seller need not give further notice under s 32(3).

2   In *Re Moore & Co and Landauer & Co* (1921), it was held that goods did not comply with their description when the contract called for 3,000 tins of fruit to be packed 30 tins to a case and the seller delivered the correct number of tins, but some were packed 24 tins to a case.

3   Lord Wilberforce in *Reardon Smith Line Ltd v Hansen Tangen* (1976) described some of the older cases as 'excessively technical', but that the need for certainty, particularly in international sales, outweighs the need for flexibility.

CIF CONTRACTS

Introduction

Under a cif (cost, insurance and freight) contract, the seller is required to arrange the carriage of the goods and their insurance in transit, and all costs of such arrangements are included in the contract price. The essential duties of a cif seller are to obtain a bill of lading, a policy of insurance and any other document required by the contract, and to forward them to the buyer who pays on the invoice when he receives the shipping documents.

Shipping documents play a central role in cif contracts, particularly where documentary financing is concerned. Because the buyer in international sale contracts has two rights of rejection, he retains his right to reject the goods on arrival if they do not conform with the terms of the contract, even if he has paid against shipping documents.

Cif contracts are often concerned with the sale of unascertained goods, and issues concerning the passing of risk and property are often involved. A particular problem arises where unascertained goods are lost before the cif seller has appropriated the goods to the contract.

Checklist

Students should be familiar with the following areas:

- the requirements of proper shipping documents;
- the role of the bank in documentary financing;
- the buyer's two distinct rights of rejection;
- the passing of risk and property, particularly where unascertained goods are concerned.

Question 45

Bonnie ships 10,000 tons of groundnut oil from Southampton to Hamburg via Antwerp on board *Chronicle*. Whilst the goods are afloat, Bonnie enters into the following three separate contracts:

(a) to sell 5,000 tons of groundnut oil to Marcus cif Antwerp, payment to be made by letter of credit to be issued by Marcus' bank;

(b) to sell 3,000 tons of groundnut oil to Christopher cif Hamburg, payment by cash against documents;

(c) to sell 2,000 tons of groundnut oil to Debbie ex *Chronicle*, payment in full in advance.

The voyage between Antwerp and Hamburg is beset with difficulties and the master of *Chronicle* informs Bonnie that 1,000 tons of groundnut oil have been lost. Marcus' bank accepts a bill of exchange on tender of documents which include a delivery order for 5,000 tons of groundnut oil, but Marcus refuses to take delivery of the goods, claiming that the groundnut oil is of inferior quality. Bonnie couriers the shipping documents to Christopher, who rejects them because they included a delivery order indicating that 500 tons of groundnut oil have been lost. Debbie refuses to pay Bonnie because only 1,500 tons of groundnut oil had been discharged at Hamburg.

Advise Bonnie.

Answer plan

Shipping documents have always played a key role in international sale contracts and normally shipping documents include the bill of lading. In all three parts to this question, however, a delivery order is tendered. In the absence of an express term in the contract, is the seller entitled to tender such a document where the sale involves a part of a bulk quantity?

Part (a) also involves s 13 of the Sale of Goods Act 1979. Part (b) requires you to discuss whether goods must be appropriated to the contract before loss. Part (c) involves a straightforward discussion of s 30 of the Sale of Goods Act 1979. Note, however, that the contract with Debbie is *ex* ship.

Answer

Neither the contract with Marcus nor the contract with Christopher requires Bonnie to supply goods from those on board *Chronicle*. The contract with Bonnie, however, does so require. When did the loss of the 500 tons occur? Was it before risk passed to the buyer? Risk will, however, have passed under the first two contracts (with Marcus and Christopher) when the goods passed over the rail of the ship on their way into the ship. Thus, assuming (as seems to be implied by the question) that the loss occurred during the voyage, the risk falls upon the buyer under a cif contract. Of course, that is so provided that the buyer has taken up, or has no legitimate reason for not taking up, the documents.

(a) Marcus

So far as Marcus is concerned, his bank has taken up the documents and, it being his bank, Marcus is presumably bound by what his bank has done. Thus, Marcus – although he may have been entitled to reject the documents – cannot now resile from the acceptance of the documents by his bank. To put it another way, he is estopped from rejecting the goods on any ground which would have entitled him to reject the documents (*Panchaud Frères v Etablissements General Grain* (1970)). Thus, he is not entitled to reject the documents or the goods on the ground that he should not have been tendered a delivery order, but a bill of lading. In any case, it may be that the cif contract in this case expressly or impliedly provided for the tendering of a delivery order instead of the more normal bill of lading. This may be so especially if both buyer and seller (Bonnie and Marcus) contemplated that the contract would be performed by delivery of documents relating to goods consisting of an undivided part of a cargo.[1] As already indicated, however, even if Bonnie was not entitled to tender a delivery order, the documents tendered were accepted and Marcus is estopped from relying on that non-compliance. On the other hand, a buyer under a cif contract has two rights of rejection: (i) to reject non-complying documents; and (ii) to reject goods which on arrival prove to be in breach of condition (except on any ground which would have entitled him to reject the documents) (*Kwei Tek Chao v British Traders and Shippers* (1954)). Thus, if the goods when tendered are in breach of condition, Marcus is entitled to reject them. It is possible that the groundnut oil being 'of inferior quality' means that: (i) there is a breach of an express term of the contract; and/or (ii) there is a breach of one of the conditions implied by s 14 of the Sale of Goods Act 1979 (as to satisfactory quality or fitness for purpose).[2] In the case of (i), it is only if either: (a) the express term amounts to a condition; or (b) the breach is such as to deprive

Marcus of substantially the whole of the benefit of the contract that the buyer will have a right of rejection. From the facts given, it is impossible to determine whether the goods being of inferior quality amounts to a breach of condition, express or implied.

If, in fact, Marcus' bank has accepted documents which it was entitled to reject and which it ought to have rejected, then although Marcus is estopped as indicated above, he will have a remedy against his bank if the bank has acted contrary to his instructions in accepting the documents.

(b) Christopher

Unlike Marcus, Christopher has rejected the documents. The reason which motivated him to reject the documents is irrelevant. What is relevant is whether he had a valid reason to reject the documents. He can rely on a valid reason, even if at the time of his rejection he relied upon an invalid reason, and he was unaware of the existence of the valid reason (*Glencore Grain Rotterdam BV v Lebanese Organisation for International Commerce* (1997)). There are two possibly valid reasons. First, that he was tendered a delivery order rather than a bill of lading – though, as seen above, it may be that the contract expressly or impliedly allowed tender of a delivery order. Secondly, that the delivery order showed less than the contract quantity. It is unclear whether Bonnie had appropriated[3] the lost 500 tons of groundnut oil to Christopher's contract before the goods were in fact lost. Cases such as *Re Olympia Oil and Cake Co and Produce Brokers Ltd* (1915) indicate that a seller *can* appropriate lost cargo since, in a cif contract, the buyer has the benefit of a contract of carriage and a policy of insurance so that, in the event of loss, the buyer has a claim against either the carrier or the insurer, even though the loss or damage to the goods occurred before those documents were tendered (*Manbre Saccharine Co Ltd v Sugar Beet Products Co Ltd* (1919)). There is academic opinion, however, that the seller *cannot* make a valid tender of documents after the loss of the goods unless, before the loss occurred, they had become fully identified as the contract goods. In this case, they appear not to have been fully identified. Indeed, the problem does not even state that the goods supplied to Christopher must come from the cargo on *Chronicle*. It would appear that Bonnie could have complied with the terms of his contract with Christopher by buying a cargo of groundnut oil afloat (cif Hamburg) and using that cargo to fulfil his contract with Christopher. Thus, although the matter is not free from doubt, Bonnie is advised that his tender of documents to Christopher was not valid and that accordingly Christopher was entitled to reject them.

(c) Debbie

The difference between *ex* ship and cif contracts is that in the former, documents do not stand in the place of documents so that actual delivery of the goods must be made (*The Julia* (1949)). So far as Debbie is concerned, the risk in an *ex* ship contract, unless the contract specifically provides otherwise, passes upon delivery from the ship against payment. According to s 30(1) of the Sale of Goods Act 1979, where the seller delivers a quantity less than he has contracted to sell, the buyer has the option of either rejecting them or to accept the part-delivery and pay for them at the contract rate. However, according to s 30(2A), the buyer who does not deal as a consumer will not be able to reject the goods under s 30(1) if the shortfall is so slight that it would be unreasonable for him to do so. A shortfall of 500 tons, in the present instance, is not slight. There is no question of Debbie getting her money back, since she has not yet paid the price. She has refused to pay. It seems, therefore, that Debbie is entitled to reject the goods and to refuse to pay (s 30(1) of the Sale of Goods Act).

Notes

1   Even if this were the case, the delivery order must be one issued by the ship so that the document should give the buyer some contractual rights against the ship. (Under the Carriage of Goods by Sea Act 1992, this has the same effect as a bill of lading in transferring property.)

2   It is unlikely to amount to breach of the condition implied by s 13, since the matter of quality is not normally regarded as part of the contract description (*Ashington Piggeries v Christopher Hill* (1972)).

3   'Appropriation' here is used in the sense that the seller has contractually bound himself to deliver certain goods. There can be appropriation in this sense even though the goods remain 'unascertained' because they form part of a larger bulk.

Question 46

Caesar agreed to buy the following goods under separate contracts:

(a) 1,000 tons of sugar beet cif Antwerp from Alfred.

(b) 2,000 oranges fob Portsmouth from Tara.

(c) 3,000 staves of Latvian timber cif Mumbai from Ruth.

Each contract stipulated for payment by irrevocable letter of credit at Dunnit Bank on presentation of the shipping documents, and called for shipment in August/September.

The following events have occurred and you are asked to advise Caesar:

(i) Alfred has the sugar beet ready to load by 10 September, but discovers that no credit has been opened and hence refused to load. The credit in fact was opened on 28 September and although Alfred begins to load the sugar beet, loading was not completed until 1 October. The bank refused to pay against the shipping documents, which included the bill of lading showing a shipment of 1 October.

(ii) Dunnit Bank informed Tara that the credit was opened on 30 July. Caesar contacted Tara to say that he wanted his local representative to inspect the oranges before shipment, but Tara refused to allow the representative to do so. The bank paid on presentation of the shipping documents. On arrival of the vessel, the oranges were found to have been damaged due to severe storms during the voyage. The shipment date was 10 August, but Caesar knew nothing of this.

(iii) On 7 August, the Latvian authorities announced that the exportation of timber was prohibited as from 1 September. Since the market price for timber was rising, Ruth used the prohibition announcement as an excuse for not being able to ship the contract goods.

Answer plan

Part (a) concerns the opening of credit which comes too late to enable Alfred to load the goods within the contract shipment period.

Part (b) involves a discussion as to an fob buyer's right to examine the goods. In relation to this, a comparison to domestic sale contracts must be made since in that situation, the point of delivery is the normal place of inspection, whereas in international sale contracts, there is no such rule. Was Caesar entitled to insist on an inspection at the point of shipment (which in international sale contracts is the point of delivery)? What are the effects of Tara's refusal to allow Caesar's representative to inspect?

The answer should also deal with the fob seller's statutory duty under s 32(3) of the Sale of Goods Act 1979.

Part (c) asks you to discuss whether Ruth is entitled to rely on the prohibition of timber as justifying her refusal to deliver (for instance, because the contract has been frustrated).

Answer

(a) Alfred

The general rule is that documentary credit must be opened in accordance with the terms of the contract of sale. The contract between Caesar and Alfred does not provide a date for the opening credit but it does, however, stipulate a period for the shipment of goods. It is clear from *Pavia & Co SpA v Thurmann-Nielsen* (1952) that in these circumstances, the documentary credit must be opened at the very latest on the first day on which shipment may take place. In a cif contract, the seller is not bound to tell the buyer the precise date when he is going to ship, because it is the seller who has the option as to the time of shipment. Whenever the seller does ship, he must nevertheless be able to draw on the credit. Thus, Alfred is entitled to refuse to load the goods if the credit has not been opened, and is entitled to treat the contract as discharged because of Caesar's breach. Furthermore, Alfred will be entitled to claim damages.[1]

The credit is opened on 28 September and Alfred begins to load. However, there is insufficient time before the end of the shipment period to complete the loading. *Bunge & Co Ltd v Tradax England Ltd* (1975) involved an fob contract where the buyer nominated a ship which was not ready to load until two hours before the end of the last working day of the shipment period; it was held that the seller could have rejected the nomination. Although Alfred is a cif seller, and thus has the option of when to load, his option was restricted to that part of the shipment period when the letter of credit was open. By loading part of the goods within the available period, he has not waived his right to treat the contract as repudiated because of Caesar's failure to comply with the contractual stipulations as to payment.

When Alfred tenders the shipping documents to Dunnit Bank, the documents are rejected. Since the bill of lading gives the shipment as 1 October, as far as the bank is concerned, it is not obliged to pay the seller because the documents do not comply with the terms of credit (*Equitable Trust Company of New York v Dawson Partners Ltd* (1927)). Dunnit Bank's right of reimbursement depends on it taking up a faultless set of documents and since the bill of lading indicates a shipment date outside that permitted under the terms of credit, Dunnit Bank is entitled to refuse to pay Alfred. Alfred's remedy is against Caesar for failure to have the documentary credit opened in his favour in time for him to load the goods before the end of the shipment period.

(b) Tara

Tara refuses Caesar's request for an inspection of the oranges to be carried out before shipment. Under s 35(2) of the Sale of Goods Act 1979, there is no 'right' to inspect the goods before shipment, but if the buyer had not done so, there is no legal acceptance when the goods are shipped until the buyer has had a reasonable opportunity to inspect them upon delivery.

The fact that the buyer here was not afforded an opportunity to inspect the goods before shipment does not deprive him of his right to inspect at the contractual place of examination. This means that although Caesar was not given an opportunity to look at the goods when he asks to do so, he is nevertheless entitled to ask to inspect (and be allowed to do so) at the contractual place of examination.

Where is this contractual place of examination in Caesar's case? Section 35(2) refers to the place of delivery and this reflects the rule at common law, where it was held in *Perkins v Bell* (1893) that there is a presumption that the place of examination is the contractual delivery point.

'Delivery' in this instance is to be construed according to the terms of the fob contract. Where it is a classic or strict fob case, namely, where the buyer acts as shipper of the goods, then the buyer is entitled to inspect the goods or have the local representative look at the goods before the ship sails. Where it is an fob contract with extended services, then the seller acts as the buyer's agent in shipping and hence the contractual (note: not necessarily coinciding with the statutory!) point of delivery for the purposes of s 35(2) would be at the point of arrival. So, unless the contract provides otherwise, the assumption is that inspection and examination of the oranges is postponed until the consignment arrives at the destination and that is the place for examination. Even then, if Tara knows that the oranges are being resold to Caesar's sub-buyer, then the opportunity to examine goods is postponed until his sub-buyer has had an opportunity to examine.

We will need to inquire as to whether the buyer had waived the right to inspect. If Caesar was requesting inspection at a non-contractual time, Tara was acting within her rights not to let Caesar inspect the goods. If, however, Caesar did not purport to exercise his right to inspect at the contractual time, it is possible that such an omission might be construed as a waiver (especially in the case of a non-consumer transaction). In *B&P Wholesale Distributors v Marko* (1953), when the goods arrived, the buyer was given an opportunity to inspect the goods at the docks, but the buyer did not avail himself of the opportunity. Instead, the buyer transported the goods to his depot and then examined the goods. The court held that the buyer had not lost his right to reject. He would only be deemed to have waived his right to examine the goods if he had been given a genuine and practical opportunity to make a proper examination of the goods at the docks.

If Caesar had been offered a real and practical opportunity to inspect the goods, then he may not be able to quibble with any defects or deficiencies which that inspection could have revealed. However, where the goods deteriorated as in the present case and it is possible that an inspection could not have revealed the inherent vice in the goods, then the buyer retains his statutory and contractual right to damages for unfit goods as long as the deterioration was caused by the state of the goods as they were at shipment: *Mash & Murrell Ltd v Joseph Emanuel* (1961). Deterioration caused by the sea passage shall naturally be borne by the buyer (as he is the shipper) and any claim (if any) would have to be brought against the carrier under the contract of carriage.

It is also possible that Caesar wished to inspect the oranges in order to discover matters necessary for him to take out effective insurance. There is no information in the question leading to the suggestion that Tara must have made the shipping arrangements. Unless the fob contract stipulated otherwise, Tara is not obliged to obtain insurance cover for the goods. It is Caesar's responsibility to ensure that insurance cover was in place if he required it. We are told that the goods are damaged during the voyage, but we are not told whether or not Caesar had insured the oranges. Since Caesar only knew of the date of shipment after the damage occurred, it may be that under the contract, Tara had the responsibility to make the shipping arrangements. Thus, if Caesar had not taken out effective insurance cover because he did not have sufficient information to insure, then s 32(3) of the Sale of Goods Act 1979 places the risk of damage after shipment on the seller, Tara. Although in a 'classic' fob contract, it is the buyer who makes all shipping arrangements (*Pyrene Co Ltd v Scindia Navigation Co Ltd* (1954)), it seems in this question that Tara might have made them, otherwise Caesar would have had sufficient information on which to insure the goods.

Thus, if Tara is in breach of s 32(3) by failing to give notice to Caesar and Caesar has not insured the goods, although the risk in goods normally passes on shipment, Tara bears the damage to the oranges during the voyage.

(c) Ruth

Once the contract has been concluded, a contract may be frustrated because of supervening governmental prohibition rendering the contract illegal. However, the prohibition operates as a frustrating event only if it is final and extends to the whole time still available for the performance of the contract. Ruth will not be able to rely on the prohibition of export to excuse performance, since the Latvian authorities had indicated in advance that the export of timber will only be prohibited from a future date within the shipment period.

In *Ross T Smyth & Co Ltd (Liverpool) v WN Lindsay Ltd* (1953), the contract provided for the shipment of horse beans from a Sicilian port, cif Glasgow during October/November. On 20 October, the Italian authorities announced that the exportation of horse beans was prohibited as from 1 November except under special licence. The sellers failed to ship. The court held that the buyers were entitled to claim damages, since the prohibition did not operate as a frustrating event.[2] Applying this case to the question, although Ruth has the option of when to ship, she is not entitled to refuse to ship the goods before 1 September. The prohibition merely limited her option of when to ship from two months to one month and, when the announcement was made, Ruth should have shipped the goods between the date of the announcement and 31 August. Caesar is thus entitled to claim damages from Ruth.

Notes

1   The measure of damages in these circumstances is not limited by the market price rule in s 50(3) of the Sale of Goods Act 1979, but may extend to the seller's loss of profits, provided that they are not too remote under the rule in *Hadley v Baxendale* (1854); *Trans Trust SPRL v Danubian Trading Co Ltd* (1952).

2   If the prohibition of export had been instantaneous, it would have operated as a frustrating event. If, on the other hand, the Latvian authorities indicated that an export embargo may be imposed, then Ruth would probably not be in breach if she did not ship between the time of that announcement and the subsequent date of the embargo: *Tradax Export v André & Cie* (1976).

Question 47

Mick agrees to buy 10,000 tons of horse beans from Margaret out of the 15,000 tons of horse beans currently in Margaret's warehouse in Portsmouth, cif Hong Kong. Shortly afterwards, Margaret sells to Jane the remaining 5,000 tons of horse beans, fob Bristol, Margaret to make the shipping arrangements to Hong Kong. Payment was to be in cash against shipping documents on both contracts.

Margaret ships all 15,000 tons on board *The Morning Star* and the cargo of horse beans is put into two separate holds – 10,000 tons in hold No 1 and 5,000 tons in hold No 2. The master of *The Morning Star* is hesitant in signing clean bills of lading because he knows of the rumour that the horse beans were suspect, having been lying in Margaret's warehouse for some time. The gossip is that the horse beans are unlikely to be usable by the time the cargo arrives in Hong Kong. Nevertheless, he is persuaded by Margaret and signs two clean bills of lading, one relating to hold No 1 and the other to hold No 2.

Before the ship sails, the horse beans are severely wetted due to an exceptionally heavy storm. Water penetrates into both holds due to inadequate sealing of the hatch covers. The master notes on both bills of lading as follows: 'Cargo wetted by rain after shipment.'

After the ship sails, Margaret tenders the bill of lading relating to hold No 1, with the insurance policy and the invoice to Mick who, having now heard about the rumours regarding the horse beans, refuses to pay on the ground that the bill of lading is not 'clean'. Margaret tenders the bill of lading relating to hold No 2 to Jane who also refuses to pay on the ground that because she had not been given any information about the shipping arrangements, she had not taken out an insurance policy covering the sea transit.

Advise Mick and Jane as to their legal position.

Answer plan

Shipping documents have always played a key role in international sale contracts, and the first part of this question requires you to discuss the time when the bill of lading must be 'clean'. The fact that Mick has heard of rumours concerning the cargo does not entitle him to reject the documents, but he does have the right to reject the goods on arrival. The cif buyer's two rights of rejection are separate and distinct.

As far as Jane is concerned, this is a straightforward question about the fob seller's statutory duty under s 32(3) of the Sale of Goods Act 1979.

Answer

Both Mick and Jane are refusing to pay against shipping documents. If these documents conform to the contract, then Mick and Jane must accept them, otherwise they will be in breach of contract even if the goods themselves do not comply with the contract when they arrive (*Gill & Duffus SA v Berger & Co Inc* (1984)).

Mick is refusing to pay on the ground that the bill of lading is not 'clean'. A clean bill of lading is one that does not contain any reservation as to the apparent good order or condition of the goods or the packing (*British Imex Industries Ltd v Midland Bank Ltd* (1958)). The time to which such a reservation must relate to prevent the bill of lading from being clean is that of shipment. In *The Galatia* (1980), a bill of lading was issued stating that the goods had been shipped in apparent good order and condition, but bore a notation that they had been subsequently damaged. The court held that the notation did not prevent the bill from being clean.

Applying *The Galatia* to this question, Mick cannot reject the bill of lading on the ground that the bill is not clean. The master of *The Morning Star* is neither bound to take samples of the horse beans nor to have them analysed nor otherwise investigate the cargo even if he is aware of rumours concerning the quality of the cargo. The master is justified in issuing a clean bill of lading. The note that was added referred to damage that occurred after loading. Thus, the bill of lading is still clean.

If Margaret has tendered the shipping documents (which, in a cif contract, will include an insurance policy and an invoice in addition to a bill of lading (*The Julia* (1949)) in accordance with the contract, Mick must pay against them. It seems that Mick has wrongfully refused to do so. It should be said, however, that a buyer in international sales contracts has two rights of rejection. For non-compliance with the contractual terms, he may have a right to reject documents, and a right to reject the goods on delivery where the breach is not slight (ss 13, 14 and 15A of the Sale of Goods Act 1979). These two rights of rejection are quite distinct (*Kwei Tek Chao v British Traders and Shippers* (1954)). A cif buyer to whom documents have been tendered is not entitled to refuse to pay until he has examined the goods for the purpose of determining whether the goods are of the contract quality. Even if Mick hears of the rumours and suspects that the horse beans are not in accordance with the contract, he is nevertheless bound to pay on tender of documents which are in accordance with the contract.[1]

Mick is thus advised to pay against the shipping documents because by doing so, he retains his possible right to reject the goods on arrival provided that the breach is not so slight so as to treat it as a breach of warranty (s 15A of the Sale of Goods Act 1979). Certainly, even if the horse beans are of satisfactory quality on shipment but are in such a state that they cannot endure a normal sea transit, Margaret will be in breach of an implied warranty entitling the buyer to claim damages (*Mash & Murrell Ltd v Joseph Emanuel* (1961)). This implied warranty is distinct from the implied term under s 14 of the Sale of Goods Act 1979, the former relating to an undertaking that the goods can endure sea transit, as opposed to s 14(2) and (3) which are implied terms relating to satisfactory quality and fitness for purpose. If the horse beans at the outset were of satisfactory quality and usable, then no action arises under s 14. But, because horse beans are normally capable of enduring a sea transit, Margaret will be liable for any deterioration apparent on arrival.

Even if the horse beans were of satisfactory quality at the time of shipment and were in a state that they could have endured the sea transit, the cargo was damaged due to rain penetrating through improperly sealed hatches. It may be that Mick will have an action against the carrier (but if, as we are informed, this is due to exceptionally heavy weather, perhaps the carrier might be covered by the excepted perils under the Hague-Visby Rules). It must be said, however, that in order to take the benefit of the contract of carriage, Mick must be the holder of the relevant documents and the only way Mick will be the holder of the documents is to have paid Margaret for them. If Mick does pay Margaret, Mick will have the right to sue the carrier for breach of his duty to take proper care of the goods, as is required under the contract of carriage.[2] Since Margaret is under a duty to make a reasonable contract of carriage (s 32(2) of the Sale of Goods Act), Mick will have a good action against the carriers.

Furthermore, once Mick has paid against the shipping documents, he will have the insurance policy assigned to him and he will be able to claim against the underwriter if he can show that the damage to the horse beans by heavy storm conditions is a peril insured against.[3]

As for Jane, she is refusing to pay against the shipping documents because she did not receive information from Margaret as to the shipping arrangements and thus she has not insured the cargo. In an fob contract, a seller is not obliged to obtain insurance cover for goods, but s 32(3) of the Sale of Goods Act 1979 provides that the seller must give such notice to the buyer as may enable the buyer to insure the goods during the sea transit. If the seller fails to do so, the goods are at the seller's risk during sea transit. In a 'classic' fob contract, it is the buyer who makes the shipping arrangements and thus a seller need not give notice under s 32(3) where the buyer already has enough information to be able to insure (*Wimble Sons & Co v Rosenberg & Sons* (1913)). The contract between Jane and Margaret appears to be an fob contract with additional services, obliging Margaret to make the necessary shipping arrangements. If Margaret has not given Jane notice to enable her to insure, then although the cargo will be at Margaret's risk during the sea transit, Jane is not entitled to refuse to pay against the shipping documents. Section 32(3) imposes a statutory duty and not a contractual duty. Thus, if the goods arrive safely, Jane has no cause of action because of the lack of insurance cover. As was discussed above, however, if the goods are not of satisfactory quality or unfit for their purpose, Jane may have a second right of rejection, that is, against the goods on arrival, provided she is a non-consumer and the breach is not so slight that it would be unreasonable to treat it as a breach of condition (s 15A of the Sale of Goods Act 1979).

In order to have an action against the carrier for breach of the contract of carriage, Jane must, as with Mick, have paid against the shipping documents. If Jane does not accept the documents but wishes to claim damages against the carrier in tort, the position following *Leigh and Sillavan v Aliakmon Shipping, The Aliakmon* (1986) is that she must show that at the time of the damage, she had legal ownership of the goods.[4] Because she will not be able to do so (having refused to pay against the documents), Jane does not have a claim in tort and must pursue her claim in contract against Margaret. Jane is thus advised to pay against the documents and reserve the possibility of rejecting the goods on arrival. If the cargo is damaged during the sea transit, Jane will then have a claim against either the carrier for breach of the contract of carriage or Margaret for breach of s 32(3).

Notes

1   There is a controversial decision of the High Court of Australia (*Henry Dean & Sons (Sydney) Ltd v O'Day Pty Ltd* (1927)) which suggests that a buyer may be entitled to reject documents where the documents are, but the goods themselves are not, in accordance with the contract. The sellers, when refusing to pay against documents, are taking a risk but one that was 'justified by the result'. This problem is yet unresolved in the English courts.

2   Under s 2(1) of the Carriage of Goods by Sea Act 1992, the lawful holder of a bill of lading has the right to sue the carrier under the contract of carriage 'as if he had been a party to that contract'.

3   Marine insurance is not usually found within undergraduate commercial law syllabuses and students will not be expected to discuss the implications of whether or not Margaret, who arranges the policy, has disclosed the rumours that surround the quality of the horse beans. Remember that contracts of insurance are contracts *uberrima fidei*, that is, of utmost good faith, so that even if

a non-disclosure does not relate to the loss, an insurer may decline to pay against a claim.

4   It is not clear what the position is now following the Carriage of Goods by Sea Act 1992, which seems to have done away with this requirement.

Question 48

Ernie agrees to sell to Ashok 1,500 sacks of coal, cif Singapore, shipment by 31 January, payment by Foxon Bank's letter of credit, the bank to accept Ashok's bill of exchange. Ashok arranges for the opening of the letter of credit and Foxon Bank informs Ernie of this on 25 January. Ernie arranges for *Babolat* to ship the goods and loading began on 30 January and finished on 1 February. During loading, 10 sacks of coal are dropped into the sea and five more are later damaged. The master signs three bills of lading, the first being dated 30 January, the second 31 January and the third 1 February. The total quantity shipped referred to in the bills of lading was 1,490 sacks of coal and a notation was made referring to 'five sacks damaged after loading'. Ernie tenders the documents including an insurance policy covering the goods 'from warehouse to warehouse' to Foxon Bank, which rejects them. Ernie then tenders the documents to Ashok who, hearing that *Babolat* has been involved in a collision, also refuses to pay.

   Advise Ernie.

Answer plan

Much of the question is concerned with the passing of risk in cif contracts. Normally, risk will pass to the buyer on shipment (that is, when the goods are delivered over the ship's rail), but here the seller has obtained warehouse to warehouse insurance cover for the benefit of the buyer. Does this fact alter the time at which risk normally passes to the buyer?

   When the buyer rejects documents, all rights of property (if transferred) and liabilities of risk re-vest in the seller and we will need to discuss whether Ashok was entitled to reject the documents and/or the goods. If he was, the damage to the coal which has occurred will be at Ernie's risk.

   Two further points need to be discussed: first, the effect of one of the three bills of lading being dated outside the contractual date of shipment (are the goods therefore of contract description?); secondly, the fact that a smaller quantity of goods was shipped (is a buyer entitled to reject the smaller quantity of goods tendered?).

Answer

Ernie's primary duties as a cif seller are to ship goods of the description contained in the contract, to procure the shipping documents and to tender those documents in the manner agreed (*The Julia* (1949)). Ashok's main obligation is to be ready and willing to pay the price.

The contract between Ernie and Ashok does not provide a date for the opening of the credit. It does, however, stipulate a date by which shipment must take place: 31 January. Following *Pavia & Co SpA v Thurmann-Nielsen* (1952), Ashok must open the credit within a reasonable time to allow Ernie to arrange and make shipment by 31 January. We are told that Foxon Bank informs Ernie on 25 January that the letter of credit was opened. If this does not allow Ernie sufficient time to make the necessary shipping arrangements and load the goods, Ernie is not obliged to ship the goods and is entitled to treat the contract as repudiated by Ashok and claim damages. However, Ernie has chosen not to accept Ashok's breach as discharging the contract because he ships the goods. The contract therefore remains open to the benefit of both parties.

We are told that during the loading operation, 10 sacks of coal are dropped into the sea. Normally, risk under a cif contract does not pass before shipment (*Law and Bonar Ltd v British American Tobacco Ltd* (1916)). This is based on the assumption that goods are at the buyer's risk only once insurance cover begins. In a 'classic' cif contract, the seller takes out an insurance policy to cover the goods as from shipment. In this question, however, we are told that Ernie has effected 'from warehouse to warehouse' insurance cover.[1] It may be that since cover is available as from Ernie's warehouse, this excludes the general rule that risk in the goods does not pass before shipment. It is possible, therefore, that the goods are at Ashok's risk from the beginning of the insurance cover. It should be said, however, that such a variation of the general rule should be by express agreement, and there is nothing in the facts to indicate either that Ashok agreed to warehouse cover or that, if he did agree to such cover, that was indicative of the intention to place risk on him before shipment. If the general rule applies, then any damage prior to shipment is at the seller's risk and Ernie must bear the loss of the 10 sacks of coal.

Once goods have been loaded, risk passes to the buyer. This presupposes that the buyer does accept property in the goods, that is, by accepting the documents and/or the goods. If Ashok has the right to reject the documents and/or the goods and he does so, then even if property has passed to him (and therefore risk as well), all rights re-vest in the seller (*Kwei Tek Chao v British Traders and Shippers* (1954)). The only significance of the passing of risk on shipment, therefore, is that it prevents Ashok from claiming from Ernie for loss which occurs after shipment. If the whole contract is discharged, then property re-vests in Ernie and Ashok will not bear the risk during any part of the transit.

As far as the five sacks of coal are concerned, the damage appears to have occurred after loading. Thus, if Ashok does accept the contract, he must bear the loss, although he may have a claim against the underwriters of the insurance policy and/or against the carrier for breach of duty under the contract of carriage.

The master of the ship issues three bills of lading, indicating that 1,490 sacks of coal were shipped in total. According to s 30(1) of the Sale of Goods Act 1979, where the seller delivers a quantity less than he has contracted to sell, the buyer has the option of either rejecting them or to accept the part-delivery and pay for them at the contract rate. However, by s 30(2A), the buyer who does not deal as a consumer will not be able to reject the goods under s 30(1) if the shortfall is so slight that it would be unreasonable for him to do so. A shortfall of 10 sacks, in the present instance, may be considered slight. Even if it was, Ashok is not deprived of his right to the full quantity sold merely because he accepts the smaller quantity shipped.

It seems, therefore, that Foxon Bank has rightly rejected the documents tendered by Ernie, since the bills of lading do not disclose shipment of the correct quantity of goods. Furthermore, one of the bills of lading indicates a late shipment: 1 February. This is not merely a breach by Ernie of the duty to ship the goods by 31 January, but also means that the goods tendered did not match the description by which they were sold. The requirement that goods correspond to their description, until recently, entitled the buyer to reject for quite trivial discrepancies and to do so even though the failure of the seller to deliver goods of the contract description does not in the least prejudice the buyer (*Arcos Ltd v Ronaasen & Son* (1933)). *Bowes v Shand* (1877) established that the time of shipment is part of the description of goods. In that case, a contract for the sale of rice provided for shipment in March/April. Most of the rice[2] was loaded in February and the balance in March. Four bills of lading were issued, three bearing February dates and one a March date. The court held that this was a February shipment. Applying this case to the question, since one-third of the goods was shipped too late, it is submitted that Ernie is in breach of s 13 of the Sale of Goods Act 1979 in not shipping goods complying with the contract description. However, it is arguable whether Ashok can reject the goods, since s 15A of the Sale of Goods Act 1979 provides that, where the breach is so slight that it would be unreasonable for the buyer to reject the goods and the buyer does not deal as a consumer, the breach is to be treated as a breach of warranty and not as a breach of condition. Since time is of the essence in commercial contracts, it is submitted that the breach will not be perceived as so slight for it to be treated as a breach of warranty.

It seems that Foxon Bank has rightly rejected the shipping documents. Ernie then tenders the documents directly to Ashok for payment. Ashok is entitled to refuse to accept the documents, since the contract has provided for payment by letter of credit and that the only acceptable method of tender was to Foxon Bank (*Soproma SpA v Marine & Animal By-Products Corp* (1966)). The principle of short-circuiting credits prohibits direct presentation to the buyer where the documents have been rejected by the bank. This does not mean that Ashok must reject the documents, since he is always entitled to accept defective tender, but clearly he does not wish to do so. Ashok rejects the documents on the ground that the goods may have been damaged afloat due to a collision. This of itself is not a good reason for rejecting, because the seller is not in breach by tendering documents relating to goods damaged afloat, provided that the documents themselves are in order. The giving of an improper reason for rejecting documents does not prevent Ashok from justifying his rejection, provided that there was good reason available at the time of rejection.[3]

Ernie is therefore advised that Foxon Bank was entitled to reject the documents because they revealed that an incorrect quantity of goods was shipped and that the shipment was late. In addition to these reasons, Ashok was entitled to refuse the documents, since the contract had provided for payment by Foxon Bank. Ernie is liable in damages to Ashok for non-delivery.[4]

Notes

1 Institute Cargo Clauses (on which most cif contracts are now covered) cover loss or damage from warehouse to warehouse plus 60 days after landing, and during loading and unloading.

2 8,150 bags of rice out of 8,200.

3 See Question 50 and *Boston Deep Sea Fishing and Ice Co v Ansell* (1888).

4 The measure of damages will be calculated in accordance with s 51(3) of the Sale of Goods Act 1979, that is, the difference between the contract price and the market value the goods would have had, had the documents and goods both been properly delivered.

Question 49

Joshua buys 4,000 tons of wheat from Simone, October shipment, cif Karaky. Karaky is a port in the Middle West where war had been raging continuously for many years.

The wheat is put on board *The Lasthing*. On 27 October, the master, believing the loading will have been completed by the end of October, issues a bill of lading to Simone dated 31 October. In fact, loading was not completed until 1 November.

The wheat is in good condition on shipment but deteriorates on the voyage and by the time the consignment arrives, the wheat is unsuitable for use in the manufacture of bread. The wheat would not have deteriorated on the voyage but for the fact that *The Lasthing* was forced to make a substantial detour in order to avoid hostile submarines which were known to be patrolling the area. Such detours are normal in the Middle West. The bill of lading contained a deviation clause.

Simone tenders the bill of lading and a certificate of insurance (which is customary in the wheat trade). Joshua discovers that the wheat is insured against ordinary marine risks, but not against war risks.

The general market price of wheat has unexpectedly dropped.

Advise Joshua as to whether he must accept the shipping documents.

Answer plan

This question involves the importance of shipping documents, in particular, the bill of lading and the insurance policy. The key issues in relation to the bill of lading are whether the false date of shipment and the deviation clause entitle Joshua to reject the document. A buyer of goods under a cif contract is not entitled, as against the seller, to reject shipping documents merely because the ship has deviated. The buyer's remedy is usually against the carrier. However, the problem in this question is that the bill of lading contains a deviation clause entitling the carrier to deviate. What is the effect of such a clause as between Simone and Joshua?

The part of the question involving the insurance policy requires discussion of what type of policy the cif seller is entitled to expect, taking into account what is usual in the trade in question.

Answer

If the documents tendered by Simone accord with the contract, Joshua must accept them and pay the agreed price (*Biddell Bros v Clemens Horst Co* (1912)). A wrongful rejection amounts to a repudiation of the contract: *Gill & Duffus SA v Berger & Co Inc* (1984).

As far as the bill of lading is concerned, it is clear that it must show that the goods were loaded at the time required by the contract of sale. We are told that the bill of lading is erroneously dated 31 October whereas, in fact, loading was not completed until after the contract shipment period. The general rule is that the bill of lading must be 'genuine' (*James Finlay & Co Ltd v Kwik Hoo Tong* (1929)), and a bill of lading which contains a false date of shipment is a bad tender entitling the buyer to reject the shipping documents. If Joshua is certain that he can prove the goods were not shipped until 1 November, then he has the right to reject the bill of lading.

Joshua may have the right to reject the goods themselves on the ground that the wheat was not of contract description. According to the House of Lords in *Bowes v Shand* (1877), stipulations as to the time of shipment form part of the description of the goods and that breach of such stipulations entitles the buyer to reject. Although *Bowes v Shand* was decided before the Sale of Goods Act 1893, subsequent cases have acknowledged that the time of shipment is part of the description of the goods and is within s 13 of the Sale of Goods Act (*Avon & Co v Comptoir Weigmont* (1920)). However, s 13 is affected by s 15A, introduced by the Sale and Supply of Goods Act 1994. According to s 15A, where the breach is so slight that it would be unreasonable for the buyer to reject the goods and the buyer does not deal as a consumer, a breach is not to be treated as a breach of condition but as a breach of warranty. The issue here is whether time of shipment is to be treated as a slight breach and hence as a breach of warranty. Since time is of the essence in commercial contracts, it is unlikely that the time of shipment will be treated as a breach of warranty.[1] It seems that Joshua would be entitled to reject the goods even though he previously accepts documents which were, on the face of them, in accordance with the contract. In *Suzuki & Co v Burgett v Newsam* (1922), peas were sold under a cif contract which called for shipment by January. The seller tendered a 'received for shipment' bill of lading, which was usual in the trade, dated 31 January. Although the goods had been received for shipment on 31 January, actual shipment took place in February. The court held that the buyer, who had accepted the bill of lading (which was in accordance with the contract), was entitled to reject the goods as they did not constitute a January shipment (*Kwei Tek Chao v British Traders and Shippers* (1954)). Applying this to the question, Joshua is thus advised not to reject the bill of lading unless he is sure that he can prove that the goods were in fact shipped on 1 November. He may be entitled to reject the goods themselves.

We are told that the wheat deteriorates during the voyage due to the need to make a substantial detour. Since risk in the goods passes to the cif buyer on shipment (irrespective of the time at which property passes) (*Law and Bonar Ltd v British American Tobacco Ltd* (1916)), Joshua cannot reject the goods on the basis that they have deteriorated during carriage. Objection may nevertheless be taken to the bill of lading on the ground that it contains a deviation clause permitting the carrier to depart from the route of shipment. This rule is subject to contrary custom or usage (*Burstall v Grimsdale* (1906)). It seems likely that a bill of lading relating to a shipment to the Middle West, where hostilities have been apparent for years, will contain a deviation clause permitting the carrier to make such detours as are necessary to avoid danger. If the clause is not drafted in unusually wide terms, Joshua is advised that the bill of lading is a good shipping document as the bill is 'usual and customary'. This bill of lading may be governed by the Hague-Visby Rules,[2] which allow for express deviation clauses (*Stag Line Ltd v Foscola, Mango & Co* (1932)). Under the Rules, deviation is also permitted to save life, to save property, and where it is reasonable.

Joshua is therefore required to accept the bill of lading.

It appears that there are two problems with regard to the policy of insurance: first, Simone tenders a certificate of insurance (and not a policy); secondly, war risk cover has not been obtained.

In respect of the first problem, it is established that a cif seller does not perform his obligations by procuring and tendering a certificate of insurance (*Maine Spinning Co v Sutcliffe & Co* (1917)).[3] Of course, a document may be a policy even though it does not contain all the terms of the insurance, but incorporates a reference to an identified or identifiable policy or perhaps makes reference to terms known in the trade.[4] It is unlikely that these requirements are satisfied in this question. The fact that it is customary in the wheat trade to tender certificates of insurance rather than policies is unlikely to be sufficient to require Joshua to accept the certificate of insurance tendered by Simone, unless there was an express provision in the contract to the contrary.

As for the second problem, if Simone tenders a policy which is usual or in accordance with the express requirements of the contract, it is immaterial that the policy does not cover the loss which has actually occurred. We are not told of any express terms in the contract requiring Simone to obtain war risk cover. In the absence of any contractual term, the general rule is that the seller must tender such policy as is usual in the trade to cover the goods and voyage in question (*Burstall v Grimsdale* (1906)). It is not clear if the risks covered must be those usual at the time of the contract of sale or at the time the policy is issued. In *Groom Ltd v Barber* (1915), a policy not covering war risks was held to be a good tender on the basis that at the time of the contract of sale, it was not usual to cover war risks.[5] The decision in this case makes it clear that the time of tender of the documents is not decisive, but the court did not indicate whether the relevant time is that of the sale or the time at which the policy of insurance was taken out. There was no interval between these two points in *Groom Ltd v Barber*. The better view might be that the relevant time should be the time at which the insurance policy is effected. Either way, we are told in this question that war had been raging continuously for many years in the Middle West. It would appear, therefore, that it was usual to insure against war risks. Simone's tender of the certificate of insurance is probably defective, entitling Joshua to refuse to accept the documents on the basis that a certificate (rather than a policy) is not sufficient and that Simone failed to insure against war risks. However, this will only be so on the basis that there was no express provision to the contrary in the contract.

Notes

1   Time of shipment is generally regarded as part of the description of the goods, due to the crucial role that time plays in commercial contracts. Time for both the seller and buyer is important for sorting out payment arrangements. The buyer may also wish to fulfil his contractual obligations with other parties (see Lord Cairns' judgment in *Bowes v Shand* (1877), p 463).

2   The Hague-Visby Rules will be applicable provided that the conditions set out by the Convention are met. See, for instance, Arts I(c) and X of the Rules.

3   One of the reasons behind this rule is that the certificate usually makes reference to the policy, and the person to whom tender is made will be unable to determine from the certificate what the terms of the insurance are (*Donald H Scott Ltd v Barclays Bank Ltd* (1915)). A certificate of insurance is not transferable like a policy to the buyer by endorsement, which means that the buyer will not have a right of action against the insurers (*Diamond Alkali Export Corp v Fl Bourgeois* (1921); s 50(3) of the Marine Insurance Act 1906).

4   There is, however, authority to support the proposition that an insurance certificate or other document entitling the insured to demand the formal delivery of an insurance policy will suffice. See Schmitthoff, *The Law and Practice of International Trade*, 10th edn, 2000, para 2-023.

5   Unless otherwise provided, cif policies are only for commercial rather than war risks. This is implied at common law and expressed in INCOTERMS (2000 International Chamber of Commerce Document No 560). This is also why the

Institute Cargo Clauses (now commonly used in cif contracts) have war clauses separate from, and in addition to, the other clauses.

Question 50

Edward sells 3,000 tons of maize to Beatrice, cif Southampton and 4,000 tons of wheat to John cif Swansea. Both contracts called for April shipment and stipulated for the tender of a bill of lading, an insurance certificate and an invoice. Soon after the contracts are concluded, the market price of wheat falls dramatically.

The bill of lading covering the maize is dated 30 April. On tender of the documents, Beatrice refuses to pay against them on the basis that Edward has not tendered an insurance policy. Beatrice now learns that the maize was actually shipped on 1 May.

Edward books shipping space on *Challenger* to take the wheat consignment. Due to a typing error, Edward names the ship *Challengra* in his fax to John. The wheat is delivered to the docks and loading begins in March and is completed in April. The bill of lading correctly names *Challenger* as the ship and is dated 2 April. *Challenger* deviates from the usual route in order to obtain further supplies before arriving at Swansea. John wishes to repudiate the sale if he can.

Advise Beatrice and John of their remedies against Edward.

Would it make a difference if Edward had tendered along with an insurance policy an electronic bill of lading?

Answer plan

This is another question dealing with the importance of shipping documents in a cif contract. The first part of the question raises the difficult issue of whether a buyer who wrongfully repudiates the contract may rely on a subsequent and valid right to repudiate to justify his initial wrongful repudiation. The case of *Boston Deep Sea Fishing and Ice Co v Ansell* (1888) is in point. The qualifications to the general rule will also need to be discussed.

As in Question 49, we will need to deal with deviation clauses, but in this question we are not told whether there was a specific provision in the bill of lading. Furthermore, we are asked again to reiterate the well established principle that time of shipment forms part of the description of goods.

Answer

Under a cif (cost, insurance and freight) contract, once goods are shipped, the seller performs his part of the contract by tendering to the buyer the proper shipping documents which, in the absence of express terms to the contrary, include the bill of lading, an insurance policy and a commercial invoice (*The Julia* (1949)). On tender of these documents, the buyer must pay the agreed price if they conform to the terms of the contract (*Biddell Bros v Clemens Horst Co* (1912)). However, if it subsequently transpires that the goods were defective in a way that amounts to a breach of a fundamental term or to a breach of condition, the buyer is normally entitled to reject the goods even though he has previously accepted documents which were perfectly in accordance with the contract.

Beatrice

We are told that when Edward tenders the shipping documents to Beatrice, Beatrice repudiates the contract on the ground that the insurance policy is not included. It is unclear whether Edward tenders any insurance document at all. A cif contract is an agreement to sell goods at an inclusive price covering the cost of goods, insurance and freight (*Johnson v Taylor Bros* (1920)). If Edward does not tender an insurance policy, even if the goods in fact arrive at the contract destination unharmed, Beatrice is entitled to treat the contract as repudiated. On the other hand, it may be that Edward does tender an insurance document but Beatrice's objection to it is that it is an insurance certificate rather than a policy. The general rule is that a cif seller does not perform his obligations by procuring and tendering a certificate of insurance (*Maine Spinning Co v Sutcliffe & Co* (1917); *Diamond Alkali Export Corp v Fl Bourgeois* (1921)). However, this *prima facie* rule is displaced in this question because of an express term in the contract of sale allowing the seller to tender an insurance certificate. Substitution of a policy with a certificate of insurance where expressly agreed is recognised as a good tender (*Burstall v Grimsdale* (1906)). It appears, therefore, that if Edward tenders an insurance certificate, Beatrice is not entitled to refuse to pay against the documents. In so doing, Beatrice is in breach of her primary duty to pay on tender of documents, and it is Edward who has the right to treat this breach as a repudiatory breach entitling him to recover damages.[1] Beatrice has wrongfully rejected the documents.

However, although the bill of lading gives the date of shipment as 30 April, Beatrice has now learnt that the wheat was actually shipped on 1 May. In *Bowes v Shand* (1877), stipulations as to the time of shipment were held to be part of the description of the goods entitling the buyer to reject. However, due to s 15A of the Sale of Goods Act 1979, the non-consumer buyer's right to reject is dependent on whether or not the breach is slight. Since time is of the essence, it is likely that the breach will be perceived as a breach of condition. Since Beatrice has already refused to perform her part of the bargain by refusing to accept the documents, and assuming that the time of shipment entitles the buyer to reject, can she now rely on another ground of rejection which does justify her refusal to perform? The answer seems to be yes (*Boston Deep Sea Fishing and Ice Co v Ansell* (1888)). It may be, therefore, that if Beatrice wrongfully rejected the documents on the ground that they included an insurance certificate as opposed to a policy, she might still be entitled to justify her rejection on the ground that the goods were not of the description (April goods) called for by the contract.

The general rule, however, is subject to two qualifications. First, the ground of rejection on which subsequent reliance is placed must actually exist at the time of the rejection. Applying this to the question, did Beatrice's right to reject the goods because they were not of contract description exist at the time she rejected the documents? The answer is in the affirmative. Secondly, if the seller could have remedied the defect had the buyer stated a valid ground for rejection, the buyer is not entitled to rely on the subsequent ground to justify his refusal to perform. In other words, if Beatrice had complained to Edward at the time of tender of the documents that contract description goods had not been shipped, could Edward have remedied that defect? The answer is no. The goods had already been shipped outside the contract shipment period and Edward could not do anything to put that right.

It seems, therefore, that although Beatrice wrongfully rejected Edward's tender of the shipping documents, she may nevertheless rely on the fact that the goods did not conform to the contract description to justify her rejection of the documents. In the circumstances, Beatrice may recover damages from Edward for non-delivery under s 51 of the Sale of Goods Act 1979.

As for the tendering of an electronic bill of lading, it is likely to be regarded as a bad tender. Electronic bills of lading are not in common use, even though the Comite Maritime International (CMI) has drafted the CMI Rules for Electronic Bills of Lading for incorporation by the parties. Section 1(5) of the Carriage of Goods by Sea Act 1992 empowers the Secretary of State to make provisions for the application of the Act to electronic documents. For the tender to be a good tender, it is important that the parties have agreed expressly to use a paperless bill of lading. According to cif INCOTERMS 2000, the parties may agree to use electronic equivalents of transport documentation.

John

As far as the wheat is concerned, it is unclear whether the contract of sale expressly required Edward to ship the goods on any particular vessel. This seems unlikely, since under a cif contract, it is the seller who arranges the carriage of goods (*The Julia* (1949)). Thus, Edward's error in naming the ship in his fax to John would not give John a ground for repudiating the contract.[2] The bill of lading does correctly name *Challenger*.

We are not told whether the contract of sale specified the route of shipment. If there was no express provision, the court will imply that the seller will ship the goods by the usual and customary route. We are also not told whether or not the bill of lading contained a deviation clause. If there was a clause permitting the carrier to depart from the usual and customary route, then John may reject the bill of lading whether or not the ship actually deviates.[3] On the other hand, if the bill of lading does not contain a deviation clause, John may not reject it against Edward merely because *Challenger* has in fact wrongfully deviated. Edward is not responsible for breach of the contract of carriage; John must seek his remedy against the carrier.

The bill of lading is dated 2 April, although loading of the wheat began in March. As discussed in relation to the earlier part of the question, the time of shipment forms part of the description of the goods. A buyer may reject goods if they do not correspond with the contract description, provided that the breach is not slight. In this question, shipment begins outside the contract period but is completed, and the bill of lading is dated, within it. May this be considered to be a shipment in accordance with the contract? In *Bowes v Shand* (1877), a contract for the sale of rice provided for March/April shipment. Most of the rice (8,150 out of 8,200 bags) was put on board in February and the rest in March. Four bills of lading were issued, three bearing February dates and one a March date. The court held that this was a February shipment. In relation to the wheat, a single bill of lading is issued stating that the goods are shipped on 2 April. Although part of the loading began in March, it is unlikely that this will entitle John to repudiate the sale.

It seems, therefore, that John is not entitled to refuse to pay Edward on proper shipping documents being tendered to him.

Notes

1   The measure of damages is to be calculated in accordance with s 50 of the Sale of Goods Act 1979 for non-acceptance.

2   Since the seller makes the arrangements for carriage and insurance, s 32(3) of the Sale of Goods Act 1979 does not apply to cif contracts (s 32(3) obliges the seller to give sufficient information to the buyer so that the buyer may effect

insurance cover). See Chapter 11 on fob contracts for further details on the effect of s 32(3).

3   If the bill of lading contains an 'objectionable' deviation clause, the buyer may reject the bill of lading even if the ship does not in fact deviate. This is so because the buyer does not usually know whether the ship has deviated or will deviate before arriving at the destination at the time of tender of documents.